Wellbeing in the Primary Classroom

Other titles from Bloomsbury Education

Live Well, Learn Well by Abigail Mann

Proactive Pastoral Care by Maria O'Neill

Teaching Happiness and Well-Being in Schools, Second edition by Ian Morris

The Emotionally Intelligent Teacher by Niomi Clyde Roberts

The Happy Tank by John Magee

The Wellbeing Curriculum by Andrew Cowley

Wellbeing in the Primary Classroom

The updated guide to teaching happiness and positive mental health

Adrian Bethune

BLOOMSBURY EDUCATION
LONDON   OXFORD   NEW YORK   NEW DELHI   SYDNEY

BLOOMSBURY EDUCATION
Bloomsbury Publishing Plc
50 Bedford Square, London, WC1B 3DP, UK
29 Earlsfort Terrace, Dublin 2, Ireland

BLOOMSBURY, BLOOMSBURY EDUCATION and the Diana logo are
trademarks of Bloomsbury Publishing Plc

This edition published in the UK 2023 by Bloomsbury Education

Text copyright © Adrian Bethune 2023
Photographs © Adrian Bethune 2023

Adrian Bethune has asserted his right under the Copyright, Designs and
Patents Act, 1988, to be identified as Author of this work

A catalogue record for this book is available from the British Library

ISBN: PB: 978-1-8019-9212-1; ePDF: 978-1-8019-9215-2;
ePub: 978-1-8019-9213-8

2 4 6 8 10 9 7 5 3 1 (paperback)

Typeset by Newgen KnowledgeWorks Pvt. Ltd., Chennai, India
Printed and bound in the UK by CPI Group Ltd, CR0 4YY

To find out more about our authors and books visit www.bloomsbury.com
and sign up for our newsletters

Contents

Acknowledgements

I thought that writing a second edition of *Wellbeing In The Primary Classroom* would be much easier than writing the first book from scratch. How wrong I was. Fortunately, I had the support of my editor, Emily Badger, who made sure that this edition was the best it could be. Thank you for your feedback and comments – this book is better for them.

I'd like to thank my wife, Sam, for once again reading my writing and offering a non-teacher perspective on it. Your insights were invaluable and also your encouragement when I was struggling to find the motivation to write!

I am indebted to the teachers who gave up their time to contribute to the 'Tales from the classroom' sections. These anecdotes really help the theory come to life and show what's possible, so thanks to: Sophie Tong-Smith, Rhiannon Phillips-Bianco, Ben Levinson OBE, Kate Chadwick, Cat Peterson, Holly Laceby (special props to you as you wrote your section not that long after giving birth to twins!!) and Sara Mekhari.

Thanks again to a range of experts who read my chapters, offered insights or pointed me in the right direction in terms of research and ideas: Prof. Katherine Weare, Chris Wright at the Youth Sport Trust, Louise Moore at the Children's Society, Rick Hanson, Louis Cozolino, Ruby Wax, Debbie Johnson, Mark Williamson, Vanessa King, Peter Harper, John Ratey, Emma Kell, Yvonne Biggins, Vicki Zakrzewski and Tal Ben-Shahar.

Finally, I want to thank all of the children and my colleagues, especially Charlie Reed and Lizzy Rackham, at Broughton Community Schools. You have allowed me to try ideas out, kept me laughing and inspired many of the new ideas in this book!

Foreword

When Adrian asked me whether I'd be willing to write the foreword for the new edition of his book, my first thoughts were, 'But why do we need a second edition?' (mixed with a heap of joy at being asked, of course). You see, I absolutely love the first edition of this book and have been recommending it regularly since it hit our shelves back in 2018. It felt like such a comprehensive and complete offering and was serving the needs of primary school communities so well that I was unsure what a second edition could bring. But on reading the manuscript, I fell in love with Adrian's ideas and approach anew and saw that the second edition had the possibility of bringing joy, happiness and wellbeing in its many forms to our classrooms in the current context – because so much has changed in the few years since that first edition.

Our communities find themselves reeling and looking uncertainly towards the future as we try to pick ourselves up and brush ourselves off after the wheels fell off during the pandemic. Society has changed, our children have changed, our staff are physically and emotionally exhausted and, as I write this in the spring of 2023, 'The Good Childhood Report 2022' by The Children's Society (2022) has recently been released and showed that, yet again, our children became less happy in the last year and that the thing that is making them most miserable of all is school.

It can all feel a bit bleak. But let's take a moment to focus on the positives, as Adrian teaches us to in Chapter 3. You see, in those early pandemic days, when it felt like the world stopped spinning on its axis and nobody knew what to do next, the one thing that we could rely on was our schools. Whilst many other people took cover at home, our schools remained open (sometimes only partially and sometimes only remotely, but you guys never packed your bags and jacked it in, unlike so many of us!). Schools became safe hubs right at the heart of communities. They were not just places of learning but were also sources of food, clothing, advice, love, consistency, care… all the things that really matter. In those early months, when things were at their hardest, a beautiful thing happened in schools because they were left to fend for themselves. Nobody knew what to do and so you just had to crack on without the demands of Ofsted and the next time that the children would be measured. With limited resources and no playbook, you simply had to do what felt right.

You did an amazing job.

The things that schools prioritised during the pandemic – connection, care, curiosity and calm – were exactly what our children needed at the time and, arguably, all the time. Adrian's book picks up on that – and shows you how to make these vital elements a part of your everyday so that this generation can grow through and from adversity and become stronger adults as a result. The book is a wonderful journey through the 'why' and 'how' of nurturing children to live their happiest lives, so that they can thrive both at school and beyond it.

The second edition is needed because we're living in a different world to the one for which the first edition was written. Our priorities have changed, the children coming up through our primary schools are noticeably different to their recent predecessors, and our ability to teach them (in the widest sense of the word) has been altered by our own experiences. The book is brilliant and it took me an age to read it because I took so many notes and had to go and do a tonne of thinking in between digesting ideas. It's one of those books that presents a complete set of answers if you'd like to use it off the shelf, but it also acts as the most fabulous jumping-off point if you're prepared to take some of the ideas and run with them and make them your own too. It makes you excited to get started and keen to see the impact on the young people whom you're supporting.

Personally, I am a very logical thinker and doer; I consider this one of my autistic superpowers and if you've ever watched me speak you'll have observed this in action. However, this can get in the way a little bit when reading the works of those who are less structured. This is categorically *not* a problem with Adrian's book, which will be a real gift to anyone who wants to be able to dip in and out and refer back to good ideas later.

Each chapter has a clear focus and starts with the 'Why', where you'll learn all about the theory and the research underpinning exactly why Adrian feels that this particular line of practice would be a good use of your children's learning time. You'll have all the evidence that you need to bring those less sure around, and will be reassured that you're making good choices for your curriculum. It can be easy to doubt this amongst so much talk of catch-up and closing the gap. I honestly think that finding a way to incorporate as many of the themes in this book as possible as a standard part of the everyday school culture for all children would lead to schools that our children are excited to attend, at which our staff are delighted to lead learning and in which our families are fully invested. The gap would naturally close.

I'll step off my soapbox now and return to the mechanics of the book… the 'Why' is followed with the 'How' – and hurrah for that, because theory is very interesting, but time-poor teachers need ideas about exactly how to make this work in their classrooms right away. You need to know what you can do differently tomorrow as a result of something that you've learned today, and Adrian gives you that in spades. He has also outlined dozens of case studies from schools all over the world, who share ideas and inspiration about what this looks like in practice. Each of these filled me with a warm glow and gratitude for the amazing adults creating wonderful environments for children, as well as excitement for the many more who could follow, because if they can do it, then you can too, right?

I love this book. I hope that you will too. It's one of the best weapons that you could possibly add to your armoury when trying to make a difference to the children you work with and care for. With these ideas, you can make meaningful change happen in many young lives, whether as one person trying to make a difference or as part of a wider team.

Start with something small; the changes so small that you are sure you can make them tomorrow and then the next day and the next are often the changes that make the biggest difference of all. You make more difference than you'll ever know and the passion that you pour into your work has ripples that are felt across a lifetime for the children in your care. Thank you a million times for all that you've done through these hardest of times and all that you continue to do each day for our communities, and thank you to Adrian for giving you the tools to do it even better.

Dr Pooky Knightsmith, Child and Adolescent Mental Health Expert

Pooky has a PhD in child mental health from the Institute of Psychiatry, King's College London. She is the author of several books and is a former chair of the Children and Young People's Mental Health Coalition. Pooky is a Director at Creative Education Limited and at Pooky Knightsmith Associates. Pooky is autistic; a late diagnosis has helped her to thrive following many years of anorexia, depression and anxiety.

Preface

All the world is full of suffering. It is also full of overcoming.
— Helen Keller

It is ironic that poor mental health led me to write books about wellbeing, but that is exactly what happened. Back in 2008, I had everything I needed to be happy and content – I had a good job in the music industry, a good group of friends, I was in a serious relationship and I had just bought my first flat in London (a shared-ownership flat as I couldn't afford a whole one!). But something else happened in 2008 – a world financial crisis. I started to feel uneasy about having taken on a mortgage, and I worried about what would happen if I lost my job. Anxious feelings started to dominate. It didn't take long for things to unravel for me. My sleep deteriorated badly, I lost weight because I had no appetite and my thoughts were a constant swirl of endless negativity. In the space of a few months, I was single, had fallen out with a good friend and I became lonely and depressed living in the flat on my own.

What is also ironic about that very dark period in my life is that I look back and feel extremely grateful for it. First of all, there is a huge sense of gratitude for my family and friends who helped me through the darkest times (like my best friend Joe, who shot round to my flat one night when I called him up and burst into tears). Then, there's a sense of gratitude for all of the people who gave me lots of practical ideas and insights into helping myself to get better – from colleagues who opened up about their own struggles with poor mental health to the counsellor who listened to me without judgement. Most of all, I'm grateful that the hardest time in my life (well, it's up there with the sleepless nights of becoming a new parent) has led to where I am today. I have my own family now, I teach, write and give talks about wellbeing.

I have since discovered that there is something that psychologists call 'adversarial growth' (sometimes called 'post-traumatic growth'). This can happen when people go through really stressful and difficult times in their lives and don't just bounce back (aka resilience) but actually grow from their tough times and 'bounce forward'. Typically, adversities can help people to grow in three main ways:

1. They realise they're stronger than they thought and this changes their self-concept.

2. They strengthen their relationships with others (mainly the people who helped them through their difficulties).

3. They have a change in mindset or philosophy, where they become more focused and appreciative of the present moment and more compassionate towards others who suffer.

These are all true of me. I have come to realise that nothing is more important than your physical and mental health, because they are your lens on the world and they affect how you interact with it every moment of every day. There are no qualifications, awards, accolades, prizes or sums of money that are more important than them. They are the 'ultimate currency', to borrow a phrase from Tal Ben-Shahar (2008, p. 51) – more on him later.

I think it's really important that we know about adversarial growth. Just take a moment to reflect on life now and what's happened over recent years. At the time of writing, this includes a deadly global pandemic, outbreak of war in Ukraine, climate change and a cost-of-living crisis in the UK. These issues are not going away any time soon, but rather than viewing them as catastrophes that will overwhelm us, with the right skills and mindset (and support from people around us) we can view them as challenges that will help us to grow. Throughout history, human beings have endured and recovered from unimaginable difficulties. The message that we need to be giving teachers and children is that we are no different and we can do the same.

It was a real privilege to write the first edition of *Wellbeing in the Primary Classroom*. I'd never written a book before and imposter syndrome loomed large at times. I had no idea whether teachers would read it or like it. I was blown away by the positive reception to the first edition and it was lovely to receive emails and tweets from teachers who were putting the ideas into action. This edition has been updated with references to the latest evidence and research from the science of wellbeing. There are two new chapters on the power of nature and digital wellbeing, and a diverse range of primary teachers have contributed to the 'Tales from the classroom' sections.

This book, like the first edition, aims to be a practical guide for how you can teach primary school-aged children (and their teachers) to be happier. The ideas are backed up by science and research and I have tried them in my classroom (and so have many other teachers too). This is not a one-size-fits-all book. You may need to tweak and adapt the ideas to suit your school, your class and your children. Some of the ideas may work wonderfully; others may not. The whole point is to take action and experiment (just like Sophie did – see below). If you don't, nothing changes and we are still left with the broken system that we had before.

> 'When returning from maternity leave I had a realisation – all was not well with either the children or the adults at our school. We had focused so much on our school's 'successes' that somewhere along the way we had neglected to think about what impact they were having on our school wellbeing. After sharing my concerns, it was agreed that a change in approach was required – a mammoth task that I found hard to navigate. Where should I begin? Along came *Wellbeing in the Primary Classroom*. I find it hard to pinpoint one example of how this book had a positive effect on my school because really it gave me so much more than one

activity. This book gave me a place to start, foundations to lay and practical exercises to explore and develop the wellbeing of our whole school community.'

Sophie Tong-Smith, teacher, North London primary school

There is a quote by Ralph Waldo Emerson that I love and which has informed a lot of my teaching practice and life in general: 'Do not be too timid or squeamish about your actions. All life is an experiment. The more experiments you make, the better.' (1965, p. 211) This book is a guide and an invitation to be bold and experiment with some new ideas in your classrooms. I wish you luck and success on your teaching happiness journey.

Adrian Bethune

Introduction

Educators – parents and teachers – who care about helping children lead happy lives must first themselves believe that happiness is the ultimate currency.

– Tal Ben-Shahar, 2008

There are many people who would argue that our education system is outdated and not fit for purpose. And I have to say that I would agree with them. Created during the Industrial Revolution of the nineteenth century, our school system was designed to give people skills that were essential for them to succeed in an industrial world. Children were taught how to master the technical skills of reading, writing and calculation. Although these skills are still important now, the world in which our children are growing up has changed but our school system has not. And change is continuing and rapid. We have been focusing so hard on filling our children's heads but we have forgotten about their hearts. I am in favour of a 'knowledge-rich curriculum' but is the knowledge that we are currently teaching our children what they need to lead well-rounded and satisfying lives?

High-stakes testing and an extremely narrow curriculum (with just English and maths assessed at a national level in primary schools), where all children are expected to make linear progress year after year, not only puts teachers and children under huge pressures but saps the life out of teaching and education. As Professor Sue Roffey puts it, 'What is the point of academic "excellence" for young people who are anxious, depressed, or feel life has no meaning?' (Cited in Grenville-Cleave et al., 2021, p. 38) I believe that schools could be so much more than this. They could be places of self-discovery, places of wonder and awe. Schools should nurture our young people and respect and value their unique differences. Schools should help children to uncover their immense potential and enable them to realise that they can have a positive impact on the world. I believe that teaching happiness and wellbeing in primary schools is one way in which to achieve this. Teaching happiness has benefits for teachers too. Teaching the skills of wellbeing brings humanity back to education; it can rekindle teachers' passion for educating young people and it can restore the innate meaning and purpose to teaching that comes from wanting to make a difference in children's lives.

What is happiness and wellbeing?

What happiness is and how to 'obtain' it have been debated for millennia. There are, of course, individual differences in what happiness means to people. For example, I get a great deal of pleasure and purpose from working with young people as a teacher. But, for others, the thought of working with children every day is a complete nightmare. However, research shows that there are some common themes that appear to contribute to most people's happiness, such as having strong social ties and contributing to something bigger than yourself. Psychologists can sometimes get quite technical when it comes to happiness and, rather than calling it as such, prefer to use terms like 'subjective wellbeing' and 'psychological wellbeing'. Subjective wellbeing is a person's own assessment of how well their life, or specific aspects of it, is going. Two commonly used measures of subjective wellbeing are life satisfaction and the experience of positive and negative emotions. Psychological wellbeing is concerned with people's sense of meaning, purpose and engagement with life. Working towards these may not bring pleasure (positive emotions) at the time but leads to a sense of fulfilment in the longer term. When we have high subjective and psychological wellbeing, by some definitions we may be said to be flourishing (The Children's Society, 2022, p.6).

For the purposes of this book, I'm using a definition of happiness that comes from Professor Paul Dolan, who says that happiness is 'experiences of pleasure and purpose over time' (Dolan, 2015), with pleasure meaning the experience of positive emotions (like joy, peace, love, curiosity and fun) and doing things that you enjoy, and purpose meaning the time that you spend on activities that are important and meaningful to you (but, crucially, may not necessarily be enjoyable at the time!). To be clear, I use the terms 'happiness' and 'wellbeing' interchangeably to mean the same thing.

I think it is important to point out that the happiness on which I am focusing in this book is not about feeling good all the time. This is unrealistic. We can actually make ourselves feel less happy if we're always trying to feel great, because this is an unachievable goal. We will all experience loss, heartache, anxiety and loneliness at times. These feelings are normal reactions to life's difficulties and they can help us to grow. We become wiser by learning to navigate through the rocky terrains of life. Without difficulties we cannot hope to develop our levels of resilience, which is a core part of leading a happy life.

So, happiness involves all the emotions, not just positive ones. In fact, one study showed that even negative emotions like anger can make us feel 'happy' if these are the emotions that we desire to feel at that time (Tamir et al., 2017). The lead researcher in this study, Dr Maya Tamir, said, 'Happiness is more than simply feeling pleasure and avoiding pain. Happiness is about having experiences that are meaningful and valuable, including emotions that you think are the right ones to have.' (American Psychological Association, 2017)

Importantly, our happiness is something we have to work at regularly. It is not a destination at which you arrive and that's it. You wouldn't go to the gym for a month and then sit back and relax for the rest of your life, enjoying your new-found levels of fitness. And so it is with our happiness – it takes work and effort, and it is a journey that will last us our whole rich, diverse and messy lives.

Can you teach happiness?

There used to be a commonly held belief that people's happiness levels were determined from birth and didn't really change much during our adult lives. The 'set point theory' argued that people were either born with a sunny disposition or not, and that despite good or bad events happening to you, your happiness levels would always return to their 'set point' (Lykken and Tellegen, 1996). These researchers gave examples of people whose happiness levels returned to their 'set point' after dramatic life events, such as winning the lottery or becoming a paraplegic (Brickman et al., 1978).

Although it is certainly true that genes (and our early upbringing) do play a part, the latest research shows that there is a lot that we can do to impact and change our levels of happiness and wellbeing in the long term (in effect, raising our 'set point' of happiness). Research by psychology professor Sonja Lyubomirsky (Lyubomirsky et al., 2005) studied identical twins separated at birth and raised in different places, by different parents, to see the role that genetics play in our happiness levels. If genes determined our happiness levels from birth, then the identical twins studied (who have a 100 per cent DNA match) should have been as happy as one another, but this was not the case. Lyubomirsky's research concluded that genetics only determined their happiness levels by up to 50 per cent.

Furthermore, she discovered that people's life circumstances (gender, race, where they lived, etc.), assuming that their basic needs – such as food and safety – were met, had less impact on happiness than we might think. In this study, this accounted for, on average, around ten per cent, with this relatively small amount being due to 'adaptation' to these factors. Adaptation is when people get used to a new situation or thing (e.g. the place where we live or the new car that we bought), and the joy or misery that it first provoked wanes and we adapt to it with our happiness levels returning back to our 'set point'.

However, the most interesting discovery from Lyubomirsky's research was that a whopping 40 per cent of happiness was determined by the choices and actions taken by the participants.

By monitoring very happy people, Lyubomirksy and other psychologists have been able to identify the intentional activities and strategies that work to boost and maintain people's levels of happiness (Sheldon and Lyubomirsky, 2007). There were common themes that arose when happy people's lives, behaviours and thinking were scrutinised. In general, happy people tend to:

- invest a lot into their close personal relationships with friends and family
- express high levels of gratitude for what they have
- be quite helpful and altruistic
- have an optimistic outlook when imagining their future
- savour pleasures and tend to live in the present moment
- exercise regularly
- have a clear sense of purpose in life (Lyubomirsky, 2006).

Lyubomirsky and other psychologists' research certainly suggests that you can teach happiness and that you can learn to be happier. This relatively new area of psychology is known as positive psychology (also referred to as the 'science of wellbeing') (Seligman and Csikszentmihalyi, 2000). Whereas traditional psychology focuses on illness, misery and people's 'issues', positive psychologists study how human beings flourish and what contributes to a happy and meaningful life. In short, the science of wellbeing can be described as the scientific study of what makes life worth living (Peterson et al., 2008).

In fact, many wellbeing curricular have been tested in schools and have been shown to produce positive results. For example, a very large randomised control trial devised by Dr Alejandro Adler, measured the results of a wellbeing curriculum delivered to almost 8,000 students. The results were clear – students in the intervention schools reported significantly higher levels of wellbeing and they performed significantly better on standardised national exams (Adler, 2016). More recently, a course I co-wrote called *The Seeds of Happiness* (which teaches children and their teachers about the science of wellbeing and uses many of the ideas contained within this book) was tested in a pilot study by researcher, Sean Callard, from Cambridge University's Faculty of Education. Callard found that the children who took part in the course had significantly increased levels of wellbeing and improved attitudes to learning compared to the control group (Callard, 2022). As one child explained in the study, 'I think the *Seeds of Happiness* got me really excited about my lessons. Even the ones I didn't really like before.'

Perhaps happiness is best thought of as a skill. It is something that we need to practise, to hone and to craft. As the Dalai Lama says, 'Happiness is not something ready-made. It comes from your own actions.' So, alongside the skills of reading, writing and maths, we can add skills for happiness. This book delves into these skills in more detail and shows you how to teach them to children.

Intrinsic motivation – a key to happiness

Psychologists long believed that the main drivers of human behaviour were biological (to find food, water or a mate) or extrinsic (approaching rewards and avoiding punishments). However, two researchers, Edward Deci and Richard Ryan, have become famous for challenging this old way of viewing human motivation. They developed 'self-determination theory' (Ryan and Deci, 2000), which showed that humans are also motivated *intrinsically*, meaning that sometimes we do things purely because we want to for their own sake and not because we stand to gain something or will avoid a punishment. Deci and Ryan's research showed that when motivation is driven by internal 'self-determined' forces, such as personal growth and self-development, it's associated with higher self-esteem and lower levels of anxiety and depression (Humphrey and Hughes, 2021).

The three key forces that are fundamental to being intrinsically motivated are:

- **Connection:** Our motivation increases when we feel connected to the people around us and a sense of belonging.
- **Competence:** We are more motivated when we feel that we have the knowledge and skills to achieve our goals. We need to feel that we are improving and making progress.

- **Control:** We need to feel like we have autonomy over our actions and that we are masters of our fate.

Just how important are these three Cs for our wellbeing? A massive study led by Frank Martela from Helsinki University looked at over 45,000 adults across 27 European countries and found that when people feel connected, competent and in control, it is strongly related to increases in life satisfaction and senses of meaning and purpose in life (Martela et al., 2022). As you read the rest of this book, you'll notice that connection, competence and a sense of control underpin many of the key ideas and research.

Why teach happiness in schools?

It's all very well and good that positive psychology is proving that we can teach ourselves to be happier, but why on earth should it be taught in schools? Surely schools are where academic rigour and study take place, and not where we learn how to be more grateful or more mindful? What's the point of wasting the children's time reflecting on what went well for them when they need to be learning how to use relative clauses, modal verbs and the subjunctive (five years on from the first edition and I am still not entirely sure what these are!)? There can sometimes be much eye-rolling and guffawing when you talk about teaching happiness in schools. But there are several important arguments for why it should be done.

Wellbeing and attainment

If a school wants to improve the academic performance of its pupils, it should, first and foremost, focus on their happiness and wellbeing. The simple fact is that pupils with higher levels of wellbeing generally perform better at school academically (Gutman and Vorhaus, 2012). Evidence shows that schools that put in place programmes to boost pupils' social and emotional skills see an 11 per cent gain in attainment, as well as improvements in pupil behaviour (Durlak et al., 2011). Public Health England published a report in 2014 entitled 'The link between pupil health and wellbeing and attainment', and it strongly made the case for schools placing a greater focus on the wellbeing of their pupils, especially if they wanted to raise attainment. In 2020, an evidence analysis carried out by Dr Ariel Lindorff at the University of Oxford looked at over a decade's worth of research studying the link between pupil wellbeing, attainment and other non-educational outcomes. Lindorff concluded that 'there is strong international evidence… that "whole-school approaches" to promoting wellbeing can have an effect on academic attainment and have positive effects on a wide range of other educational outcomes, including mental health, self-esteem, self-efficacy, motivation, behaviour, and decreased probability of dropout.' (Oxford Impact, 2020) Conversely, low wellbeing is linked with poor academic performance at school, and children with emotional and behavioural difficulties are more likely to be excluded from school or leave without any qualifications (Parry-Langdon, 2008).

Stress, anxiety and depression in young people (and in staff)

Since the first publication of *Wellbeing In The Primary Classroom* in 2018, the mental health and wellbeing of children and teaching staff in the UK has got worse. According to comprehensive NHS Digital data (2021), rates of probable mental health disorders in six- to 16-year-olds increased from one in nine (2017) to one in six (2021). This is a significant increase. The Children's Society (2021a) 'The Good Childhood Report 2021' reported that children's happiness with life as a whole, friends, appearance and school was significantly lower in 2018–19 than when the survey began in 2009–10. Indeed, their report in 2020 showed that children in England were some of the unhappiest in Europe, scoring lowest for life satisfaction and sense of purpose (The Children's Society, 2021b).

The picture isn't much brighter for teachers either, with the latest Teacher Wellbeing Index figures showing that 77 per cent of staff experienced behavioural, psychological or physical symptoms due to their work, 72 per cent feel stressed and over half considered leaving the sector over the past two years, due to pressures on their mental health and wellbeing (Scanlan and Savill-Smith, 2021). The teaching profession in the UK has an alarming drop-out rate, with almost a third of teachers leaving the profession within the first five years of qualifying, according to government figures (this hasn't improved at all since the first edition!) (DfE, 2022a). Teacher stress is bad for pupils too, because burned-out teachers can't teach and care for them as well as they might, and so this in itself means that pupil attainment falls (Black, 2001).

A note on the pandemic

There is no doubt that the COVID-19 pandemic that took hold in 2020 has exacerbated an already troubling situation with regard to children and teachers' wellbeing. Schools in the UK remained open throughout the pandemic to look after keyworkers' children and vulnerable children during the lockdowns, often with little or no protective clothing or equipment. I certainly felt my levels of anxiety creeping up when I had to go into school – worried about whether I would catch the virus (especially before any vaccines were available) and worried about bringing it home to my family. At the peak of the pandemic, it was a very unsettling time for everyone, but especially for those working on 'the frontline' in supermarkets, hospitals, public transport and schools. However, despite the fear and uncertainty, it would be wrong to paint the picture that the pandemic worsened everyone's wellbeing.

A fascinating study by researchers at Cambridge and Oxford Universities (Soneson et al., 2022) used the OxWell Student Survey to speak with 17,000 students and their parents. It found that about one in three students' mental wellbeing stayed the same as before the pandemic, one in three found that their wellbeing worsened and one in three reported that their mental health and wellbeing actually improved during the lockdown measures. Emma Soneson, a PhD student at the Department of Psychiatry, University of Cambridge, said: 'The common narrative that the pandemic has had overwhelmingly negative effects on the lives of children and young people might not tell the full story. In fact, it seems as though a sizeable number of children and young people may have experienced what they felt was improved wellbeing during the first national lockdown of 2020.' (Quoted in University of Cambridge Research, 2022)

Why did wellbeing improve for a large group of children? Compared with their peers, a higher percentage of students reporting better wellbeing also reported decreases in bullying, improved relationships with friends and family, less loneliness, better management of schoolwork, more sleep and more exercise during lockdown compared with before.

What this shows us is that events affect people differently. It shows us that, even in terrible situations, most children and adults cope OK and some can even learn to thrive. It also shows us that we can, in the words of the researchers, learn some 'lessons from lockdown' – namely that we should be listening to children more about what works for them in terms of their learning and wellbeing.

The purpose of education and the purpose of life

When you ask parents what they want most for their children, more often than not, they will answer along the lines of 'I want them to be happy'. Indeed, YouGov polls have shown that the vast majority of parents believe that wellbeing is more important than academic attainment and that their children's wellbeing is their main priority when choosing schools (Youth Sport Trust, 2021). And, if you think about it, we as adults want the same thing for ourselves. In fact, all humans want to be happy. Regardless of race, gender, age or any other distinguishing factor, all people are striving for that aim. British philosopher David Hume argued that 'the great end of all human industry is the attainment of happiness. For this were arts invented, sciences cultivated, laws ordained, and societies modelled.' (Hume, 1826, p. 167)

So, if happiness is the thing that we all want, and we know that we can learn to be happier, it follows that schools should help to teach children the skills to live a happy life. Shouldn't this goal, above all else, be the purpose of education? A child's happiness is bigger and more important than just their academic grades. Research backs this up. One longitudinal study by the London School of Economics tracked people from childhood through to adulthood. The study wanted to work out what the best predictors were in childhood of adult happiness. The study concluded that 'the most powerful childhood predictor of adult life-satisfaction is the child's emotional health… The least powerful predictor is the child's intellectual development.' (Layard et al., 2013, p. 2) In essence, the grades that a child gets at school do not predict a happy life. Similarly, PISA (Programme for International Student Assessment – a worldwide study by the Organisation for Economic Co-operation and Development of 15-year-old school pupils' performance on mathematics, science and reading), who have started to gather data on student wellbeing for the first time, found that 'top-performing students are only slightly more satisfied with their life than students who perform at an average level. There is no clear relationship between study time and life satisfaction.' (OECD, 2017)

But if children's emotional health is key to them growing up to be happy adults, can primary schools and teachers actually influence this crucial aspect of their lives? The answer is a resounding 'yes'! In their book *The Origins of Happiness*, Clark and his colleagues present evidence that shows that 'Primary and secondary schools have major effects on the emotional wellbeing of their children… These effects of primary schools and teachers persist throughout the following five years and longer.' (Clark et al., 2018, pp. 192–3) I believe that our education system has been barking up the wrong tree for many years. With our singular obsession with academic performance data, we have lost sight of what education should really be for, and are squeezing much of the meaning and pleasure from our schools. By teaching happiness and wellbeing at school, we teach children how to: love learning; focus and work hard; look after themselves and the people around them; deal with life's difficulties; and reach their full potential. This in turn adds a greater sense of meaning and purpose to teaching and so enhances teacher wellbeing too.

Well Schools – a movement for change

There appears to be the beginning of a shift in our education system right now. Children, teachers and parents are calling for wellbeing to be at the heart of schools more and more. People are beginning to wake up to the damage that a relentless focus on exams and academic performance does to our children. A new movement called Well Schools launched in 2020. It's a grassroots movement of schools that place wellbeing at the heart of their curriculum, coming together to support one another, collaborate and share best practice. It's powered by the Youth Sport Trust and Bupa Foundation and the whole premise is that if we want the education system to change, then we must bring about that change ourselves. I'm very proud to be the Deputy Chair of the Well Schools Board, working alongside some other fantastic teachers and school leaders, including the Chairs, Lisa Fathers and Ben Levinson. I would highly recommend joining Well Schools (www.well-school.org) and being part of the movement for change.

The chief medical officer of England makes the case for Well Schools very clear: 'promoting physical and mental health in schools creates a virtuous circle reinforcing children's attainment and achievement that in turn improves their wellbeing, enabling children to thrive and achieve their full potential.' (Public Health England, 2014, p. 5) The concept of Well Schools really is a no-brainer.

How to use this book

Each chapter of this book takes a concept from fields such as positive psychology, behavioural science or neuroscience and breaks it down into two sections: 'In theory' and 'In action'.

In theory shares with you the latest scientific research and evidence behind the concept. It will show how it impacts on people's happiness and wellbeing levels. This section answers the question 'Why should I do this?' and also gives you, should you need it, evidence to show to headteachers or governors to convince them that trying these ideas is a good thing to do.

In action gives you practical ways in which you can bring the theoretical ideas to life in a primary classroom. Many of the practical ideas have come from my own teaching practice but some have come from other teachers. This section answers the question 'How can I do this?'. As you read this section, it is worth reflecting on how you could apply the lessons to your own life as well. I also share some real-life stories in the 'Tales from the classroom' sections, which come from my own or other teachers' practice, but all names have been changed to protect the identities of the children involved.

You can choose to read this book from start to finish or, if a particular idea or theme appeals to you, feel free to jump to that section of the book and try out some of the ideas in your classroom. Chapters 4, 5 and 6 are best read together, though, as they all deal with the theme of teaching children how they learn and how best to achieve their full potential.

There are also accompanying resources available to download from www.teachappy.co.uk/resources-and-downloads. Here you will find assembly PowerPoints linked to each chapter that will enhance your teaching and learning around these topics, plus a Happy classroom poster. This poster summarises 10 of the key ideas included in the book. Print it off for your classroom to remind you of what really matters!

As with any new ideas for the classroom, you may need to tweak them to suit your children, and also give them time to embed. For example, don't expect to see immediate and dramatic results when you first start to incorporate mindfulness meditation into your daily routine. Give yourself and the children time to get to know the activities and be patient. Most of all, approach any changes that you introduce with an attitude of experimentation and curiosity. In the 'Further reading and recommended resources' section of the book, I give some guidance on how you can attempt to measure pupil and staff wellbeing in your school. Not only is this useful data to collect, but it can also help you to measure the impact of the interventions that you have introduced in your class.

The aim of this book is to equip primary school staff with the knowledge and ideas to start to put wellbeing at the heart of your classroom, and also to inspire you to take action. As Tal Ben-Shahar's quote at the start of this chapter notes, if you want children to lead happier lives, you first must believe that happiness is the most important thing there is (or the 'ultimate currency', as Ben-Shahar calls it). We can either wait for our education system to change or we can begin to positively change it ourselves from the ground up. Who knows what may happen as a result?

Chapter 1
Creating a tribal classroom

If everyone is moving forward together, then success takes care of itself.

– Henry Ford

Chapter overview

In this chapter, we explore the work of psychology professor Louis Cozolino, who created the concept of the 'tribal classroom'. When we tap into our pupils' primitive social instincts, he argues, it can have powerful effects on their wellbeing and ability to learn.

In theory:	In action:
• Understand our tribal roots	• Design a team flag
• The tribal classroom	• Greetings and endings
• Sense of belonging	• Teaching social skills
• Stories and tribes	• Humour and games
• The social brain	• Residential and outdoor trips
• Attachment-based teaching	
• Adverse childhood experiences	
• Positive relationships	

In theory

Understand our tribal roots

Before we look at what tribal classrooms are, we need to understand more about our tribal history. As a species, human beings really haven't had enough time to evolve and move away from our tribal past, according to Louis Cozolino (2013). For the majority of the last 100,000 years or more, it is thought that modern humans lived in hunter-gatherer tribes of between 50 and 75 individuals. These small communities would forage for food and resources and they were held together by family relationships, rituals and the need to cooperate in order to survive (Richerson and Boyd, 1998). Tribal groups were small, based on values of cooperation, equality, fairness and cohesiveness, decision making was democratic and there were shared responsibilities. More recently, in the last 5,000 to 10,000 years, Western culture has moved from tribal- to agricultural- to industrial-based societies. It may seem that 10,000 years is a very long period of time but in terms of biological evolution it is a nanosecond.

In our modern industrialised societies, we tend to live in larger groups (in towns and cities), our society is based more on values like individualism and competition, and there tends to be more of a hierarchy and imposed rules (just look at modern schools with their CEOs, deputy CEOs, executive heads, heads, deputy heads, etc). Cozolino believes that our modern cultures often clash with, and are mismatched to, our basic social instincts and even our neurobiology and that this causes us stress, anxiety and unhappiness.

At our core, we are a tribal species and we function best and are happiest when we live and work in tribes. By creating tribal classrooms, we are able to fulfil some of our pupils' core physical and emotional needs. Therefore, Cozolino states that 'Teachers who are able to tap into the primitive social instincts of their students through attachment relationships and build tribal classrooms succeed in seemingly impossible educational situations.' (Cozolino, 2013, p. xxiv) Children's brains literally get turned on when they feel part of a tribal classroom.

The tribal classroom

But what exactly is a tribal classroom? Well, Cozolino believes that a tribal classroom would embody tribal qualities such as democratic leadership, cooperation, teamwork, equality, fairness, trust and strong personal relationships. In a tribe, everyone feels valued and has a role to play. A tribe is essentially a big family, and if we can create this atmosphere in our classrooms then children can really begin to flourish. Cozolino explains that 'Tribal teachers become loving and protective parents to their pupils, who in turn become caring and supportive siblings to one another.' (Cozolino, 2013, p. 245) This familial environment would be full of positive relationships that foster secure attachments between teacher and pupil, which in turn promote the release of the bonding hormone and neurotransmitter oxytocin (more on this later, p. 24). Therefore, teachers are central to establishing a tribal classroom environment. You would be like a tribal elder – wise, experienced, brave and fair.

Many of the pupils whom we teach have incredibly stressful home lives, so tribal classrooms purposefully create a calm, safe environment. Ridicule and shame have no place in a tribal classroom but humour and light-heartedness do. Teachers who can incorporate appropriate humour into their teaching practice can counteract the inevitable stress and tension of our education system. Tribal classrooms also include a lot of play. Research has shown that exploration and play are a core part of our natural learning and are essential to neuroplasticity (the ability of our brain to grow and change). Play activates the release of other 'happy hormones' like dopamine, serotonin and endorphins, which boost feelings of wellbeing, aid learning and foster social connectivity (Cozolino, 2013).

Sense of belonging

At the heart of the tribal classroom is having a sense of belonging. Your job as the tribal leader is to help your children to feel like they belong to something bigger than themselves. When children feel that they belong, then they will feel safe to explore and take risks. Research has shown for a long time that a sense of belonging at school is fundamental to learning (Ryan and Powelson, 1991), but a recent study by UCL (2020) showed that pupils who experience a sense of belonging tend to be happier and more confident too (as well as doing better academically, as demonstrated by previous research). Professor Kathryn Riley from UCL's Institute of Education explained that their research found 'Much about the enjoyment of learning. The emphasis is on relationships. Interventions are purposeful… We found that intentional whole-school practice can help create a climate of welcome and belonging in school for all.' (Quoted in UCL IOE, 2020)

Daniel Coyle believes that a sense of belonging is one of the key ingredients in any highly successful group. In his book *The Culture Code* (2018), he explains that in order to feel a sense of belonging, people must feel safe, connected to the people around them and that they share a future together. Importantly, he says that belonging cues (little signals that you send out to let people know they belong, such as close physical proximity, physical touch, humour, politeness, etc.) need to be continually refreshed and reinforced. In other words, fostering a sense of belonging is a constant work in progress.

Stories and tribes

Stories and storytelling are also a core feature of tribal classrooms. Storytelling is woven into the fabric of our nature and has a deep evolutionary history. The role of storytelling in tribes was for memory storage, emotional regulation and social cohesion (Cozolino, 2013). Clearly, storytelling has as much relevance for children today as it did for our ancestors. Stories enrich children's emotional vocabulary and allow them to learn from characters' moral dilemmas. In the writing and telling of their own stories, children also get to express themselves and better understand the world around them.

One recent fascinating study showed the power of stories on children's health and wellbeing (Brockington et al., 2021). Researchers studied the effects of storytelling on the physical and psychological health of children being treated in an intensive care unit. They found that, compared with an active control condition, one storytelling session with hospitalised children led to an increase in oxytocin, a reduction in cortisol and pain, and an increase in positive emotions. All of that from a single storytelling session with children in intensive care! Imagine the power that the daily storytelling sessions have on children's wellbeing in the classroom.

The social brain

It is a widely held view amongst psychologists and neuroscientists that humans possess a social brain. What this means is that our brains are shaped and sculpted significantly by our nurture and social relationships. In fact, there are certain parts of the brain, like the amygdala (see Chapter 2, Mindfulness, and Chapter 3, What went well?, for more on the amygdala), that have neurons in them that will only fire in response to other people's reactions (Ratey, 2003). Additionally, the discovery of mirror neurons by neurophysiologist Giacomo Rizzolatti also supports the idea of the social brain. Mirror neurons fire when we carry out an action or witness someone else carry out an action, and they might move us to imitate what we observe. Mirror neurons are also thought to be partly responsible for our ability to empathise with other people and feel what they are feeling. For example, when someone else laughs at a joke, even if we haven't heard the joke, we feel the urge to laugh too. Or if someone bangs their head, we might grab *our* heads and go, 'Ouch!' It is clear that our brains change in response to other people and our interactions with them.

Looking further into our evolutionary past, we begin to see why. As primates began to live in increasingly larger social groups, their brains started to get larger and more complex. These larger social groups were able to provide more dedicated childcare, stimulation and challenge to the brain, which supported its growth further (Dunbar, 1992). This laid the foundations for the development of our language, problem-solving skills and complex thinking abilities. The brains that humans have today have been grown and moulded over hundreds of thousands of years by the social groups and tribes in which they were raised.

The implication of all of this is that *how* we look after the children in our care will have a far bigger impact on their development than anything that we explicitly teach them. Psychology professor Alison Gopnik goes as far to say, 'Children actually learn more from the unconscious details of what caregivers do than from any of the conscious manipulations' (Gopnik, 2016, p. 90). In starting to design your tribal classroom, it is important to bear in mind that we need to give the children in our care something good to imitate and that the atmosphere in your tribe is crucial for their brain development and wellbeing. As tribal leaders, teachers can have a significant impact on their tribe's lives.

Attachment-based teaching

Psychologists call love 'attachment', I guess, because it sounds less problematic than 'love' and is maybe easier to measure. Either way, attachment psychologists study how young children feel about their caregivers (normally mothers in these experiments) and one way in which they do this is by separating one-year-olds from their caregivers, whilst leaving them in a room with a stranger, and then reuniting them. Generally, the children will fall into one of the following four categories of attachment:

1. securely attached
2. avoidantly attached

3. anxiously attached

4. disorganised attached.

The 'secure' children will show distress when their caregiver leaves and joy when they return. The 'avoidant' children look away when their caregiver leaves and appear ambivalent even when they return. 'Anxious' children get very distressed when separated and then continue to be inconsolable when reunited. 'Disorganised' children will often display strange behaviour like spinning around in circles or collapsing to the ground. These children often have parents who display frightened or frightening behaviour to their children and, as a result, the inner turmoil in the child causes their coping skills and even motor skills to become disorganised. Also, the worrying thing noted by psychologists about 'avoidant' children, who on the surface seem fine and not really bothered when left alone, is that when their heart rates are monitored they are actually very upset but have learned to hide their true feelings.

Attachment styles are important because they affect children's wellbeing, their ability to learn and their behaviour. They tend to follow us into adulthood too and shape our future relationships. The behaviour of insecurely attached children can often be the expression of anxiety and fear. So, what looks like disobedience and 'bad' behaviour on the surface may actually be their way of coping with difficult feelings and an inability to regulate their emotions (Cozolino, 2013). Our classrooms will be full of an array of children (and teachers) with varying attachment styles, but the good news is that tribal teachers and classrooms can create a secure base for all children so that they feel supported and safe. Cozolino says that 'Children learn best when they feel protected and connected. The goal of attachment-based teaching is to have each child move from feeling vulnerable, frightened and unimportant to feeling protected, cared for and valued – a state… that optimises learning.' (2013, p. 241) Tribal classrooms are essential for promoting secure attachments amongst their pupils because they foster strong, positive relationships where children feel safe and cared for.

Adverse childhood experiences

When children don't come from secure and loving homes, or when their early lives are blighted by trauma or severe adversity, they are more likely to develop insecure attachments styles and suffer poorer outcomes generally. Adverse childhood experiences, or ACEs, can be things like growing up in a home with domestic violence, experiencing substance misuse, parental separation or growing up in poverty. ACEs can underpin poor educational attainment, health-harming behaviours and anti-social and criminal behaviour in adolescence, and can significantly increase the chance of developing a mental illness. When a child experiences ACEs, their future can look particularly bleak.

However, some reassuring research came out from Bangor University in conjunction with Public Health Wales, looking into what protective factors developed children's resilience in the face of multiple ACEs (Hughes et al, 2018) . They discovered that if children had certain protective factors, their risk of developing a mental illness was more than halved, which is a huge buffer against the stressors that they were experiencing. The main protective factors were:

- having a relationship with at least one safe, trusted adult
- supportive friends
- regular participation in sports.

These are all things that schools provide children with on a regular basis and are at the heart of tribal classrooms, and it shows what a huge source of support good schools can provide to children with the greatest need.

This was a point emphasised by Peter Fonagy, Chief Executive of the Anna Freud National Centre for Children and Families, in an interview with the *Times Education Supplement*. He was asked what teachers can do for children who experience trauma and adversity and seem shut off to learning. He explained that 'there's no point in any teacher becoming an amateur counsellor or psychotherapist… Even when a child is mentally unwell, you're not there to heal them. That's not your role.' (Fonagy, in Amass, 2022) Instead, he states that the best thing that teachers can do is to be calm, to listen and to have a well-organised classroom where there is connectedness and where hope, happiness and optimism are cultivated. I find Fonagy's final piece of advice very reassuring, and it's something that we all need to remember: 'Just by your class functioning well, you're actually helping these kids to structure their own minds. You can just do your job and you're helping.' (In Amass, 2022)

Positive relationships

Ultimately, creating a tribal classroom is about establishing and investing in positive relationships between the teaching adults and the children, and between the children themselves. These are relationships based on trust, honesty, support, kindness, love, friendship and teamwork. Positive relationships have been a core part of our survival as a species and the backbone of tribes. Writing in the late nineteenth century about human evolution, Charles Darwin stated that 'those communities which included the greatest number of the most sympathetic members would flourish best and rear the greatest number of offspring' (Darwin, 1871, p. 163). To foster positive relationships, we need to be mindful about how much criticism we give children in relation to the amount of praise that we give them. Studies by relationship expert John Gottman show that successful relationships have an average ratio of five to one in terms of positive to negative interactions (Gottman, 1994). The Institute of Child Education and Psychology (ICEP) notes that, for children, this ratio should probably be even higher for them to flourish, and we should aim for about seven or eight positive interactions for every negative one (ICEP, Module 2, p. 13).

Not only do positive relationships aid survival in our species, but they also positively impact our health and even help us to live longer. Studies show that just being around supportive others can have a huge impact on our health and can reduce blood pressure, stress hormones and the risk of getting ill (Cozolino, 2013). Positive relationships also promote the release of the 'happy hormone', oxytocin, in our brains. Oxytocin is often called the 'love' or 'tend and befriend' hormone and is fundamental in creating secure attachments between children and their caregivers. Mothers' bodies are flooded with oxytocin when they give birth, as it helps them to bond with their newborn babies and is necessary for the production of breast milk. It promotes feelings of trust and empathy, and has been shown to reduce levels of anxiety. People who are administered oxytocin seem to be more trusting, and it makes them more willing to share and cooperate (Gopnik, 2016). There is no doubt that positive relationships would have been key in the development of our social brain and in the survival of our tribal ancestors, and they are crucial for tribal classrooms today.

In action

I am certain that many great teachers naturally create tribal classrooms without even realising that this is what they are doing. It is instinctive for these teachers to create tribal classrooms for the very reason that it is woven into our DNA. It just feels right and natural to create a sense of belonging in your classroom. What I am proposing is that, rather than this being a happy by-product of good teaching, we make this a conscious, intentional and planned part of our teaching practice. Taking Cozolino's messages on board, here are a few ways in which you can create a tribal classroom in your school.

Design a team flag

Developing a sense of team in your class can be a great way to bring out children's tribal instincts. Here's how you could do this by creating a team flag:

- At the beginning of a school year, get your new class to think about what makes a good team (this is your version of a tribe). Discuss some ideas and then show a video montage of one of the most successful teams around – Team GB. The great thing about Team GB is that it is full of inspiring role models from both genders and is culturally diverse.

- After watching a highly emotive Team GB montage (there are quite a few on YouTube, but my new favourite is: **www.youtube.com/watch?v=yS0iSnVx-Xc&t=1s**), brainstorm the qualities and values that a good team needs. Typically, the children come up with ideas like 'teamwork', 'friendship', 'kindness', 'effort', 'love', 'trust', 'honesty', 'perseverance' and 'resilience'.

- Scribe these on the board as the children call them out. Then tell your class that, like Team GB, they are a team. 'We are now Team XXXX,' I normally proclaim proudly. (Team Year 4 Green, Team Year 2, Team Picasso and Team Monet are some of my previous teams.)

- Tell them that any great team needs a team flag and that they are going to make their own. Then ask each child to choose one value from the board that really means something to them and to write it in bold on a piece of paper, and fill their page with colour and patterns. You want this to be as eye-catching as possible, as this is your team flag and it represents who you are!

- It really doesn't matter if more than one child writes 'love' or 'teamwork', but I do try to encourage children to choose something else that they like if I can see too many instances of 'kindness' in the room (not that you can ever have too much kindness, of course). Once each child has finished their part of the flag, piece all of the parts together and you have one large, eye-catching, unique team flag! See Figure 1.1 for an example.

Now, the flag is just the beginning but it represents the values of your new team and family, and gives your tribe a sense of identity. It's what some experts would call a 'symbol of unity'. When I teach,

Figure 1.1: *Team Year 4's flag*

I will constantly refer to our flag and our team. Every time I want my class's attention, I'll say, 'Right, Team Monet, listen up!' I do this to remind each team member that they are part of something bigger than themselves, and that they belong. I also use the team flag to address poor behaviour choices and to reinforce the positive values and behaviours that I want to see. The flag stays up throughout the year on display in our class, as a symbol of our values and that every member has a part to play in the success of our team.

Tales from the classroom

'Who's that, Mrs Chadwick?' piped up Iris, the first to be brave enough to ask.

It was the first day of autumn term and my new Year 2 class were charged with nervous excitement. Iris was referring to the slightly mournful stuffed giraffe that was sat on the edge of my desk.

'This is Jeremy. I thought he might like to join our team – what do you think? Shall we have him as our team mascot?' I asked.

The class exploded with enthusiasm! I hadn't expected this reaction to what, in my eyes, was a rather sad-looking stuffed giraffe, but I was delighted. A rather dysfunctional Year 1 had left these kids wobbly. They weren't ready to trust each other and didn't have the skills to be a team yet. As a school, we had taken Adrian's suggestion to start the year building team values, which was why I had introduced a stuffed giraffe to my class.

He quickly became our hero, our comfort blanket, our glue. My excitable and loud Year 2 class began to gently carry him to all our important moments: the Daily Mile, where he was bounced along between the kids as they ran; team photos; our first class trip; birthday assemblies for the children who shied away from attention. He was the subject of stories, given hand-made gifts at Christmas and when 'mislaid' (gone in the washing machine!), missing-in-action posters were created. Our team flag had him front and centre. The teacher should hold a pivotal role in the team culture, but so too should their sidekick. Jeremy was mine and he brought the very best empathy, resilience and strength out of my class in a way that I could never have imagined. When lockdown hit, I used the daily adventures of Jeremy to keep our spirits up and to keep the kids entertained. Some of their best writing was in the form of letters telling Jeremy all about their lockdown experiences. When I got the same class back in Year 4, the children fondly embraced him back into the team. They were stronger now and didn't need him to endorse them, but every now and again when their strength wavered they could be found sitting reading a book in the book corner with one arm wrapped around his neck, calm and happy.

Kate Chadwick, teacher, primary school in St Albans

Greetings and endings

If we're trying to establish a sense of family in our tribal classrooms, I feel that it is really important for all of your pupils to experience a warm and positive greeting in the morning and a fond farewell at the end of the day. These are examples of 'belonging cues' that need to be continually reinforced every day. Why not try these ideas when greeting your class in the morning?

- Greet your pupils at the door of the classroom with a smile and by saying their name. Not only are smiles contagious, so it is an easy way to spread some positivity throughout your tribe at the start of the day, but they also signal to the children that they are safe and that you can be trusted. Using their first names is a powerful way of connecting with individual tribe members and signals to them that they have been noticed and that they matter.

- You can mix your greetings up with a handshake, a 'high-five' or a 'fist-bump', as the power of touch can be really important (you work in a primary school so you're allowed to have fun with your tribe!). Remember the happy hormone, oxytocin? Well, it can be released when people touch hands together, so greeting your pupils in this way can release the hormone that helps them to feel calm, secure and connected. A positive greeting in the morning sets the tone for the rest of the day.

Endings are crucial too, especially when the day has been difficult for some of your tribe. If people's days end on a negative, even if it was largely positive overall, they will generally rate it and remember it as a bad day. Conversely, 'peak-end' theory demonstrates that if endings are positive, people will rate the overall experience as positive even if, on average, the experience was neutral or even negative at times (Kahneman et al., 1993). So try to end your day positively by experimenting with these ideas:

- End your day reading a chapter or two from a great story. Nothing conjures up an image of a tribe more than being gathered around a campfire, listening to tales of the past, so always bring your class together for a story. It's great when a chapter ends with a cliffhanger, as your tribe will be desperate to find out what happens next and will look forward to story time again with anticipation!

- You could play live music videos or a funny performance poem (Michael Rosen is my go-to) to end the day – just to get their positive emotions pumping and to end the day on a high.

- If one of your tribe has not had such a great day in terms of their behaviour, it is really important to remind them of the team flag and the values that they are expected to uphold, but also that tomorrow is a new day and a fresh start. Putting your arm around their shoulder and reminding them of the positive choices that they had made in the day reinforces the fact that you care about them, that their day was not entirely bad and that you have high expectations of them to which you know they can rise. This allows you to maintain boundaries but you're doing it in a positive way.

Teaching social skills

There will be children in your tribe who regularly make poor choices and who find it difficult to fit in. The most important thing for these children is not to give up on them. Yes, they will take up most of your time. Yes, they will push your buttons. And yes, they will keep making the same mistakes despite pep talks, encouragement and constant reminders about making the right choices. But, as the saying goes, 'the children who need the most love will ask for it in the most unloving ways'. Often, these children simply have not had the nurture, upbringing or positive role models in their lives to help them to develop the social skills to thrive in a tribal classroom.

Helping these children find their way and feel part of the tribe will be far more important and useful for their lives than teaching them how to use subordinate clauses. In such circumstances, it has been shown to be beneficial to directly teach social skills to children (Ratey, 2003), and you could try these ideas:

- Set aside time each week for your class to play card and board games. All children will learn and practise the skills of taking turns, sharing, listening and responding, as well as how to win and lose graciously. Games are also great for developing cognitive skills, as children have to learn the rules and then develop strategies to win.

- Use drama and role-play to act out different social situations. It could be practising how to politely ask others to join a game in the playground, or how to deal with another child who is being mean to you. When children are put in role-play social situations and then rehearse their different responses, their brains are learning how to handle those situations in the future.

- When reading your class story at the end of the day, be sure to discuss any social situations in which characters find themselves, where they may be experiencing a problem or dilemma. Get your children to put themselves in the characters' shoes and ask: 'What would you do in that situation?' Getting children to see others' perspectives is a key part of developing empathy, a crucial social skill.

Humour and games

Successful tribal classrooms definitely incorporate fun and laughter in an appropriate way into the school day. I think it is important that teachers don't take themselves too seriously, and find opportunities to laugh with the children and at themselves. I'm certainly not proposing that you become the class clown and just try to make wisecracks all day, but having a sense of humour shows that you are human, and by sharing laughter with your tribe, you can bring everyone together in an inclusive way. Here are three simple games to play with your class:

- **Call my bluff**: This is one of the best getting-to-know-you games to try at the start of the year. Each child and adult in the classroom writes down two lies about themselves and one truth. The lies shouldn't be too obvious, like 'I once flew to the moon wearing a Donald Trump onesie'. Everyone takes a turn to read out their three personal 'facts' and the teacher has to guess which one is the lie. If the teacher gets it wrong, one point to the class, but if they get it correct, one point to the teacher. The children then get to guess their teacher's lie. This game can be really funny and is a great way of finding out more about your tribe. You also get to know who the really good liars are, which can be insightful! You can play this game at various points in the year, when it should be harder to hoodwink your tribe as they get to know you even more.

- **Pass the hug**: When teaching a tribe of six-year-olds, I created a game called 'pass the hug'. The children sat in a circle with their eyes closed. I would touch someone on their shoulder and they had to pass a hug to the person next to them. The hug would get passed round until it reached the start person again, who then called out 'Stop!'. The children then had to guess who had passed the first hug. Now it's not the most challenging game, but I invented it because I knew that hugging releases oxytocin, and that the children found it hilarious to hug one another. Seeing the children beaming with smiles, anticipating the hug, and then giggling away when someone hugged them was great. The children often asked to play this game – usually at the start of a maths lesson! It's a nice game to play near the end of a busy week.

- **Bounce buzz**: Another popular game that I play with the children is my version of the maths game 'Fizz buzz'. In 'Bounce buzz', the children stand in a circle and someone starts with a large, soft, bouncy ball. As the ball gets passed around the circle, each child says a number in sequence, starting from 'one'. When they get to a multiple of five, they don't say the number; instead, they bounce the ball, say 'bounce' and pass the ball to the next person, who carries on with the counting. When they get to a multiple of ten, they don't say the number; instead, they bounce the ball twice, saying, 'bounce buzz'. If you make a mistake (e.g. by not bouncing the ball or by saying the number instead of 'bounce' or 'bounce buzz'), you sit down and are out of this round. As the children get good at playing this version, start to make the game harder. You can move to passing the ball randomly around the circle (if it's a poor throw or you drop the ball, you're out). You can then introduce rules, like you can't pass to the person next to you or pass back to the person who just threw to you. You could change the multiples by using threes and sixes.

You can then move onto 'Super-speed bounce buzz', where the children are given very little time to catch the ball and pass it on to the next person whilst correctly saying the right number or phrase. The game can end when there are, say, five people left in, or it can go down to having a single winner. The great thing about this game is that it is fast, frenetic and fun. It definitely improves children's numerical, throwing, catching and coordination skills. Plus, everyone can succeed at this game – the children who win are not always the best mathematicians or throwers and catchers. And if anyone really dominates in this game, you can always ask them to put their stronger throwing hand behind their back and get them to play one-handed.

Humour and games can be a great way in which to punctuate your day. They can galvanise a tribe together, raise morale and reduce any stress or tension. I would recommend that all teachers add more of these elements into their teaching practice.

Residential and outdoor trips

Another way in which to bring the inner tribesperson out of you and your class is to go on a residential trip. These trips often involve lots of time spent outdoors in natural settings, with various activities such as canoeing, abseiling, den building, orienteering and team building.

They are a fantastic way to bring your tribe together and push them out of their comfort zones (see Chapter 5 for more on this). Not only do the children become more physically active and get back in touch with nature, but they also get to learn in a novel and non-conventional way. The children always learn lots about themselves on these trips and discover talents and inner resources that they never knew they had. I often see sides to my children that I didn't know existed when on residential trips, and it is often the children who struggle academically and behaviourally in class that really shine. Figure 1.2 shows some of Team Monet posing for the camera en-route to a nearby stream for pond-dipping. I am a big advocate of residential trips and have enjoyed every single one I have been on.

Figure 1.2: *Team Monet on their residential trip*

If you don't feel that your class is old enough for a residential trip (the youngest age group I have taken away is a class of nine-year-olds) or budgets won't allow it, then a day trip to an outdoor activity centre can be a great alternative. Here, the children may get to experience activities like high-rope tree climbing, where they navigate around a course with various obstacles in the way (like cargo nets and zip-wires). Again, the point is to get children outdoors and back in touch with the hunter-gatherer in them. The shared experience of getting around what can be quite a scary obstacle course will foster the tribal spirit amongst your team.

What do tribal classrooms feel like from a child's perspective?

A teacher from the British School in the Netherlands, Rhiannon Phillips-Bianco, contacted me to say that she had been doing a lot around fostering a sense of team in her class. They had made a team flag with their values and every day they worked on bringing those values to life. She wanted to share what a nine-year-old child in her class had written about her experience of being in that class: 'When people think of a class, they think of a room of children in a school. I think of my class at JSL as much more than that. The children I sit next to, we have a bond. We trust each other, we help each other, we learn together. We know we can ask each other for help. We are definitely more than a room of children.' I think that perfectly sums up what it means to feel part of a tribal classroom.

Key points

- Humans are an innately tribal species. Our ancestors lived in tribal communities based on familial ties, cooperation and cohesion. We still have our roots firmly planted in our tribal past.

- Tribal classrooms tap into children's primitive social instincts and create safe and secure learning environments, where children feel that they belong and are able to take risks, play and explore. This turns on their brains for learning and fosters wellbeing.

- Adverse childhood experiences can hamper children's wellbeing and ability to learn, but trusting relationships with adults, supportive friends and regular participation in sports can develop resilience and protect against poor mental health.

- Create a sense of tribe in your classroom by discussing the values and attributes of good teams and making your own class flag. Work towards becoming a good team.

- Ensure that your day starts with a positive greeting and ending. Even if behaviour has been challenging, find ways in which to address the behaviour that show that you have high expectations and that you care.

- You may need to directly teach social skills to some children but, ultimately, the best teaching comes from modelling the behaviour that you wish to see. Your tribe will imitate the example you set as the tribal leader.

- Play more games with your class to galvanise your tribe, inject some fun into your day and reduce any stress or tension that may arise in the school week.

- Tap into your pupils' inner tribespeople by taking them on an outdoor residential trip if time and budget permit. At the very least, get them outdoors more and back in touch with nature.

Chapter 2
Mindfulness

*If every eight-year-old in the world is taught meditation, we will
eliminate violence from the world in one generation.*
    – His Holiness the Dalai Lama

Chapter overview

There has recently been an explosion in mindfulness
interventions in schools, workplaces and business. But does
mindfulness live up to the hype? In this chapter, we will look
at what mindfulness is, how it can benefit your pupils and
how you can authentically introduce mindfulness practices
into your classroom.

In theory	In action
• Origins of Western mindfulness	• Embodying mindfulness
• What is mindfulness?	• Children's response to mindfulness
• Autopilot and mind-wandering	• Meditating with your children
• Looking inside the brain	• Mindfulness practices:
• The stress response – fight or flight	◦ *Breathing buddies*
• Anxiety, depression and mindfulness	◦ *Tummy and chest*
• Children and mindfulness	◦ *Walking and listening*
	◦ *Taking a quick selfie*

In theory

Origins of Western mindfulness

In Massachusetts Medical School in the late 1970s, a radical doctor named Jon Kabat-Zinn was experimenting with a new way for treating patients who suffered with chronic pain, illness and stress. His patients had largely been failed by modern medicine, which hadn't been able to alleviate their acute suffering. Kabat-Zinn had created an eight-week course, *Mindfulness Based Stress Reduction (MBSR)*, which involved patients meditating, performing mindful movement exercises and relating to their thoughts, feelings and body sensations in an entirely new way. Surprisingly, the MBSR course had profound positive effects for the patients, and they were at last able to regain some control of their health and attain some peace of mind. Although mindfulness has its roots in 2,500-year-old Buddhist teachings (and other contemplative traditions of Asia), Kabat-Zinn's MBSR course was entirely secular and it has spawned an explosion of mindfulness-based courses and interventions in the West. One such variation of MBSR is *Mindfulness Based Cognitive Therapy (MBCT)*, which was developed by three scientists who wanted to help treat people with recurrent depression.

The fact that MBSR and MBCT courses were introduced into Western medicine by doctors and scientists rather than spiritual yogi-type figures (like Transcendental Meditation, for example) might explain why it has been so well received and accepted into mainstream Western culture. MBSR courses are now subject to numerous clinical trials and studies around the world, and the University of Oxford set up the Oxford Mindfulness Centre in 2008, which offers training in and research into mindfulness interventions. The National Institute of Health and Care Excellence in the UK (NICE – a body that advises the NHS on which drugs and interventions to use) recommended MBCT in 2004 to treat people with depression, and in 2009 the recommendation was updated and given 'key priority' status. There is even the Mindfulness All Party Parliamentary Group (MAPPG) in the UK government, which was set up in 2014 to review the evidence and best practice of mindfulness and how it can affect policy decisions based on its findings. With so much time, effort and money being invested into mindfulness on a national and global scale, there is no doubt that mindfulness interventions are firmly part of mainstream Western culture and that it is here to stay and not just a passing fad.

What is mindfulness?

Mindfulness has become very on-trend in educational settings in recent years and is becoming more mainstream. However, some mindfulness practitioners worry that a 'McMindfulness' culture is taking root and that quick fixes are being introduced by teachers who have no proper training or background in mindfulness. Although teachers may be meditating with their classes, they do not know exactly what mindfulness is, the critics argue.

One of the best definitions that I have come across that neatly sums up what mindfulness is comes from Mindful Nation UK (a report published in 2015 by the MAPPG), which states that:

> 'Mindfulness means paying attention to what's happening in the present moment in the mind, body and external environment, with an attitude of curiosity and kindness. It is typically cultivated by a range of simple meditation practices, which aim to bring a greater awareness of thinking, feeling and behaviour patterns, and to develop the capacity to manage these with greater skill and compassion. This is found to lead to an expansion of choice and capacity in how to meet and respond to life's challenges, and therefore live with greater wellbeing, mental clarity and care for yourself and others.' (MAPPG, 2015, p. 13)

So, in its simplest form, mindfulness is about being aware of what is happening in the here and now. To 'be mindful', according to Rick

Hanson, means 'having a good control over your attention: you can place your attention wherever you want and it stays there; when you want to shift it to something else, you can.' (Hanson, 2009, p. 177) Now this may sound very simple, but the fact is that our minds do not just stay where we want them to. They drag up memories from the past or they fast-forward to the future and, often, we do not take in what is happening right now. Therefore, mindfulness can also be seen as a type of mind-training, which strengthens the attentional- and emotional-regulating parts of the brain.

Autopilot and mind-wandering

Our minds have an amazing ability to automate many parts of our lives using habits. If we did not have this ability to learn from repetition, we'd still be trying to remember how to dress ourselves every time we woke up in the morning. When we operate on 'autopilot', it means that we can do things automatically like driving our cars or eating our food, with our minds free to think about other things (like that lesson after break that we haven't planned yet!). But, over time, we can give over too much control to autopilot and we can end up living most of our lives without full awareness of what we are doing. We can miss a lot of life's richness, and many small moments, like the smile of a grateful pupil or a reassuringly warm summer breeze, can simply pass us by.

When operating on autopilot, we often enter a state known as 'mind-wandering' – with our minds not focused on what we are doing. Two psychologists at Harvard University, Matthew Killingsworth and Daniel Gilbert, discovered that, on average, people spend about 47 per cent of their waking hours in a mind-wandering state (Killingsworth and Gilbert, 2010). More importantly, they found that this mind-wandering depletes us and lowers our levels of happiness: 'A human mind is a wandering mind and a wandering mind is an unhappy mind.' (Killingsworth and Gilbert, 2010, p. 932) Numerous studies have shown that mindfulness meditation is an antidote to this mind-wandering malaise. By strengthening certain parts of the brain, mindfulness helps to bring us back into the present moment more often and gives us greater control over our attention.

Looking inside the brain

One of the most interesting discoveries about mindfulness is how it can physically change our brains. With the benefit of MRI scanners and EEG machines, neuroscientists are able to track what happens inside the brain when people take part in mindful meditation practices. One of the leading neuroscientists in this field is Professor Richard Davidson. By spying inside our brains, Davidson found that when people were angry, upset, worried or depressed, an area of the brain known as the right pre-frontal cortex lights up (the neurons in this part of the brain are firing away). However, when people are in a positive mood, joyful, enthusiastic and upbeat, Davidson saw that there was more neural activity in the left pre-frontal cortex (Davidson, 2004).

Davidson and Kabat-Zinn teamed up to monitor what might happen to a group of biotech workers' brains after they had taken part in an eight-week MBSR course (Davidson et al., 2003). Amazingly, there had been a significant shift of brain activity towards the left pre-frontal cortex, so these workers reported feeling happier and far less stressed than the control group. Another unexpected consequence of the MBSR course was that the workers' immune systems became significantly stronger too – they had more antibodies in their blood when given a flu jab, compared to the control group.

The stress response – fight or flight

A tiny yet extremely powerful part of the brain, known as the amygdala, is often behind a lot of our stress and unhappiness. When we sense a threat or we're fearful or anxious about something, the amygdala kicks in and prepares us to either fight the threat or run away from it. The amygdala is a 'primeval' part of our brain and would have been crucial for keeping us alive during our hunter-gatherer days (see Chapter 3, What went well, to find out more) but it also means that it can be very simplistic in how it interprets danger. For example, it makes no distinction whatsoever between a real threat, like a dangerous dog trying to attack you, or an imagined threat, like the thought about a looming deadline. It treats both scenarios in exactly the same way and prepares your body for the stress response, often referred to as 'fight or flight'.

The stress response broadly works as follows: a threat is sensed by the amygdala and it sends signals to other parts of the body to prepare for 'fight or flight'. Our heart rate increases to pump more blood and oxygen to our muscles. The adrenal glands release the stress hormone cortisol into our blood stream. Cortisol makes you hypervigilant; it halts your immune system, stops your ability to learn and prevents you from relaxing. According to psychotherapist Sue Gerhardt, it is as if cortisol is having the following conversation with other bodily systems: 'Stop what you're doing, guys! This is an emergency! Don't waste time fighting bugs. Don't waste time learning or connecting new pathways. Don't relax! I want all your attention on this problem!' (Gerhardt, 2014, pp. 61– 62) This works brilliantly when the threat is real and it enables us to escape from it and, therefore, to survive. Once the threat has passed, our bodies can return to normal – the extra cortisol is reabsorbed into the body, our heart rate slows back down and we can think clearly again. Except that this doesn't always happen. If we continue to feel stressed or threatened, the stress response keeps working and cortisol stays in our system. If too much cortisol is released, or when it is released unnecessarily, it can cause damage to our brains and bodies, even killing brain cells (Davidson and Begley, 2012).

You can see how the everyday stresses of home and school life can mean that many of our pupils may be operating on a kind of 'fight or flight' basis for a lot of their lives. Imagine a pupil who hasn't done their homework and thinks that they will get in trouble. Or a pupil about to sit a maths test who feels unprepared and worried about failing. The amygdala will be firing away with these threats, even though they are not life-threatening. Over time, if we stay in this hypervigilant state of arousal, it can deplete us. We start to get ill more frequently, we struggle to learn as well and we can start to feel that we don't have the inner resources for the challenges of our lives. If we're not careful, we can end up suffering periods of acute anxiety and depression.

Anxiety, depression and mindfulness

But it is not all doom and gloom. More and more studies are showing that mindfulness can really help us to cope with the increased stresses of daily life.

In the UK, one of the leading experts in mindfulness-based interventions is Professor Mark Williams. Williams was one of the three scientists who adapted Kabat-Zinn's MBSR course and created MBCT to help patients who suffer with anxiety and depression. Williams and his colleagues have found that MBCT can significantly reduce the chances of suffering depression (Williams and Penman, 2011). Impressively, it reduces the chance of a relapse of depression by about 40 to 50 per cent in people who have experienced three or more previous episodes of depression. Another study showed that people who came off their antidepressants and did an eight-week MBCT course instead did as well or better than those who stayed on their medication.

Why does mindfulness have such a positive effect on levels of stress, anxiety and depression? Well, it has a lot to do with the physical changes that take place in the brain when you meditate regularly. As we discovered earlier, there is a shift in brain activity away from a part of the brain that processes negative thoughts and emotions. If our thoughts can be a trigger for the stress response, and if we are having fewer negative or worrying thoughts, then we will not be reacting in the 'fight or flight' mode so much. Davidson also believes that mindfulness can create new neuronal pathways in the brain that change how we respond to stress, so that when we experience a stressful situation, it will get processed in our frontal cortex but fewer of the signals reach our amygdala (Davidson and Begley, 2012). In fact, studies have shown that there is less overall activity in the amygdala in experienced meditators. Over time, this boosts our levels of resilience and our ability to cope with stress, rather than being overwhelmed by it.

Children and mindfulness

There is one big caveat to the research above, and that is that it was all performed on adults and not children. But there is a growing body of research and evidence showing the positive effects of mindfulness on young people in line with the adult evidence.

One study looked at the impact of an eight-week MBSR course on 102 children aged four to 18 with a wide range of mental health issues, and they reported significantly reduced symptoms of anxiety, depression and distress, and increased self-esteem and better-quality sleep. At a three-month follow-up, the pupils who practised the most showed improved levels of anxiety and depression compared to those who did not (MAPPG, 2015). With mindfulness, the adage 'practice makes progress' holds true. Another study by Professor Willem Kuyken in 2013 reported that teenagers who had completed a mindfulness intervention course (the *.b curriculum* created by the Mindfulness in Schools Project) had significantly lower levels of depressive symptoms and stress and greater wellbeing (Kuyken et al., 2013).

Alongside this, when cognitive neuroscientist Dusana Dorjee was at Bangor University, she studied the impact of a mindfulness course for primary school children (the *Paws.b curriculum* created by the Mindfulness in Schools Project). Dorjee's findings show that a mindfulness intervention at primary school can significantly reduce negative emotions and improve metacognition (i.e. higher-order thinking skills or the ability to be aware of your own thoughts)

(Vickery and Dorjee, 2016). More recently, Dorjee's research has shown that children in Year 6 report that mindfulness gives them an increased ability to regulate their emotions (Hutchinson et al., 2018). Indeed, I took part in a mindfulness research project at the primary school in which I teach. Portsmouth University psychology undergraduate Emily Main conducted the research, which showed a significant positive correlation between a mindfulness intervention and increased emotional self-regulation, compared to the control group (Main, 2017).

Dr Darren Dunning at Cambridge University's Cognition and Brain Sciences Unit carried out a meta-analysis of randomised controlled trials into whether mindfulness-based programmes improve the cognitive skills, behaviour and mental health of children and teenagers (Dunning et al., 2022). He and his colleagues found that mindfulness training, when compared to passive control groups (business as usual), showed benefits in reducing anxiety, stress and negative behaviour, and in improving attention, executive functioning and social behaviour. When comparing mindfulness training to active control groups, positive results were confined to reducing ratings of anxiety and stress only. Dunning concluded that mindfulness training shows promise in terms of improving anxiety and stress, and future research should involve young people in co-designing mindfulness programmes that are accessible and engaging.

The MYRIAD Project

In 2022, one of the largest ever randomised control trials looking into the effects of mindfulness-based interventions in secondary schools published its results. This was a six-year study involving around 28,000 teens, over 100 schools and 650 teachers at baseline. News outlets were quick to write headlines, like the following from the BBC, when the results were released: 'School mindfulness lessons don't work for teens, study finds' (Roberts, 2022). This was unhelpful because it didn't paint the full picture at all. This is what the MYRIAD Project actually found:

The positives

- Mindfulness seemed to improve the school climate and a better school climate is associated with improved mental health.
- Teachers who received the mindfulness training showed improved wellbeing and experienced less burnout.
- Mindfulness worked best for those students who engaged with the practices inside and outside of school.
- The best teachers of mindfulness had students who practised more and enjoyed improvements in their mental health.

The negatives

- Over 80 per cent of the teenagers didn't engage with the mindfulness practices outside of the lessons.
- Overall, mindfulness was shown to be no more effective than normal PSHE lessons.
- Mindfulness was shown to be hard to implement well in secondary schools.
- The mindfulness lessons were unhelpful overall for teens with pre-existing mental health problems.

What should we take from this study? I believe that it highlights what we have known for a long time about good teaching, regardless of the subject: namely, that high-quality teacher training is important for having competent teachers who can deliver curricula to a high standard; that one size does not fit all; that knowing our pupils well means that we can tailor our curriculum and delivery to ensure that we do no harm and ensure a high level of pupil buy-in; and, finally, that to benefit from something and improve, being engaged and practising regularly are essential.

In action

Good teachers have always incorporated 'quiet' times during their day, so children have a chance to be still and reflect. But as primary education has become more pressurised and exam-focused over the years, this 'quiet time' can easily become lost as schools view it as lost 'learning' time. Below I give some practical ways to incorporate more stillness and mindfulness into your day to support children's learning and emotional wellbeing.

Embodying mindfulness

The best way in which to incorporate mindfulness into your classroom is to establish your own personal mindfulness practice. My first experience of mindfulness was during my first year of teaching. This was an incredibly stressful time for me – not only was I juggling the demands of university projects and deadlines but I was also teaching a very lively group of ten-year-olds and, if I'm perfectly honest, I didn't have a clue what I was doing! So, I undertook a four-week online mindfulness course (**www.bemindful.co.uk**) run by the Mental Health Foundation UK. At the start of the course, I had to take a stress test and scored 21 out of 40. My stress levels were slightly below the average, which was 23 out of 40. I couldn't believe that my stress levels were deemed average – I was struggling to sleep at night, my appetite had gone and I dreaded going into school most days! But, according to Mark Williams, stress levels that were deemed 'chronic' in the 1950s are deemed 'average' now (Williams and Penman, 2011, p. 52). Sadly, to be chronically stressed is now the norm.

However, as I was to discover, the mindfulness course dramatically changed my relationship with my stress. I followed the programme (which was a condensed version of an eight-week MBSR course) and meditated daily, performing body scans and mindful movement (a body scan is where you slowly scan through

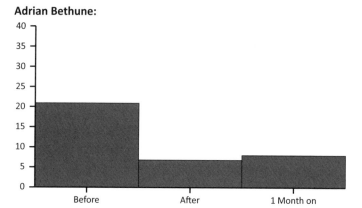

Adrian Bethune:

Figure 2.1: *A graph showing a dramatic fall in my stress levels after completing my mindfulness course (reproduced with kind permission from Wellmind Media)*

various parts of your body, bringing your full attention to each part, and you notice what sensations are there; mindful movement exercises are normally based on hatha yoga practices – you move slowly and deliberately, bringing your full attention to your body as it moves), and sometimes kept a record of the positive and negative thoughts and feelings that I was having. By the time I had completed the course, I was invited to take the stress test again and my stress levels had dropped by an impressive 66 per cent (see Figure 2.1). I was also sleeping better at night, my appetite had returned and, best of all, I was enjoying teaching and felt happier. Wider research confirms mindfulness could be exactly what teachers need to help them deal with the complex demands of teaching. A systematic review of mindfulness interventions for school staff by Yoon-Suk Hwang et al. (2017) showed staff experience reductions in stress and burnout and improvements in wellbeing. Hwang concluded, 'Those who practice mindfulness are better for it'.

So, my advice to teachers is to give mindfulness a go yourselves. You have nothing to lose. There is also the little matter of authenticity. You cannot hope to cultivate a greater sense of awareness and calm in your class if you are flapping around wildly at school, stressed out of your mind. Claire Kelly, Director at the Mindfulness in Schools Project, puts it well when she says, 'If you are not living the mindfulness principles yourself, the kids will know. If you teach them a lovely mindfulness lesson and then go and kick the photocopier in the corridor, they will notice.' (Quoted in Jenkin, 2014)

Children's response to mindfulness

From my experience of meditating with children, the response from them and their parents has been overwhelmingly positive. Here is some of the feedback from the children whom I have taught:

> 'I feel relaxed and that I'm not going to get into trouble.' Mojeed, 6
>
> 'I feel really good because I relax my brain.' Nancy, 7
>
> 'I feel happy because it calms me down.' Dexter, 6
>
> 'I like it because I'm normally sleepy in the morning but it wakes me up.' Lara, 7
>
> 'Mindfulness helps me when I get nervous or when I can't sleep.' Olivia, 9
>
> 'Whenever I meditate my day is calm, and so am I.' Jamie, 9
>
> 'I love meditation, it helps me do my work.' Lucy, 8
>
> 'It helps me a great deal when I struggle with my work and at home.' Zak, 9
>
> 'I feel calm and relaxed, like I don't have a worry in the world.' William, 9

You may also find that your children start to meditate outside of school as well. I have had many children tell me that they meditate at night to help them get to sleep. I often hear from parents too, who tell me about the positive difference that they notice in their children once they have started meditating.

Figure 2.2: *Children pause mid-lesson for a moment of mindfulness*

This doesn't mean that every child will love it. In one class that I surveyed, three children said that they found it 'boring' and that they didn't like it. However, I would argue that, given that moods are contagious, if the 27 other children in my class are meditating and cultivating a peaceful state of mind, then everyone in the class gets to benefit, whether they choose to join in or not. It is such a great way to start the day and can be used at various points throughout the day as well (Figure 2.2 shows children taking a 'mindful moment' mid-lesson).

Tales from the classroom

Every morning, my Year 2 class starts the day with a mindful minute ritual to foster their ability to check in with how their bodies, hearts and minds feel. At the start of the year, Skylar, a new student to the country and school, who had missed our initial discussions about the purpose of mindfulness and our daily check-ins, asked: 'Ms Peterson, why do we do the mindful check-in? And what is mindful? Is that when your mind is full of things? Because my mind gets full of things all the time!' I explained to Skylar that the mindful minute enabled us to know how we're feeling in the morning, and that it helped us to set the tone for the rest of the day. As for the definition of mindful, I promised Skylar that he would come to understand it with time and through practice, briefly sharing with him a poster that illustrated the concept of the self-discovery journey on which he was about to embark!

As the first term progressed, Skylar was always keen to lead the class through the mindful minute by regularly volunteering to ring the mindfulness chime, helping to choose a breathing technique or creatively coming up with his own ones. It wasn't until parents' evening came around that I learned how much of an impact a couple of months of mindful check-ins had had on him. As we sat together with his parents, Skylar was invited to reflect on his strengths and areas for improvement. Skylar confidently asserted that learning to be mindful had helped him to focus better when undertaking class tasks, and that he used his 'dragon' and 'star' breathing to help soothe him from the nightmares he had at times. His parents smiled, as did I, as we sat in the company of this confident, wise six-year-old.

Cat Peterson, teacher, international school in West Africa

Meditating with your children

I think that it is quite important for any adult guiding meditation practices for the first time to have realistic expectations. Your children may fidget and squirm and be distracted, and that's

OK. This is a new skill that they are learning and it will take time before they get used to it. It is useful to let the children know that you cannot fail at mindfulness. They may or may not get frustrated that their mind keeps wandering off. But each time they notice that their mind has wandered off, that *is* the meditation. That's the point! It may also be useful to debunk some myths about mindfulness meditation. You are not trying to stop your thoughts, as this is impossible. You are simply becoming more aware of your thoughts and letting these go when you choose to. As thoughts pop into your mind, you notice them and then watch them drift by like clouds in the sky. The children may come to the wonderful realisation that 'thoughts are not facts' and they don't have to believe them. One final point: the aim of mindfulness is not to become more calm or relaxed. Relaxation may be a pleasant side-effect of mindfulness but it is not the goal.

Your attitude as teacher is key, so try to cultivate a light-hearted and kind mindset when meditating with your class. The aim is to give the children a taste of what mindfulness feels like, so we don't want to turn them off it at such a young age. If a practice doesn't go as planned, no big deal. There is always tomorrow. Once, during a lovely listening meditation, a boy in my class accidentally broke wind. He burst out laughing, as did I and the rest of the class. So, we had a laughing meditation instead that day. Try to make meditating with your class an enjoyable experience rather than feeling like a chore.

Here are some tips for meditating with your class:

- **Posture:** Ensure that your pupils embody a strong, confident posture, either sitting or standing with a straight spine and shoulders relaxed – like a king or queen on their throne: alert and dignified.
- **Eyes:** Their eyes can be closed or looking down.
- **Hands:** Encourage them to keep their hands still – resting on their knees or in their laps.

- **Three deep breaths:** They can start by taking three big, deep inhalations that fill their lungs with air. In through the nose, out through the mouth. This begins a virtuous circle of calm in the body.

- **Curiosity and kindness:** It is helpful to cultivate a sense of being curious about what they notice during a practice, and also kindness towards themselves if their mind is very busy with thoughts.

- **Singing bowl:** I start and end my meditations by ringing a singing bowl. It is a pleasant way in which to start and end a practice. I also get the children to take turns to ring the bowl so that they feel part of the teaching. You could also use chimes or prayer bells.

- **Regular practice:** Try to practise every day at the same time. Mornings work best, as it sets you and your class up for the day. Having a routine means that you're less likely to forget to do it.

- **Short and sweet:** Keep the meditations short to begin with (one to two minutes) and build from there.

- **Inclusivity:** Make sure that your practices are inclusive and are adapted for children who need it. One boy found it almost impossible not to fidget and tap the table when we meditated, so I gave him a pad of paper and pencil and he doodled during the practices. He found that it helped him to focus.

Mindfulness practices

Below, I have suggested five simple mindfulness meditation practices to explore with your class. Your job is to guide your class through the meditations, giving them the instructions. Although you can join in with the practices, you will need to keep your eyes open to ensure that the atmosphere and behaviour are conducive for meditating. There are many practices out there that you can try, and I have listed some specialist mindfulness for children books in the 'Further reading and recommended resources' section of this book (p. 269).

It is important to remind the children that, in essence, mindfulness meditation practices are about resting your attention, awareness or focus on one thing at a time. Every time you notice that your mind has wandered off (which it will do constantly), you gently bring your attention back to focus on the thing on which you had intended to focus. You keep repeating this focus, mind-wandering, back to focusing, for the duration of the practice. This is what strengthens the parts of the brain that control the attention and emotional self-regulation.

Breathing buddies

This is a good one to start with for very young children (three to six years old). I once taught this to my god-daughter when she was feeling quite frantic, and she loved it and said that it calmed her down.

Choose a cuddly toy that will be your 'breathing buddy'. Now, find a space to lie on the floor and place your breathing buddy on your belly. As you breathe in normally, watch as your belly rises and your breathing buddy goes up. As you breathe out, notice your breathing buddy going back down as your belly falls and relaxes. Keep noticing the rise and fall of your breathing buddy as you breathe in and out. If your mind wanders off, that's OK – just focus back on your breathing buddy going up and down, up and down.

Tummy and chest

This is a practice inspired by the *Paws.b* course created by the charity Mindfulness in Schools Project (see p. 44). You can perform this practice either sitting – on the floor or on a chair – or standing in 'mountain pose' (standing tall, arms and hands relaxed by your side, feet shoulder-width apart).

Start by taking three deep breaths – in through your nose and out through your mouth. Then, as you begin to breathe normally, slowly place one hand on your tummy and one hand on your chest. Feel the breath coming into your body as your chest rises and expands. And then feel the breath leaving your body as it falls away and relaxes. Where do you feel the breath the strongest – in your tummy or in your chest? Are the breaths long or short? Are they deep or shallow? Just notice your breathing with friendly curiosity. See whether you can be with the whole of the in-breath and the whole of the out-breath. Be curious about the pause between each in-breath and out-breath. Every time your mind wanders off into thinking mode, simply notice that it has wandered, and gently bring it back to focus on your hands, resting on your tummy and chest. Let any thoughts drift away like clouds in a bright blue sky. Breathing in… and breathing out.

Walking and listening

If you do this practice indoors, it feels nice to do it without any shoes on. This practice is about walking slowly and deliberately.

Starting in mountain pose with your eyes closed, take your attention down into the soles of your feet. Feel where they connect to the floor, helping you to feel grounded and stable. What sensations are in your feet? Is there any tingling or fizzing? Is there any sense of heat or coldness? Be aware of your whole body standing here in mountain pose. When you're ready, open your eyes and focus on your right foot. Slowly peel this foot off the floor. Feel the weight of the foot as you lift it, move it through the air and then place it slowly down. Notice the weight of your body in this foot as you shift your weight, ready to lift your left foot. Now, slowly peel your left foot off the floor, feel the weight of this foot as you lift it, move it through the air and slowly place it down. As you continue to slowly and deliberately walk, see whether you can notice what other parts of the body are involved in helping you to walk. Each time your mind drifts off into thinking mode, gently bring your attention back to

*focusing on the feet. [Allow a few minutes of mindful walking.] And
then, come back to stand in mountain pose for a few moments.
Gently close your eyes, as you become aware of how your body feels,
standing here, breathing.*

Listening meditation

This listening practice is inspired by Eline Snel's *Sitting Still Like a
Frog* (2014). You can do this seated or standing, and it is a lovely
practice to do outside when the weather is nice.

*Start by taking three deep breaths. As you begin to breathe normally,
bring your attention to sounds [leave short pauses between each of
the questions to allow the children to notice]. What sounds can you
hear in this moment? Are the sounds nearby or far away? Are they
high- or low-pitched? Are the sounds pleasant or unpleasant? You're
not trying to think lots about the sounds; you're just noticing the
sounds. Are the sounds outside of yourself? Can you hear any sounds
inside yourself? Can you hear yourself breathing? If you're really quiet,
can you hear your own heart beating?*

Taking a quick selfie

This is a lovely short practice shared with me by mindfulness
expert Professor Katherine Weare. It uses the language of selfies
but really this is a practice about checking in with how we're
feeling in the here and now. What follows here is an invitation to
practise, and not a set of commands. If any of it makes pupils too
uncomfortable, remind them they can stop, raise their gaze and
come back to the room. The practice can be as short as two or
three minutes or as long as ten.

*Gently and kindly pause in whatever you are doing, come to rest,
standing or sitting. Close your eyes if you like or just rest your gaze
comfortably on the floor in front of you. I invite you to 'take a
quick selfie' – lightly taking note of what is happening right now*

in mind and body. What thoughts are here? What feelings? What bodily sensations? No right or wrong, nothing to change, we're just noticing. Maybe gently adding one-word labels for what you find (e.g. lightness, tired, relaxed, tense, comfortable, etc.). Move the attention to the points of contact between the body and the floor, the feet on the floor, the seat under you. Notice the sense of contact, of weight, of heaviness. Turn the attention to the physical sensations of the breath in the body, wherever you feel it most clearly in the body right now. Just breathe steadily, nothing to change. Now gently expand the awareness out across the body as a whole, being here just as you are, breathing just as you are. Return now to the mind and body, and take a second internal 'selfie'. What is happening now in mind and body? Maybe the same, maybe something has changed, shifted slightly? Either way, just notice. Gently open the eyes and gradually return now to what you were doing. Maybe there is a small increased sense of calm, clarity, space, wisdom. Maybe not.

Key points

- Our primitive brains often find it hard to cope with the everyday stress of modern life and they can get stuck in a stress–response cycle. Over time, this can exhaust and deplete us and can lead to anxiety and depression.
- Mindfulness-based interventions have proven very effective in helping people to lower levels of stress, anxiety and depression, whilst boosting their immune systems and increasing their levels of resilience and happiness.
- Introducing mindfulness practices into your classroom is fairly simple, but to make it authentic, it helps if you have your own personal mindfulness practice.
- It often works best to meditate with your class at the start of the day, and establishing a regular practice, little and often, is key.

Mindfulness

- For younger children, 'Breathing buddies' is a great meditation to start with (see p. 54). It is a fun way in which to help children to learn how to focus on their breathing.
- Experiment with guiding your class through sitting, listening and walking meditations. Keep an open mind and a light heart when you start – meditation is a skill that children will develop the more they practise. Don't lose faith if some meditations don't go to plan and try to have fun with it.

Chapter 3
What went well?

*When you arise in the morning, think of what a precious
privilege it is to be alive – to breathe, to think, to enjoy, to love.*
— Marcus Aurelius

Chapter overview

In this chapter, we'll better understand why brains have
a negativity bias and look at powerful ways in which we
can begin to actually rewire children's brains to notice and
savour the positive in their lives more.

In theory	In action
• Negativity bias • Teflon™ for good and Velcro™ for bad • Positive emotions • Emodiversity • Rewiring our brains • Three good things • Gratitude • Savouring the past and the future	• What went well? • Be an emotions detective • Thank you letters • Savouring meditation • Counting your blessings • Mental time travel

In theory

Negativity bias

Have you ever noticed how the news is full of negative stories and we can't help but be drawn to them? Or how when your headteacher is giving you feedback, you'll forget all of the positive bits and just remember the one negative? According to psychologists, this is because our brains have an innate negativity bias. This is an evolutionary hangover – our ancestors needed to be hypervigilant on the savannah in order to survive. In short, those hunter-gatherers who spotted the dangers quickly could avoid them (and therefore survive and pass on their genes) but those who stopped to smell a rose or admire a beautiful vista were more likely to be gobbled up by a lion. So, our brains are primed to look out for bad stuff more than they are tuned to notice the good stuff.

Although it was essential for our hunter-gatherer ancestors to hunt and forage for food, if they didn't find food one day, they could always go searching the next day. However, if they were not paying attention to all of the many threats that were out there too, their hunting days would be over for good. According to neuropsychologist Rick Hanson, the number one rule in the wild is: 'Eat lunch today – don't *be* lunch today.' (Hanson, 2014, p. 20) Despite the lack of life-and-death situations for many of us in our modern lives, our brains still react in a very primitive way to threats, as we saw in Chapter 2 (p. 37). Our brains will likely react in a negative way in stressful situations like traffic jams, lesson observations, arguments and even first dates!

The fact is that your brain constantly scans its environment for threats. Even when you're feeling calm and content, without you being aware, your brain is scanning away, looking for negative things. This is why negative stimuli are perceived more quickly than positive stimuli, and why we recognise angry faces more easily than happy ones. Our brains are trying to notice the bad stuff rapidly so that we can then take evasive action. And it is our old friend the amygdala (see Chapter 2, p. 37) who is largely responsible for our negativity bias by triggering the 'fight and flight' response when we sense danger. Every time your amygdala responds to a negative situation, it becomes even more sensitive to negative situations in the future. A vicious circle can arise because when your amygdala triggers the release of the stress hormone, cortisol, it can weaken and inhibit an area of the brain known as the hippocampus. Hanson points out that this is a problem because 'The hippocampus puts things in perspective while also calming down your amygdala.' (Hanson, 2014, p. 23) When our brains are caught up in a negativity-bias loop, it can become very hard for us to regain perspective and appreciate the good things that are going on in our lives as well.

Teflon™ for good and Velcro™ for bad

Fear plays a huge part in our brain's negativity bias. Hanson (2014) notes that our ancestors could have made two types of mistake in the past:

1. believing that there was a lion hiding in the bushes when there wasn't actually one there

2. believing that there wasn't a lion in the bush when actually there was.

The first mistake means a bit of needless anxiety, but the cost of the second mistake would have been death. Therefore, our brains have evolved to make the first mistake over and over again to avoid making the second mistake even once. You can see why, when we are fearful, our minds can easily run away with negative thoughts about future events because, in many ways, this is what they are designed to do. There are even parts of the amygdala specifically designed to prevent the unlearning of fear, especially from childhood events (Hanson, 2014).

Furthermore, your brain tends to be 'stickier' when it comes to bad experiences. Hanson explains: 'Your brain is like Velcro for negative experiences and Teflon for positive ones.' (Hanson, 2014, p. 27) When you experience something negative, unpleasant, sad or stressful, these implicit memories are hardwired into your brain. We generally learn much faster from pain than from pleasure, whereas positive experiences tend to wash over us without leaving much of a trace. We might remember them but they aren't as powerful as our negative memories.

Positive emotions

If our brains are designed to have a negativity bias, then what role do positive emotions play in our lives? Positive emotions are those that feel good or pleasant when we experience them. They range from the feelings of peace that we might experience during a walk in the woods to the feeling of joy when our favourite team wins a match. Psychologist Barbara Fredrickson (2013) has conducted extensive research in this area and believes that the top ten positive emotions that people experience the most are:

1. love
2. joy
3. gratitude
4. serenity
5. interest
6. hope
7. pride
8. amusement
9. inspiration
10. awe (Frederickson, 2013).

Based on her research, Fredrickson developed her 'broaden and build' theory. Whereas negative emotions narrow our focus so that we can pay close attention to a specific threat, positive emotions tend to have the opposite effect. When we're in a positive emotional state, we tend to *broaden* our horizons, notice more options open to us, become more creative and flexible in our thinking and solve problems better. We also *build* greater social bonds, which in turn helps us to build greater physical and intellectual capabilities. Many studies have shown that people who experience more positive emotions tend to do better in life overall. Professor Paul Dolan explains:

> 'Those who experience better emotions tend to live longer, are in better health, recover from viruses more quickly, take less time off work, are more successful in their careers, are generally more productive, and have happier marriages. In a study of siblings, kids who have a sunnier disposition are more likely to get a degree, get hired and get promoted. Good emotions also… improve our ability to resolve conflicts. Furthermore, those of us who are seen to be in a good mood are thought of as more attractive, which means getting better grades at school and more money at work.' (Dolan, 2015, p. 82)

So, in a nutshell, negative emotions helped to keep us alive, but positive emotions improve the *quality* of our lives.

Emodiversity

Biologists know that biodiversity is good for ecosystems because when an ecosystem has a wide range of different types of organisms, it can adapt and survive in a variety of changing environments. Biodiversity protects and even strengthens ecosystems because no single predator or disease can wipe everything out in one go. Psychology teacher and author Aidan Harvey-Craig argues that, in a similar kind of way, experiencing a wide range of human emotions is good for wellbeing. This is known as emodiversity, and it means that the more emotions we experience and get used to, the less likely it is that any one emotion will dominate and overwhelm us. Emodiversity promotes a sort of emotional homeostasis – an ability to self-regulate our emotions so that we maintain stability and adapt to our surroundings, allowing us to thrive. One of the key ways in which we develop our emodiversity, Harvey-Craig explains, is to simply learn how to name our emotions. In fact, neuroscientist Dan Siegel coined the expression 'name it, to tame it' (Siegel and Bryson, 2012, p. 83) – that is, our emotions lose some of their intensity when we are able to articulate what it is that we are feeling. This is because when we name our emotions, we're engaging our pre-frontal cortex (our rational, decision-making part of the brain) and not our amygdala (the reactive, emotional centre of the brain). So, a key in enhancing our wellbeing is learning to name, be with and regulate our more uncomfortable and difficult emotions, because the more emotions that we experience, the better.

Rewiring our brains

Just because our brains have a negativity bias, it does not mean that it has to stay this way. Neuroplasticity is the brain's ability to change, adapt and rewire, and we can not only train our brains to notice the positive in our lives more, but actually hardwire these experiences in our brains (Chapter 4 looks at neuroplasticity in more detail, p. 79). Hanson (2014) believes that in order for us to do this effectively, we need to stay with positive experiences for longer than normal (for example, maybe ten to 30 seconds). He calls this 'taking in the good'. So, if we are enjoying a nice meal out with family or friends, we have to consciously take in this experience by really noticing what is going on in our minds and our bodies, and savour the experience almost as if it is filling us up from our core. Clearly, becoming more mindful will help with the skill of becoming more aware of those positive present-moment experiences. And by taking time to appreciate and savour the good in our lives, we increase the amount of positive emotions that we feel. Good feelings experienced today increase the likelihood of experiencing good feelings tomorrow. And each time we stop to appreciate and take in the good in our lives, we grow more neural structure in our brains. Over time, Hanson believes that this 'will change your brain, and how you feel and act, in far-reaching ways.' (Hanson, 2009, p. 77)

By regularly looking for chances to take in the good, you can prime the brain to keep on the lookout for positive experiences. These will promote the release of happy hormones, such as dopamine, which in turn make your brain more receptive to positive experiences in the future. This can create a virtuous cycle and even make your brain 'stickier' for positive emotions. Shawn Achor notes that in studies of people who practised taking in the good, 'The better they got at scanning the world for good things... the more good things they saw, without even trying, wherever they looked.' (Achor, 2011, p. 101)

It is important to note that we are not talking about putting a happy, positive spin on everything or ignoring the hard aspects of our lives. This isn't 'positive thinking' – that is, trying to convince ourselves that life is great when the reality is the opposite. Taking in the good is about noticing what is already there. Hanson notes, 'It's about nourishing wellbeing, contentment, and peace inside that are refuges you can always come from and return to.' (Hanson, 2009, p. 76) This is more about levelling the playing field rather than our brains being biased towards either negative or positive experiences. There are several exercises that you can do to take in the good, which we'll look at now in more detail.

Three good things

A simple yet powerful technique used to train our brains to notice the good stuff more is called 'three good things'. This is often an activity attributed to the godfather of positive psychology Martin

Seligman. The research shows that when people write down three things that went well for them each day, it can have a profound effect on their levels of wellbeing. In a famous study carried out by Seligman and his colleagues, participants were asked every evening for one week to write down three things that went well for them, and what caused them. A measure of the participants' wellbeing was taken before they started the activity, immediately after it and then up to six months later. The results showed that the activity gradually increased people's happiness levels and decreased any of their depressive symptoms over a six-month period. Even though they were only asked to write down their three good things for one week, some of them continued. Those who continued showed the greatest improvement in wellbeing. For those who stopped the exercise, they still remained significantly happier and showed higher levels of optimism (Achor, 2011). This shows not only that this exercise is very potent but also that practising regularly changes your brain the most.

This is a great example of 'taking in the good'. Rather than letting good experiences pass through our minds like water through a sieve, the 'three good things' exercise forces us to recollect a positive experience, write it down and savour it. Every time this exercise is done, it is likely that more neural structure will be built in the area of our brains that processes positive emotions, lessening the effect of our negativity bias.

Gratitude

Showing gratitude and appreciation for the good things in our lives has been shown to have very positive effects on our levels of happiness. Gratitude expert Robert Emmons has shown that by regularly practising gratitude, people can:

- experience more positive emotions and generally feel happier
- experience fewer negative emotions
- increase their levels of optimism

- boost their immune system
- sleep better
- increase their levels of generosity towards others
- get fitter by exercising more (Emmons, 2010).

Emmons recommends keeping a daily or weekly gratitude diary and writing down things that we've appreciated or were grateful for. If you've had a bad day at work and don't feel that anything went particularly well, you can still be grateful that you have a roof over your head, that you have supportive friends or that your children are healthy. Emmons believes that the act of writing is important and helps to really internalise the good in our lives.

Another gratitude exercise is known as the 'gratitude letter'. This is where you stop to consider someone in your life who is really important and whom you would like to express your gratitude towards. You then write them a letter expressing your thanks and deliver it to them in person. Studies by Seligman and others show that this exercise has significant immediate results in terms of boosting happiness and has positive lasting effects one month later on (King, 2016). The power comes not just from reflecting on the positive impact that someone has had on your life and consciously expressing your gratitude, but also from the act of sharing it with them. It can be a deeply connecting experience, helping to foster positive relationships (which Chapter 1 shows are extremely important for growing happiness, p. 15), and expressing gratitude can also be seen as an act of kindness, which also causes a host of positive changes to our happiness levels (see Chapter 7, p. 145).

Savouring the past and the future

Although it is important to savour the present and 'take in the good' as it happens, we certainly shouldn't miss the opportunity to relive those moments again. We can savour the past and derive more happiness from it. One study showed that people who spent 15 minutes a day for three days thinking about happy memories from the past showed increased wellbeing one month later (Smith et al., 2014). Another study showed that when participants were put in a stressful situation, the group that were asked to think of a happy memory for 14 seconds after the event had 15 per cent less cortisol in their bodies than the control group (Speer and Delgado, 2017). Remembering happy memories, it seems, goes right to the heart of the psychological stress response. It can even help to do this exercise with a friend or in a group, and then share your happy memories afterwards. You can then benefit from 'the doubler effect' (Slatcher and Pennebaker, 2006), which is where you derive as much pleasure from sharing your story as you did from the original experience – effectively doubling its impact.

And let's not miss opportunities to think positively about the future either. When you have a holiday coming up, or a party or special event, have you ever noticed how you can get lots of enjoyment from looking forward to the event? This is known as 'anticipatory enjoyment savouring'. Studies show that positive mental time travel into the future can boost happiness levels and reduce anxiety (Quoidbach et al., 2009).

In action

Children (and teachers!) can be very quick to point out what's going wrong. The following activities flip that tendency around and teach children that there's always something or someone that we can appreciate or be grateful for, and that our lives are often full of many small and wonderful things that are actually going well. I have found that these practices can be very powerful, especially for more vulnerable children, and they can help to foster a culture of gratitude amongst your team.

What went well?

'What went well?' is my take on 'three good things'. When I introduced the 'what went well?' board in my classroom, it was one of the simplest but most effective things that I have done in terms of promoting my class's wellbeing. In practice, it is very easy. Here is how you could do it:

- At the end of the week, give each child a sticky note and ask them to reflect on their week in school. Take a few minutes to remind the class of all the positive experiences that they've had and then ask them to write down three things that went well for them. Children have written things like 'We had a fun PE lesson playing dodgeball!', 'I had a good playtime playing with my friends' and 'I enjoyed making models of teeth in science'.

- Each child gets to choose to share one of their 'what went wells' with the class (so benefitting from 'the doubler effect') before handing you their sticky note to put up on your 'what went well?' display (see Figure 3.1 for an example).

- You can download a free 'what went well?' display banner using the following link: **www.teachappy.co.uk/resour ces-and-downloads**

- Give your positive week a cheer and a round of applause and then it is home time!

- You could also create a big 'what went well?' book (see Figure 3.2), where all the sticky notes are saved each week. Store the book in your book corner. Children often choose to read it to remind themselves of the previous good times that they've had as a class.

This idea can work beautifully at home too. One parent told me that her son had told her about 'what went well?' and that her family had started to share one good thing from their day before

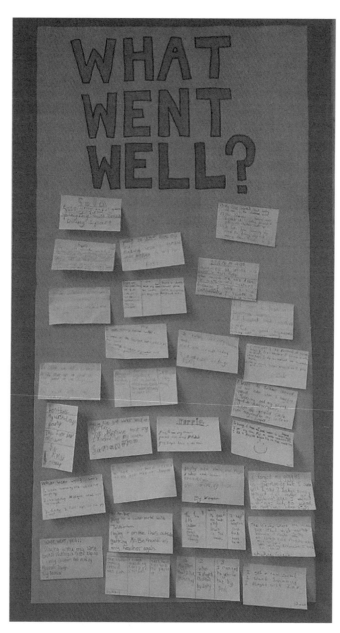

Figure 3.1: A 'what went well?' display

Figure 3.2: *Team Picasso's 'what went well?' book*

they ate dinner. It had such a positive effect that she introduced it into her workplace – before any meeting that she chaired, she would ask her team what had gone well for them that day. It changed the tone of her meetings for the better!

I love doing 'what went well?' for many reasons. Firstly, it is great to hear the small things that my class have enjoyed or are grateful for. Secondly, it is such a lovely sharing experience, in which your class members get to share and listen to each other's positive experiences (which often include the other class members). Thirdly, I know that bit by bit I'm helping to rewire my own and my children's brains to spot the positive more and savour those experiences. Fred, aged nine, summed it up nicely when he said, 'I like "what went well?" because even if I have a bad Friday, it makes me reflect on the week and find something good, so I always leave school for the weekend feeling positive.'

Tales from the classroom

The 'Journal of Joy' was born out of a desire for my students to recognise each other's positive actions and to make others smile. Quite simply, it was a notebook, decorated with stickers and a magnificent (their words, not mine) gold pen, that they could contribute to as and when they wanted. At the time, I felt that my class was divided in their friendships and attitudes towards each other and spent a lot of time trying to foster a positive tribal classroom.

One day, there was a positive interaction in the playground where a few students recognised the helpfulness of one of their classmates. They wanted to share it with the rest of the class and it led to a discussion on how we could celebrate each other more. The Journal of Joy was born. The book benefitted not only the students but also myself. By sharing and savouring so many happy moments together, our learning time became fuss-free and so much more fun. We were finally becoming a team.

Holly Laceby, teacher, international school in Malaysia

Be an emotions detective

To encourage children to get in touch with the full range of human emotions, it can help to get them to be 'emotions detectives'. What this means is that you get them to try to spot and name different emotions in lots of different situations. The following ideas can help with this:

- Whether you're reading your class a story or watching an inspiring clip of Team GB, ask them to name the emotions that they notice. Ask them whether they think those emotions might feel pleasurable or uncomfortable, and whether they've ever felt them as well.

- Create an emotions word bank. Every time a new emotion or feeling is named, add it to the emotions bank. Encourage children to use those emotions when describing characters' feelings in their own creative writing.

- Keep a mood diary. You could get your class to jot down how they feel at different parts of the school day (first thing in the morning, after break, just before lunch, late afternoon, etc.) over the course of a week. This would be just a quick check-in (taking a 'quick selfie', as described in Chapter 2) and the point is to show that how we feel changes constantly throughout the day. This can be a good activity to show that no feelings stick around forever and we don't need to be afraid of our feelings.

Thank you letters

The thank you letter exercise is an effective way in which to help children to practise gratitude more regularly. Why not try this with your class at various points in the year?

- Show your class a short video on gratitude from the BBC 'Happiness Challenge' series (a short collection of videos that investigate whether carrying out certain activities could make you happier). You can find the video on YouTube here: **www. youtube.com/watch?v=JsIPXwr9BQE**. It shows two people sharing their gratitude letters with important people in their lives and it is quite moving (I never fail to well up when watching it!). Not only does the video provide a good opportunity to discuss why doing nice things for others can make people feel 'emotional', but it also explains why writing gratitude letters can boost your happiness levels.

- Give your class a moment to think of someone in their lives who does a lot for them and to whom they'd like to show gratitude. Then ask them to write a letter thanking that person for everything that they have done. It helps if they give specific things for which they are thankful (e.g. helping them with their homework, being cooked delicious dinners, listening to their worries, etc.). The children's task then is simply to give their letter to their special person.

- As an alternative, children can write a gratitude postcard, which you can download using this link: **www.teachappy. co.uk/resources-and-downloads**

This is a really lovely activity to get children to do. Some children choose to write letters to their friends in the class, some write them to parents or grandparents, and some even choose to write them for their teachers (I have kept every gratitude letter that I've ever received). The children benefit from the act of reflecting and appreciating all of the people who are important to them, plus they get to experience how powerful it can be to let someone know that they are appreciated. This teaches children the art of cherishing and investing in their positive relationships.

Savouring meditation

I have guided my classes through savouring meditations at various points in the year. They are nice exercises to do to show the children that they have the ability to recall happy memories whenever they need to. Happy memories can be like an inner refuge to which we can retreat when we need to give ourselves a boost.

Try the following guided savouring meditation with your children, and afterwards see who would like to share their happy memories:

Sitting like a king or queen on your throne, ensure that your spine is straight but your shoulders are relaxed. Start by taking three deep breaths into your belly. Breathe out slowly. As you begin to breathe normally, bring to mind a happy memory from your past. It can be any memory where you feel safe and happy. Maybe it's a meal, a party or a celebration. What can you see as you look around? Are you by yourself or are other people there? If you're with others, notice what their facial expressions are like – are they laughing and smiling? What sounds can you hear? Is there music playing or are there people talking? Are there any strong smells about – the aroma of food, the smell of nature or people's aftershave or perfume? Don't be afraid to smile as you relive this happy time from your life. Notice how you feel in your body – are there any strong sensations present? Really turn the volume and brightness up on your happy memory, making it louder and brighter in your mind. Stay with this memory and imagine it filling up your whole body as if it were an empty vase. Every time your mind wanders off, just bring your attention back to your happy memory and all of the feelings that come with it.

- Ask the children whether anyone would like to share their happy memories. Notice whether any themes come up, such as the fact that a lot of our happiest times involve other people, and discuss why this might be with your class (most of the happiness research shows that close personal relationships are one of the biggest factors that contribute to our happiness).
- As an extension, see whether your class can identify which of the top ten positive emotions they experienced during the meditation (pp. 62–63).

- Just be mindful that this activity can trigger negative emotions if a pupil has lost a loved one who was part of their happy memory. This happened to me once when a boy in my class said he felt sad remembering a happy time with his grandad, who had died a year ago. I thanked the boy for his courage in sharing his feelings and acknowledged that it can be sad remembering loved ones whom we have lost. I also shared that I felt very sad when my own grandad died several years ago but, with the passage of time, I'm able to remember him now with fondness and savour our happy times together. I reassured my pupil that time will help him to do the same too.

Counting your blessings

An effective way in which to shift your pupils' attention away from what they don't have and onto what they do have is to get them to do the following 'count your blessings' exercise:

- Give the children a sheet of paper and ask them to make a list of all of the things in their life for which they are grateful or lucky to have, and that maybe other children around the world lack. You could do this as a timed activity and see how many things they can write down in two minutes.

- Ask the children to share their lists with a partner.

- As a whole class, ask whether anything surprising appeared on the list. For example, children might be surprised that they could show gratitude for having comfy slippers! Draw out the fact that we can be grateful for the smallest thing that makes our lives that little bit more comfortable, safe and enjoyable.

Mental time travel

We don't just have to savour the past. We can savour and positively anticipate the future. This next practice has been inspired by

Vanessa King's fantastic 2016 book *10 Keys to Happier Living* (which in turn was inspired by research led by Jordi Quoidbach (2009) at the University of Liège). Why not have a go with your class and see what impact it has?

- Spend five minutes at the end of the day trying to imagine three positive events that could reasonably happen tomorrow. They can be small things, like anticipating a fun maths lesson, a good playtime playing with friends or watching TV on the sofa snuggled up with family.
- Once they have thought of three things, ask them to jot them down on a piece of paper.
- Try this experiment for one or two weeks and after the time period is up ask the children: 'Did it make you feel any happier?'

Not only does this activity help the children's day to end on a positive note (remember that 'peak-end' theory from Chapter 1, p. 15, shows us that if our days end well, we will largely rate the whole day as positive), but it is also good to help them to positively anticipate small things that could happen the next day at school or at home.

Key points

- Our brains have developed a negativity bias that looks for bad stuff and stores it quickly in our memories, so we can try to avoid those situations in the future. This has aided our survival but sometimes undermines our happiness.
- Conversely, positive emotions enhance our quality of life. They help us to be more creative and lead to a host of benefits, such as increased levels of happiness, better health, stronger relationships and longer lives.
- We can retrain our brains to notice the positive more by taking in the good. By regularly noticing and savouring what is

going well in our lives, we create more neural structure in the positive regions of our brains.

- Every week, get your children to do the 'what went well?' exercise. Get them to reflect on three things that went well for them and share one of these with the rest of the class.

- Become emotions detectives by encouraging your class to spot and name different emotions in stories, in films and in themselves.

- Throughout the year, encourage your class to write thank you letters to important people in their lives. Expressing gratitude boosts your levels of wellbeing and physical health too.

- Guide your class through a savouring meditation so that positive experiences from the past can be relived, and they get to experience the happy hormones again in the present.

- Get your children to do a 'count your blessings' two-minute exercise. How many things can they show appreciation for in such a short space of time?

- Time-travel with your class into the future by spending some time thinking about three positive things that could happen the next day. Do this for a week to see whether worries decrease and happiness increases.

Chapter 4
Neuroplasticity – your elastic plastic brain

The brain is wider than the sky.

– Emily Dickinson

Chapter overview

Our brains are arguably the most powerful and important organ in our body. Yet relatively little is known about the brain and how it functions compared to other parts of the body. In this chapter, we'll take a peek inside our heads to see what the latest findings in neuroscience can reveal about this mysterious orb, so that we can teach children more about how it works, how it contributes to their happiness and how they can best look after it.

In theory	In action
• The elastic brain	• Mini neuroscientists
• Old-fashioned computer brain	• Brain goals
• The science of learning	• Retrieval practice
• Neural Darwinism	• Plastic(ine) brain
• Some basic brain facts	• Brain health
• Happy hormones	• Happy hormones
• Brain health	

In theory

The elastic brain

It used to be thought that after childhood, people's brains were fixed in terms of their form and what they could do. This idea has been proved to be completely wrong. Neuroscientists are now certain that all brains, young and old, are plastic. By that, they mean that our brains can be shaped, influenced and moulded by our thoughts, actions and experiences – not just once, but over and over again. Old dogs certainly can be taught new tricks (it might just take them a few more attempts to master them than their puppy counterparts). Neuroplasticity is the term used to describe this, and it means that our brains have the ability to change their structure and function in significant ways.

It's possible to peer inside our brains using MRI scanners, and this technology has shown, for example, that the brains of virtuoso violinists have larger areas of the brain that control the fingers and have way more neural activity in these parts of the brain. Similarly, London taxi drivers who complete 'the knowledge' (memorising 60,000 streets in London and over 100,000 places of note) show a significant growth in their hippocampus – an area of the brain associated with creating spatial memory (Maguire et al., 2000). Once these taxi drivers retire, their hippocampus shrinks back to 'normal' size again. Interestingly, people who are born deaf perceive objects in their peripheral vision in their visual cortex (the part of the brain that helps with sight) but also in their auditory cortex – the part of the brain that would normally process sound. Richard Davidson explains: 'It is as if the auditory cortex, tired of inactivity from receiving no signals from the ears, took upon itself job retraining, so that it now processes visual signals.' (Davidson and Begley, 2012, p. 167) Indeed, studies even show that as we become happier, the left region of the pre-frontal cortex becomes more active and can grow in size (Davidson, 2004). Our brains are amazingly fluid and versatile. They are in a constant state of flux and can literally change shape.

Old-fashioned computer brain

Scientists used to believe the idea that our brain is like a computer, but this is an outdated concept now. Dr John Ratey says that the brain is 'more like an ecosystem than a machine' (Ratey, 2003, p. 11). Unlike a computer, with its predictable outcomes depending on what you program into it, the brain is so complex and malleable that, according to Ratey, 'it is virtually impossible to predict how a given factor will influence its state' (Ratey, 2003, p. 11). The computer-brain analogy also implies that brains are devoid of emotions and that they plan, remember and process in very mechanical ways, but this simply is not true. In fact, in his book *The Emotional Life of Your Brain*, Davidson argues that all brain processes pass through the parts of the brain that handle your emotions *before* they then are dealt with by the more 'logical' parts of your brain (Davidson and Begley, 2012). In essence, all logical thought has been influenced by your emotions first. Davidson shares Ratey's view that brains can be unpredictable, and he strongly argues against a 'one-size-fits-all' approach when trying to understand how people respond to different life events. Davidson and Begley state, 'I've seen thousands of people who share similar backgrounds respond in dramatically different ways to the same life event.' (Davidson and Begley, 2012, p. 2)

Any teacher or parent will know that children's brains work in mysterious ways! You teach the same lesson to a class of 30 children and you will sometimes get 30 different responses and interpretations. Psychologist Alison Gopnik argues that there's a very good evolutionary reason for why children behave and learn in often very unique ways. By producing a 'wide, variable and unpredictable mix of children', each with a distinct brain, temperament, set of skills, strengths and weaknesses, Gopnik believes that it has allowed the human species to adapt to an unpredictable and changing culture and environment (Gopnik, 2016, p. 27). Our breadth in variety has allowed humans to flourish on Earth because, within a tribe, there will be someone whose unique personality and traits will suit any given situation. This is a useful reminder to teachers. Children's brains are not computers to be uploaded with data. Children behave, think and learn in unique and varied ways because that is what they are meant to do.

The science of learning

There has been an explosion of interest in the science of learning in education recently, driven by the research from the field of cognitive science. Cognitive science aims to help us to understand how people actually learn, mentally organise information and remember things. A recent review of the cognitive science literature by the Education Endowment Foundation (EEF, 2021) summarised some of the key findings from the field as follows:

- **Spaced learning:** Spacing out lessons and opportunities to retrieve what has been learned over a longer period of time (rather than concentrating them in 'massed' practice) can help people to learn better.

- **Interleaving:** Switching between different types of problem or different ideas within the same lesson can improve learning.

- **Retrieval practice:** Using a variety of strategies to recall information from memory – for example, flash cards, practice tests or quizzes, or mind-mapping – can enhance our ability to retain information.

- **Managing cognitive load:** Our working memory is limited (we can only hold a few bits of information in our heads at once), so if students are presented with too much information or there are too many distractions, their cognitive load can be overwhelmed. Instead, we can focus pupils on key information without overloading them – for example, by breaking down or 'chunking' subject content, or using worked examples or 'scaffolds'.

- **Dual coding:** Using both verbal and non-verbal information (such as words and pictures) to teach concepts helps us to understand and remember them more easily.

Above is an extremely succinct summary of these findings, and there is a lot more to the ideas than I have summarised. One thing that the EEF summary cautions, though, is that very little of the research has been conducted or tested in real-world classrooms. Although the strategies have evidence to show that they can work in laboratory conditions and with certain subjects and age groups, the report states that: 'The effectiveness of strategies is likely to depend on factors including the age of learners, learner prior knowledge, the nature of the subject and learning outcomes, and whether the approach is practically feasible.' (EEF, 2021, p. 8) As with a lot of the ideas in this book, experiment with them, see what works with your class and adapt where necessary.

Neural Darwinism

There is a theory developed by Nobel laureate and neurologist Gerald Edelman about the brain that is similar to Darwin's theory of 'natural selection' and it's called 'neural Darwinism'. The theory explains why neuroplasticity even exists – that is, why our brains are able to change to suit our environment and experiences, and why our brains can learn something and then unlearn it. Edelman explains that some neurons form connections that stay intact and become strong, whereas others do not and die off in a process that resembles natural selection. It's as if neurons form connections and compete with other neurons for survival. The strongest and most adaptable neurons and connections survive in a battle of survival of the fittest. This theory gave rise to the saying 'neurons that fire together, wire together'. This means that the more we rehearse certain actions and thoughts (from practising penalty kicks to learning our lines in the school play), the more those neurons will fire and form connections that can become hardwired in the brain.

On the other hand, the phrase 'use it or lose it' explains how if you don't keep exercising those neurons and connections, they can slowly weaken and could be lost. In this way, our brains work just like a muscle. The more that we work out in the gym, the bigger and stronger our muscles get. The moment that we stop exercising, we begin to lose that muscle mass and our fitness levels decline. And so it is with our brains. The more that we exercise them, the more neural connections that we make, and certain parts of the brain grow. But once we stop practising or exercising them, those brain regions begin to shrink back to their previous sizes.

Some basic brain facts

Our brains are fascinating organs and neuroscientists are discovering more and more about them all the time. Below are some of the brain facts that they have discovered:

- The adult brain is about 1.5 kg of tissue containing, on average, 86 billion neurons.
- A neuron is a cell in the brain that sends and receives signals to and from other neurons.
- Each neuron has one axon (axons are the main way by which neurons pass information on and *teach* other neurons) and up to 100,000 dendrites (which are the main way by which neurons get information and *learn* from other neurons).
- The theoretical number of different connections possible in a single brain is 40 quadrillion (or 40,000,000,000,000,000).
- It is believed that most learning and development in the brain is through the process of strengthening and weakening these connections.
- A neuron receives signals from other neurons usually as a burst of electro-chemicals called neurotransmitters. These signals tell a neuron whether to fire or not. In turn, this neuron will send signals to other neurons, telling them whether to fire or not.

- Our brains actually produce small amounts of electricity when these signals are sent. Some believe that it is enough to power a dim lightbulb!

- Even though your brain makes up only two per cent of the body's weight, it uses up to 25 per cent of the body's oxygen and glucose.

- Your brain never really switches off – it uses about the same amount of energy when you're asleep as when you're trying to work out how to explain neuroscience to a seven-year-old!

Happy hormones

There are many chemicals released by the human body that contribute to human happiness and wellbeing. They fall under various neuroscientific labels such as neurotransmitters, neuromodulators and neuropeptides. For simplicity, I will refer to them as 'happy hormones'. Below is a very brief summary of some of the key happy hormones that affect our wellbeing:

- **Serotonin:** This regulates our mood, sleep and digestion. Humans have higher serotonin levels in their digestive system than their brains. Therefore, our diet can affect our levels of serotonin, as can our exposure to natural light. Eating well and getting outdoors are two ways in which to help regulate our serotonin levels.

- **Dopamine:** Often called the 'learning neurotransmitter' (Ratey, 2003, p. 122), it helps us to pay attention. Dopamine is involved in our 'reward system' – that is, when something good happens to us, we get a rush of dopamine that makes us feel good and want to repeat the experience. It gets released when we achieve something and motivates us to approach situations where we believe that we will benefit from some kind of reward.

- **Endorphins:** They help to protect us against stress, reduce our experience of pain and produce pleasure. They are often released during intense exercise, hence the 'high' that runners feel after a run. Belly laughs that cause internal convulsions actually stimulate endorphin release.

- **Oxytocin:** This promotes prosocial behaviour and bonding between people. It helps us to be kind and show empathy towards others. It often gets released when you hug or hold hands with someone you like, or even when you stroke a pet. It can also get released when you are kind to others and when you feel like you belong to a safe, trusting group (like a tribal classroom!).

There are other happy hormones, such as **noradrenaline** and **endocannabinoids**, but for the sake of teaching children, I stick to the above four.

All of the happy hormones listed above are types of neurotransmitters, meaning that they help our neurons to communicate with each other and, therefore, they help us to learn better. They also positively impact on our health, lowering stress levels and boosting our immune system. Feeling good does us good.

Brain health

As with other major organs in our bodies, for the brain to work optimally, it is essential to take care of it. According to Ratey, 'Almost anything we do, eat, or drink can affect the brain' (Ratey, 2003, p. 6), which means that we need to be careful about what we do, eat and drink in order to affect the brain positively. Let's take a look at a few ways in which to keep your brain in tip-top condition.

Water

It is believed that around 75 per cent of the brain is made up of water. This means that drinking healthy levels of water is important to maintaining your brain function. Studies have shown that dehydration can impair short- and long-term memory and affect our ability to focus and concentrate. If you do not drink enough water, your neurons start to become less efficient (Gowin, 2010). Dr John Biffa claims that 'Dehydration is quite simply one of the biggest, under-recognised drains on performance.' (Briffa, 2014, p. 102) How much water is enough? Well, many factors will affect the amount that you need (such as age, gender, the weather, physical activity, etc.) but generally children need to aim for six to eight cups of fluid a day, in addition to the water that they'll naturally get from foods (British Nutrition Foundation, 2021). One of the best indicators of how hydrated you are is the colour of your urine (thirst is often a later sign that we might be dehydrated) (Briffa, 2014). If your urine is straw-coloured or pale yellow, that is a good sign that you are well hydrated. Dark yellow urine is a sure sign that you need to get straight to the tap!

Diet

Dr Eva Selhub, an expert in mind–body medicine, explains that 'just like an expensive car, your brain can be damaged if you ingest anything other than premium fuel' (Selhub, 2022) – premium fuel being a balanced diet consisting of a wide variety of vitamins, minerals and nutrients. Hanson believes that 'More than anything, this means eating lots of protein and vegetables.' (Hanson, 2009, p. 228) Carbohydrates are important too, though, as they increase the amount of an amino acid in the brain called tryptophan, which is the building block for the neurotransmitter serotonin. Serotonin is possibly the most important chemical in your body for maintaining a good mood. Sugar intake should be minimised wherever possible. Although the brain uses a large amount of the body's glucose to function, ingesting sugar can cause glucose spikes, followed by a sugar crash where glucose levels fall dramatically, leaving your brain feeling sluggish and tired. In fact, too much sugar can actually be toxic for the brain. As with most things in life, balance is the key.

Sleep

A good night's sleep is not only good for maintaining brain health, but it can also help to regulate your emotions and even help you to learn better. When people experience rapid eye movement (REM) sleep (rapid eye movement sleep is when active dreaming takes place), memories get moved from their short-term memory (what you learned and experienced that day – also known as your 'working memory') into their long-term memory (so that you can retrieve that information tomorrow and into the future). When you are dreaming, it is as if your brain is rehearsing what it has learned that day, and this rehearsing strengthens the neurons involved in that activity. However, poor sleep negatively affects people's concentration, coordination, memory and mood. Sleep also affects our negativity bias, as sleep expert Professor Russell Foster explains: 'The tired brain is much more likely to remember negative, rather than positive, associations.' (Foster, 2022, p. 209) Mindfulness expert Jon Kabat-Zinn adds: 'When we are sleep deprived, our thinking, our moods, and our behaviour can become erratic and unreliable, our body becomes exhausted and we become more susceptible to getting sick.' (Kabat-Zinn, 2013, p. 363) Many experts believe that one of the biggest barriers to children getting a good night's sleep is the use of electronic devices near bedtime. These devices emit blue light, which tricks the brain into thinking that it is daytime, therefore slowing the release of the sleep-inducing hormone melatonin. Even with blue-light reduction apps turned on, our devices stimulate our minds, making us feel less sleepy. Perhaps a book in bed would be a better choice than a tablet.

Exercise

Movement is good for the brain. When we exercise, our heart pumps more blood and oxygen to the brain. Our brains thrive on blood and oxygen, as they need it to think, function and learn. Exercise boosts our mood and releases happy hormones like endorphins and dopamine. We'll look at the effects of exercise on our brains and bodies in a lot more detail in Chapter 10 (p. 199) but, for now, get moving to keep those neurons firing and wiring!

In action

Without question, when I started teaching my classes about the brain, those lessons were easily some of the most engaging lessons that I have taught. That's partly due to my natural interest and passion for learning about neuroscience but it's also because I believe that most young children are budding neuroscientists. As soon as you start to teach children about the brain, they will ask so many thoughtful questions, for which you simply won't have the answers! Children love discovering more about the brain because, ultimately, it allows them to understand themselves and the people around them. In my opinion, this is one of the highest forms of learning and helps to develop their emotional intelligence.

Mini neuroscientists

Teaching mini neuroscience lessons to your children may sound daunting (especially if you don't know much about neuroscience), but the basics explained above are really all that the children need to know for now, and there are some excellent resources online to help you out. A great place to start is the BBC Brainsmart videos (although the BBC have archived this resource now, the videos are still available online). Here's how you can help your pupils to become mini neuroscientists:

- Show the video *Meet Your Brain* (**www.bbc.co.uk/program mes/p005m333**) to your class, as it neatly sums up the fact that our brains are capable of amazing things and, through effort and practice, our brains form new connections and learn new things. This also introduces the children to the idea of 'neuroplasticity', and teaches them that, like a muscle, we can grow our brains. This is a great way in which to pique the children's interest, and the visuals show what neurons look like and how they form connections.

- You could follow up with a session on stress by showing the Brainsmart video called *Managing Stress* (**www.bbc.co.uk/ programmes/p00hylmg**). You could discuss with your class what stress is and why we need it in small amounts (like in the stretch zone to help us focus and learn – see Chapter 5, p. 101), but also how too much is not good for our health or the brain. Talk about the strategies for managing stress from the video but then ask the children whether they have any other stress-busting techniques.

- Invest in some books about the brain for your book corner and allow the children to do their own research. They could share with the class any interesting facts that they discover. It was a pupil who taught me that babies' brains have more neurons than adults' brains! See 'Further reading and recommended resources' for some recommended books about the brain for children (p. 269).

Brain goals

Once you have taught your first neuroscience lesson and shown the *Meet Your Brain* video, you could try the following brain goals exercise:

- Ask your children to think of the things that they are good at. It might be things in school like writing stories, knowing their times tables or reading, or maybe it's things outside of school like doing tricks on their BMX or singing their favourite pop songs. Then ask two questions:

  1. Were you always good at those things?
  2. How did you get good at those things?

The children invariably conclude that it was through practising and putting in effort that they improved at those things.

- Next, ask them to think about three things that they either can't do now or aren't very good at, but that they wish to improve at with effort and practice. Maybe suggest that two of the things be school-related and one can be something outside of school. It helps if they are fairly specific because then it is easier for them to tell if they have achieved that goal at a later stage (e.g. 'I want to learn how to do neat joined-up handwriting' is more specific than 'I want to get better at English').

- Then give each child an outline of a brain and ask them to write down their three brain goals and colour in the brains to make them eye-catching. These brains could go up on a 'brain power' display that you could make for your classroom (see Figure 4.1) or your stretch zone display (see Chapter 5 for more on this, p. 101).

- You can download a 'brain power' display banner using this link: www.teachappy.co.uk/resources-and-downloads.

- At the end of the term, take the brains down and reflect on the goals to see whether the children have achieved them. Has our handwriting improved? Do we know our eight times table? Can we do a wheelie on our BMX? You can celebrate the things that they have achieved and tick them off (our brains normally release dopamine when we tick things off our to-do lists or achieve our goals), and they can think about what they need to do next if there are some goals they are yet to achieve.

This is a simple yet effective goal-setting exercise that can be done at the start and end of each term. Unlike the often arbitrary targets that teachers set for their pupils, these goals are more meaningful to the children because they have chosen them. This

Figure 4.1: *A 'brain power' display with brain goals attached*

activity reinforces to the children the fact that their learning is their responsibility and that to achieve anything requires effort, persistence and practice.

Retrieval practice

Whatever lesson you're teaching is an opportunity to utilise some form of retrieval practice. The idea is to help pupils to recall information and knowledge that they've been taught before, which, in turn, helps to strengthen their future recall of that information. From a wellbeing perspective, I'd emphasise the fact that any retrieval should be fun (to cultivate positive emotions) and low-stakes (to keep children in the stretch-zone sweet spot of mild-to-moderate stress). Here are a few ideas to get you started:

- **Tell a story:** Explain to your class that we remember things better when told in a story. Get pupils to recall key information from a lesson in the form of a story. For example, when recalling the water cycle, a child could say, 'Early one morning, the sun rose and began to heat the ocean. The water began to evaporate into vapour and drifted slowly upwards and gathered with its friends to form a cloud. Eventually, the cloud got too heavy. It began to fall and rain dropped over the mountains and ran down the hills….' You could break this type of retrieval task down by getting a different child to tell the next part of the water cycle story.

- **Quick-fire quiz:** When getting children ready to go out for lunch or to line up at the end of a lesson, I'll have them do a quick-fire quiz at their tables. I'll ask quick questions about previous learning (from that day or earlier in the term) and the children can confer at their table before offering their answer. If they get it right, they line up. If not, they can attempt another question (making it a table/group task encourages teamwork and takes the heat out of any one individual answering in front of the whole class).

- **Summarise:** This technique takes a bit more thinking time, but children are asked to summarise something that they have read or learned. So, you could ask children to summarise what happened in the last chapter from your class story or why the Romans left Britain. The aim is to be concise and to focus on the key points without too much waffle.

Plastic(ine) brain

One of the key messages that you want to get across to the children is just how malleable our brains are. When children begin to understand that their brains (and intelligence) are not fixed, and that they have the power to shape them through focus, effort and practice, they really start to develop more of a growth mindset (more about that in the next chapter). In any lesson that I teach, I will usually refer to the brain and how the children's neurons will be connecting up each time they learn something new or repeat a new skill.

I try to bring the brain into all areas of the curriculum. For instance, in art, when working with clay, we decided to make models of our brains. We had learned that our brains have two halves (hemispheres), connected by a thick band of nerve fibres (the corpus callosum). Amazingly, we discovered that our left side of the brain controls movement on our right side of the body, and the right side of the brain controls movement on the left side of our body. So, using the clay, we made these two hemispheres and made them the size of our two clenched fists put together (which is roughly the size of your brain). It was a fun way in which to learn more about the brain and to get the children to think about this amazing tool that they have within their skulls! It also reinforced the idea that our brains are plastic and malleable, because we literally moulded our brains out of clay. If clay sounds too messy, then you could use Plasticine™ or play dough.

Tales from the classroom

One class that I taught, Team Picasso, were so enthusiastic about the brain that we decided to do our class assembly on it (we sacked off the Romans, which was our topic that term, and focused on the brain instead). We used our computing lesson time to use the laptops and tablets to carry out our research. I organised the children into groups and then gave each group a topic to research – happy hormones, amazing brain facts, mindfulness and the brain, sleep, exercise and diet. With their research and ideas, we co-wrote a script, dressed up as neuroscientists in our white lab coats (our parents' and carers' white shirts – see Figure 4.2), and delivered an amazing assembly called 'Brain Power'. The assembly was a real hit and now every teacher in the school teaches mini neuroscience lessons to their classes at various points in the year.

Figure 4.2: *Team Picasso after their neuroscience assembly*

Brain health

It is all very well teaching children about their amazing brains but, unless they are looking after them, they may not actually be able to remember all of this cool new neuroscience stuff! Therefore, an essential part of teaching children about their brains is teaching them how to look after them. Try these ideas to encourage your pupils to take good care of their brains:

- Show your class the BBC Brainsmart video *Look After Your Brain* (**www.bbc.co.uk/programmes/p0074vst**). It covers the areas of diet, water and exercise, which you can then look at in more detail.

Diet

This is such an important part of maintaining brain health and optimising functionality.

- A great online resource that teaches children about what a balanced diet looks like is **www.foodafactoflife.org.uk**. It reinforces three key facts: food is a basic requirement of life; people choose different types of food; and we need a variety and balance of food to stay healthy. There is a fun, interactive game that the children can play online where they sort foods into different food groups, and there is a teacher's guide with lesson plans and ideas if you want to do a whole unit of work around food (see 'Further reading and recommended resources', p. 269).

- Another good idea is to share a healthy breakfast in your class. Maybe once a half-term, either ask parents and carers to donate fruit, cereals (healthy ones that are low in sugar), breads and spreads, or see whether the school budget will stretch, and have a class breakfast. It is such a nice way to start the day and helps to foster that sense of tribe and family in your classroom, whilst letting the children experience different types of food.

- You could also set up a cookery club at your school – get children preparing food, trying new foods out and learning about food hygiene.

Water

I fully understand how frustrating it can be when you want to start a lesson and several children want to get up to have a drink (especially if they've just come in from playtime, when they had access to several water fountains!), but without that water their brains may not be in the best condition to learn what you're about to teach them anyway. Rather than being specific about how much water your children should be drinking, allow them to self-regulate but teach them to check the colour of their pee! Every time they have a loo break, if their pee is pale yellow they're all good. If it's darker yellow, encourage them to have a drink. Get into the habit of including regular drinks breaks at the start of and during lessons. If your children have water bottles in school, allow them to keep them on their tables. Little and often is best but keep those brains hydrated!

Exercise

To maximise your children's ability to think and learn and be healthy and happy, we need to give them opportunities to exercise every day. Get them moving during lessons by trying the following:

- Have little breaks and do star jumps.
- Stop a lesson and get your class to do a lap of the playground before carrying on.
- Introduce the 'Daily Mile' to get your children running every day (see Chapter 10, p. 199).
- Set up some lessons in the day where the children need to get out of their seats and move around the class, either to get information from other tables or so that they can progress to the next part of the lesson. Make sure that the movement

facilitates learning (rather than the children moving around but not really learning anything in the process!).

Don't just wait for your weekly PE lesson to get the children moving – it needs to be a daily activity. Chapter 10 has a lot more ideas on how to incorporate exercise seamlessly into your daily routine (p. 199).

Happy hormones

In the classes that I teach, the children know what happy hormones are and some of the things that cause them to be released in our bodies. I think that this is important because it teaches the children that they can directly affect how they are feeling by taking some action. Feeling a little glum? Try going for a walk or a run outside to release serotonin and endorphins. A bit stressed? Try a mindfulness practice or ask a friend for a hug to release oxytocin. This is another means by which you can get children to acknowledge and recognise how they are feeling and decide whether they need to take any action. This complements the mindfulness practices very well. It means that children are not powerless in the face of difficult feelings or moods.

- Why not create four posters in your class with the main happy hormones (see pp. 85–86), explaining how the hormone affects your happiness and what activities help that hormone to be released?

- Refer to the posters when you think that hormone might have been released. For example, after some exercise with your class, you might refer to the endorphins poster and say, 'We know that exercise releases endorphins into our bodies, so enjoy that feeling of your stress levels reducing and any feelings of pleasure.'

The point is to get the children thinking about how their behaviour and actions can positively affect how they feel.

Key points

- Our brains are amazingly plastic, meaning that they can adapt and change. All of us, young and old, can learn new things and master new tricks with practice and effort.

- We learn when our neurons grow stronger connections with each other.

- Cognitive science shines a light on what strategies can help our neurons to connect together more and learn better, such as spaced practice, interleaving, retrieval practice, managing cognitive load and dual coding.

- Happy hormones are released by the body, which can help to boost our mood, reduce stress, protect the immune system and make us feel good. These hormones (also called neurotransmitters) help our brains to learn better and grow.

- We must look after our brains by staying hydrated, eating a healthy and balanced diet and exercising regularly.

- Children show a natural fascination when learning about the brain, and this enthusiasm helps to turn them into budding neuroscientists.

- Teach children more about their brains. Reinforce the key message that their brains are not fixed and that they can strengthen and grow them just like a muscle.

- Use retrieval practices to help children to recall key information in lessons and make it fun!

- Help children to look after their brains by having regular water breaks in class, sharing breakfasts and healthy food at school, and getting your children off their seats and moving more.

Chapter 5
The stretch zone

Success is dependent on effort.

– Sophocles

Chapter overview

In this chapter, we'll look at what it takes to help children to leave the safety of their comfort zones so that they can fulfil their potential. We'll understand why their brains learn better in the 'stretch zone' and how it contributes to fostering a 'growth mindset'. We'll even look at the paradox of how experiencing some stress and discomfort can actually contribute to children's overall sense of wellbeing.

In theory

- The stretch zone
- Stress and the stretch zone
- Struggle
- Growth mindset
- Teaching about the brain
- Praise
- The mouse in the maze

In action

- Stretch zone display
- Tailor your feedback
- Beautiful mistakes
- The panic zone
- 'Flearning'
- Be like the penguin
- Youcubed.org

In theory

The stretch zone

Harvard psychologist Tal Ben-Shahar developed the concept of the 'stretch zone'. He believes that by getting people to step outside of their comfort zones and into their stretch zone, they can function optimally and achieve to their fullest potential. Figure 5.1 illustrates the three zones of learning and growth. In the centre is the comfort zone. When we operate in our comfort zone, the work is not challenging us. This means that our brains are not being stimulated that much, neural activity will be low and we don't really learn anything new here. Our comfort zone is not a bad place to be (in fact, it can be very restorative and good for our wellbeing to spend time here) but, in terms of learning, it can be a bit of a cul-de-sac. You get to the end of the road and there's not much there.

In the stretch zone, however, our brains really come alive. To continue with my road analogy, the stretch zone is like being on a wide, open road with little traffic – it can take you to places that

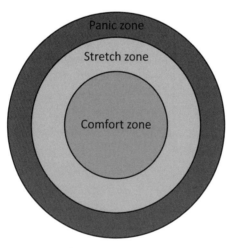

Figure 5.1: *The different zones of growth and learning*

you've never been before, you'll see some amazing sights and the journey can be really exciting. Your neurons will be firing and wiring, happy hormones will be flooding your system and learning becomes intrinsically rewarding and motivating.

The 'panic zone', though, is like being on a Formula One racetrack on a bicycle with no helmet. Quite frankly, it's just plain scary. Your brain shuts down as you enter into 'fight or flight' mode. You don't learn anything new here, apart from to avoid this scenario in the future at all costs.

The job of the teacher, therefore, is to help their pupils to spend more time in the stretch zone, by coaxing them out of their comfort zones and supporting them when they stray into the panic zone.

Stress and the stretch zone

The stretch zone by its very nature involves children leaving a place where they feel comfortable and doing work, performing tasks and operating in a place where they will feel discomfort and a certain level of stress. Now this may seem counterintuitive when trying to boost the levels of wellbeing in your pupils. However, Louis Cozolino agrees that teaching children to handle a certain level of stress is good for their development and is where their brains really begin to flourish. Cozolino notes, 'Keeping students in a neuroplastic "sweet spot" of arousal is a core element in the art of teaching.' (Cozolino, 2014, pp. 81–82)

Figure 5.2 illustrates where this 'sweet spot' occurs. Two psychologists, Robert Yerkes and John Dodson (1908), published a famous paper on the relationship between learning and stress, and their findings became known as the 'inverted-U learning curve'. Their research showed that for people to learn at optimal levels, the level of challenge, stress or arousal needs to be not too low or too high. If the challenge is too easy, children get bored and switch off (comfort zone), but if the challenge is too hard, children can enter the 'panic zone' and the level of stress inhibits any learning. It turns out that moderate levels of stress (characteristic of the type

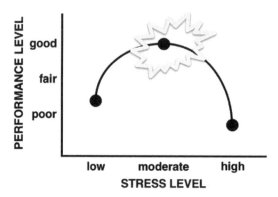

Classic inverted-U curve

Figure 5.2: *The classic inverted-U curve graph showing where the 'sweet spot' of performance occurs (reproduced with kind permission from Professor Daniela Kaufer from her 2011 presentation 'What can neuroscience research teach us about teaching?')*

that people experience in the stretch zone) lead to maximum levels of learning and performance.

When Yerkes and Dodson carried out their research in the early twentieth century, the ability to scan people's brains didn't exist, but modern neuroscience now backs up their findings. It turns out that at moderate levels of stress and arousal, our amygdala releases small amounts of hormones (such as cortisol and norepinephrine) that are crucial to learning. These hormones stimulate the hippocampus (which is a core part of the brain involved in forming memories) and neural plasticity is maximised (McGaugh, 2004; McGaugh et al., 1993). However, when we become too anxious about the task at hand, the amygdala floods our system with these same hormones, which then inhibit the hippocampus and stop new learning from occurring. If children are too stressed or anxious, they simply cannot learn.

Teachers really need to carefully manage stress levels in the classroom. By allowing just the right amount of stress, you take your class on a journey into the stretch zone, and there anything becomes possible.

Struggle

When we are in the stretch zone, the task, whatever it may be, will be challenging to us and we will inevitably struggle at times, but when we struggle there is a real opportunity for deep learning to occur. By making tasks harder for children, by introducing what some psychologists call 'desirable difficulties' (Bjork and Bjork, 2011), we actually increase the chances of learning hardwiring into their long-term memories. Ben-Shahar warns parents and teachers against protecting children too much from struggle. He notes, 'Educators, especially parents, confuse struggle with pain; wanting to protect their children from pain, they cater to their children's every wish and rescue them from every challenge.' (Ben-Shahar, 2008, p. 88) Likewise, in her book *What Mental Illness Really Is… (and What It Isn't),* psychologist Dr Lucy Foulkes explains that if a child is anxious about giving, say, a presentation, excusing that child from giving presentations can make things worse: 'One of the main ways in which anxiety is maintained is by avoidance.' (Foulkes, 2022, p. 8) Therefore, teachers need to allow their pupils to struggle with tasks in the classroom and, at times, with life in the school community. This means not rescuing pupils when they are struggling with a problem in a lesson or trying to solve a falling-out with a friend in the playground. Of course, you should be there to offer support and guidance, but it is about allowing your pupils to struggle and find their own way through. This allows children to 'discover that perhaps it isn't as bad as they fear or at least learn ways to cope – two key ways of reducing future anxiety.' (Foulkes, 2022, p. 8)

Again, this may seem contradictory when we are trying to foster our children's levels of happiness. Why wouldn't we rescue our children when we can see that they are struggling? But to rescue them denies them a crucial aspect of learning. Only when we allow our children to struggle with a problem will they experience the deep satisfaction that comes from overcoming challenges. Ben-Shahar goes on to say, 'Struggles and hardships and challenges are a necessary component of an emotionally rich life; there are no easy shortcuts to happiness.' (Ben-Shahar, 2008, p. 89) So the stretch zone involves struggle. In fact, it actively seeks out struggle. It is designed to stretch your pupils beyond what they can currently do, and in doing this, their brains are turned on for learning and they get to experience the joy of overcoming an obstacle and rising up to a challenge.

Growth mindset

The stretch zone supports and complements psychologist Carol Dweck's theories on mindset. Dweck's research shows that in certain areas of our lives we may either have a 'fixed mindset' (where we believe that our talents, abilities and intelligence are set in stone) or a 'growth mindset' (where we believe that, with effort and practice, we can improve at something).

For example, a child with a fixed mindset when it comes to maths will see their ability in maths as something with which they were born. If they are not very good at maths, they will say things like, 'Oh, I'm just not a maths person.' These children will give up easily when they do challenging maths work and will see their mistakes as confirmation that they can't do maths and won't ever be good at it. Even if they are good at maths, these children will think that they just 'get' maths and don't necessarily need to try hard at it. They often try to hide their mistakes (which contradict their self-belief about their innate ability in maths) and are driven by a fear of failure, rather than a love of the subject. In the fixed mindset, pupils seem preoccupied with how they will be judged. They fixate on performance and guard against the risk of failure by avoiding opportunities to learn if they know that they will make mistakes (Nussbaum and Dweck, 2008). Children with a fixed mindset tend to stay very firmly in their comfort zone, not wanting to take risks or make mistakes.

In contrast, take the child who has a growth mindset when it comes to maths. They see maths lessons as an opportunity to learn and grow. Whether their current ability in maths is low or high, they say things like, 'I can't do this yet but I'm going to practise to get better.' If they come up against a challenging problem, they enjoy getting stuck in and trying different solutions. If they get answers wrong, they don't hide their mistakes but seek out advice and help on where they went wrong; they correct their mistakes or adapt their problem-solving strategy (Blackwell et al., 2007). These pupils increase their efforts when they encounter a setback and they don't give up easily (Nussbaum and Dweck, 2008). Children with a growth mindset tend to inhabit the stretch zone. They seek out challenges, they embrace their mistakes and they enjoy the thrill of being outside their comfort zone.

Clearly, helping children to develop a growth mindset is good for their learning, as it encourages them to spend more time in the stretch zone where they learn the most. But how exactly do you help to foster a growth mindset in children?

Teaching about the brain

It turns out that teaching children about the plastic nature of their brains goes a long way in helping to develop a growth mindset. In one study, two groups of pupils around the age of 12, who were all doing badly in maths, were randomly assigned to workshops on study skills. The control group received standard study skills lessons. The second group were essentially given a mini course in neuroscience. They were taught about the malleability of the brain, how intelligence isn't fixed and that our neurons form new connections every time you learn something new. The results were impressive – the maths scores in the neuroscience group improved, whilst those in the control group actually got worse (Blackwell et al., 2007). The research shows that teaching pupils about how they can exercise their brains to grow bigger and stronger motivates them to learn (Dweck, 2007).

Praise

How we praise children also has a tremendous impact on whether they go on to develop a fixed or growth mindset. As a parent myself, it feels almost instinctive to say 'Clever boy!' every time my five-year-old son masters some new skill. But, inadvertently, I may be reinforcing a fixed mindset in him. Dweck's research shows that praising children's intelligence is more likely to develop a fixed mindset and undermine their resilience (Dweck, 2007). When children are praised for being 'clever', it can actually make them less likely to attempt new challenges because any mistakes that they make will conflict with this view that their parent or teacher has of them. They are more likely to work in their comfort zone, attempting work that they know they can do and score highly on, thus upholding the image that they are 'intelligent'.

However, when children are praised for the effort that they put in or their determination or persistence with a challenge, they are much more likely to learn more and perform better. This is known as 'process praise' (i.e. praise for focus, resilience, improvement, strategies, etc.) and, according to the ICEP, 'puts students in a growth mindset and fosters hardy motivation' (Institute of Child Education and Psychology, Module 3, p. 19). Dweck believes that process praise lets pupils know what they have done to be successful in their learning and what they need to do to be successful in the future (Dweck, 2007).

Tal Ben-Shahar would agree that we need to be mindful about what we praise. Schools tend to focus on praising and rewarding achievements such as high grades in tests or passing exams. The problem with this, according to Ben-Shahar, is that 'In emphasising achievements (which are tangible) over the cultivation of a love of learning (which is intangible), schools simultaneously reinforce the rat-race mentality and stifle children's emotional development.' (Ben-Shahar, 2008, p. 85) So, schools and teachers need to take heed. If we want to develop a growth mindset in our children, where they are more willing to step inside the stretch zone, embrace challenges and learn to love learning, praising the process rather than the end result may be the best way in which to achieve this.

The mouse in the maze

Part of the challenge for the teacher is encouraging children to leave their comfort zones. If their mindset is particularly fixed, it can be hard to convince them that making mistakes and doing work at which they will struggle is good for their development! Therefore, *how* you present work and challenges in your classroom is vitally important. In *Mindfulness*, Mark Williams and Danny Penman share an experiment that was carried out at the University of Maryland, involving a mouse in a maze (Williams and Penman, 2011). Two groups of pupils were asked to navigate a cartoon mouse through a maze, with a slight difference in the puzzles presented. One group had a maze with a delicious-looking piece of cheese awaiting the mouse at the exit. This is known as a 'positive' or 'approach-oriented' puzzle (Williams and Penman, 2021). The second group had no cheese in the maze but, instead, there was a predatory owl, ready to swoop and gobble the mouse up at any moment. This is known as a 'negative' or 'avoidant-oriented' puzzle (Williams and Penman, 2021). Both groups solved the puzzles easily in around two minutes, but the after-effects of the puzzles were very revealing. After completing the maze puzzle, all pupils were asked to complete an apparently unrelated test that measured creativity. Williams and Penman noted, 'When they did these, those who had avoided the owl did 50 per cent *worse* than those who'd helped the mouse find the cheese.' (Williams and Penman, 2011, p. 113)

It transpired that avoidance triggered the fear instinct in the first group of pupils. Their minds' 'aversion' pathways were activated, leaving them feeling vigilant and cautious. They became less creative when operating from a place of fear and avoidance. But the pupils helping the mouse to find the cheese displayed the complete opposite effect. They became more open to new experiences, and were more relaxed, playful and eager to experiment. The lack of fear meant that they became more open-minded. All of this leads Williams and Penman to the important conclusion that 'The spirit in which you do something is often as important as the act itself.' (Williams and Penman, 2011, p. 114)

With this in mind, it is vital that teachers use the stretch zone in the classroom in a positive way. Not only can teachers make working in the stretch zone sound exciting and appealing, but they can also make the fear of failure or making mistakes seem less scary. This is why having a safe and secure classroom environment for your tribe, like the ones that we explored in Chapter 1 (p. 15), is so important for giving children the confidence to step outside their comfort zones. Cozolino points out that 'A secure classroom allows students to cope with the stress of new learning and to regulate their fear of failure with the support of their teachers and fellow students.' (Cozolino, 2013, p. 82) A mindfulness practice also gives your pupils a tool for processing and being with the sometimes uncomfortable feelings of putting themselves in the stretch zone and leaving their place of comfort.

In action

Unless teachers can encourage children to leave their comfort zones and take risks, limited growth and learning will take place. The stretch zone can act as a great metaphor that enables children to push themselves and start to fulfil their true potential. It works most effectively when teachers walk the walk and model what risk-taking looks like by experimenting in the classroom, sharing their own mistakes and trying new things (like writing the second edition of a book! Arrgggh!). The following activities will help you to bring the stretch zone to life so that more children inhabit this zone, more of the time, and experience the thrill of taking risks.

Stretch zone display

The first thing I do to introduce the stretch zone is to teach my first mini neuroscience lesson (see Chapter 4, p. 79). This teaches the children that their brains have a huge capacity to learn new things and improve at any task with effort and practice. That lesson definitely helps to foster a growth mindset. You could then try the following:

- Create a stretch zone display in your classroom (see Figure 5.3). It needs a comfort zone in the middle (with phrases like 'Easy', 'Know it already' and 'Boring') and then a stretch zone outside (with phrases such as 'Hard', 'Tricky', 'Make mistakes', 'Exciting', 'Fun' and 'Flow'). You don't have to include a panic zone, but I would certainly talk about it in relation to the other zones of learning.

- You can download a 'stretch zone' display banner using this link: www.teachappy.co.uk/resources-and-downloads

- Explain that the comfort zone is a place where we know what we're doing. It feels nice there because the work is fairly easy and we don't feel stressed because the work isn't challenging. The comfort zone is a nice place to be but if we spend too much time there, we start to get bored. It might be good to get the children to identify work or activities that are currently in their comfort zones.

- Communicate to your class that when they step outside of their comfort zone, they enter the stretch zone! Here, they'll encounter tricky work. The tasks will be hard, they may leave them confused and they will definitely make mistakes. In fact, making mistakes is a good sign that they're in the stretch zone! However, if they really focus in the stretch zone, try their best and don't give up, they start to be able to do work that they couldn't do before. It can feel really fun in the stretch zone and exciting when they're able to do something difficult that they could not do before!

Figure 5.3: *A 'stretch zone' display with brain goals attached*

- Explain that their brain grows the most when they work in the stretch zone, as their neurons fire and wire together. They will even start to experience a state called 'flow', which is where they become so absorbed in their work that time rushes by and they don't think about anything else (see Chapter 6 for more on 'flow', p. 123).

- Get the children to share activities inside and outside school that are in their stretch zone (e.g. speaking in front of an audience, doing backstroke in the pool or using watercolours in art).

- Finally, collect the children's brain goals from your neuroscience lesson and put these up on the 'stretch zone' display. Remind your class that working towards their brain goals will put them in their stretch zone.

The idea is to get the children excited about being in the stretch zone. You want to make it sound appealing, challenging and absorbing. Whenever you see children challenging themselves, struggling with work and persisting, praise them for working in the stretch zone!

Tailor your feedback

In a blog about feedback, Professor Dylan Wiliam explains that one of the most important factors is the relationship that you have with your pupils. He says, 'When you know your students and your students trust you, you can ignore all the "rules" of feedback. Without that relationship, all the research in the world won't matter.' (Dylan Wiliam Centre, 2014) This links us nicely back to ideas around creating a tribal classroom, fostering a sense of belonging and the importance of having a trusting relationship with an adult. To help children to learn and make progress, Wiliam explains that it's about knowing your children well and tailoring your feedback to the individual. These ideas can help with this:

- **Know when to nudge and when to back off:** Every child will have a different comfort, stretch and panic zone, which means that you need to be really attuned with the children in your class. Over the year, learn what makes them tick and tune into their micro-expressions. This will help you to know when they need nudging out of their comfort zones and when you need to back off because the pressure is getting too much.

- **Tap into their strengths:** We'll learn more about this in the next chapter, but get to know your children's unique character strengths (e.g. humour, love of learning, kindness, perseverance) and encourage them to use their strengths to overcome challenges.

- **Draw on previous successes:** Children can be quick to forget the times in the past when they overcame a setback, so keep a bank in your mind of their previous successes. If they're currently panicking about their performance in front of the whole school, remind them of the time they nailed their lines in the school play. They did it then, so you know that they can succeed on this occasion too.

Beautiful mistakes

A key facet of the stretch zone and growth mindset is about communicating to children that mistakes and failure are key parts of learning and growth. Too often, children view mistakes as a sign that they aren't good at something and that they never will be. Mistakes can demoralise some children and force them to give up and retreat back to their comfort zones. It is crucial that teachers create a classroom environment where mistakes are shared, talked about and celebrated. Why not try the following?

- Host a 'share a mistake' part of your lessons, where children volunteer to share with the class a mistake that they have made. They could share it and ask the class for help, with other children then assisting with correcting the mistake. Alternatively, they could share the mistake that they made and explain how they corrected it themselves.

- You could have a 'mistake of the week', where you put up a maths problem or passage of writing, with mistakes that the children have to identify and solve. Children could put up their various solutions on sticky notes, particularly if the problem or mistake has more than one solution.

- When you inevitably make mistakes in your teaching, be sure to share these with the children. Not only does this show humility but it also models the fact that mistakes happen to everyone and there is no need to be ashamed of them.

Creating a culture where mistakes are valued helps the children to realise that mistakes are actually essential for learning and that if we share them with others, we all get to learn from those mistakes.

The panic zone

Several years ago, when I was teaching Year 4, I had the pleasure of teaching a young girl named Andrea. Crystal Palace Diving Club had come to our school the year before and selected a handful of children, including Andrea, to join their dive school. I remember Andrea talking enthusiastically about her diving training and competitions in my class. Well, fast-forward to 2022 and Andrea Spendolini-Sirieix is a two-time national champion, two-time Commonwealth champion, two-time European champion and junior world champion at the ten-metre platform and ten-metre synchronised platform events.

I was surprised to hear that, at the start of 2022, Andrea shared in a BBC interview that she became so scared of diving that she considered quitting the sport for good. I reached out to interview her to find out how she went from being in her panic zone and almost walking away from diving to having her most successful year ever (the full interview can be found at **www.teachappy. co.uk/post/interview-with-andrea-spendolini-sirieix**). Andrea explained that, ultimately, it was the people around her who helped her the most – her coach, her family and friends. 'I was ready to give up on myself but they weren't ready to give up on me,' she shared. It highlights the importance of tribal classrooms and those supportive relationships. Remember self-determination theory from the introduction? This is about *connection*. Andrea went on to say that she was honest with her coach and asked to take a break (*control*). Her coach let her go back to basics in training and they went over the most straightforward dives and aimed to develop a high level of consistency (*competence*). Finally, she said that her coach remained really positive and would praise Andrea even if she did the simplest of dives.

The rest, as they say, is history, and I have no doubt that Andrea will go on to win Olympic medals and many other accolades. Her example shows that whether you're a child in a classroom panicking about giving a speech or an elite athlete standing on a ten-metre diving board, when you enter the panic zone the following principles are essential:

- Support children and let them know that you are there for them.
- Allow children to have a break and help them to feel like they are in control.
- Stay positive and give encouragement.
- Go back to basics to build confidence.
- Remember that self-determination theory and intrinsic motivation is about connection, competence and control.

Tales from the classroom

Andrea is a very sociable, friendly and cooperative member of the class. She has a good group of friends. In class, Andrea always tries her best and she works very hard. It is down to her effort and hard work that she has made such good progress this year. She works very hard during our Fit 4 Life sessions and has improved her levels of speed, strength and coordination. I have been impressed by her dedication and success outside of school with her diving. She has the focus and determination to achieve anything she puts her mind to and I have no doubt Andrea could represent Team GB (or France or Italy!) at the Olympics if she put her mind to it. I have really enjoyed teaching Andrea this year and it has been great seeing her develop and grow. Well done, Andrea, for all your hard work and I wish you the best of luck in Year 5!

Year 4 school report of Andrea Spendolini-Sirieix, Team GB member, Commonwealth, European and Junior World Diving Champion

'Flearning'

A powerful way in which to encourage children to put themselves in the stretch zone is by showing them their role models stretching themselves, embracing challenges and making mistakes. Our school had a visit from BMX superstar Mike Mullen. Mike is a former World Masterclass BMX champion and current UK Pro Half Pipe Champion. He runs the BMX Academy (www.bmxacademy.com), which teaches growth mindset through BMX. In his assembly to the children, he shared his story about how he went from anxious, worried schoolboy to world BMX champion. Mike explained how he had a fixed mindset at school and believed that he simply wasn't good at certain things. It was only when he got a BMX for his birthday that he started practising tricks.

At first, he couldn't do them and would keep failing. But, unlike at school, Mike kept persevering with mastering his BMX tricks. He realised that every time he failed, he learned something new about what to do to get better at the trick. Eventually, through repeated failure and continued learning, Mike mastered the tricks! He then coined the phrase 'failure + learning = Flearning'. The children were so inspired by his message that 'flearning' has now become a catchphrase in our school when we make a mistake.

It can be so inspiring to invite people from the top of their field to come and share their stories of success and failure with the children. But even if this is not possible, you can share the many stories of successful people whose journeys are littered with mistakes and failures. Basketball player Michael Jordan was dropped from his school basketball team because he wasn't good enough. Not only did he go on to be the most successful basketball player of all time, but he shares this message about his success: 'I've missed more than 9,000 shots in my career. I've lost almost 300 games. 26 times, I've been trusted to take the game winning shot and missed. I've failed over and over… And *that* is why I succeed.' (Quoted in Goldman and Papson, 1998, p. 49)

Be like the penguin

Sometimes children don't like the feeling of making mistakes and they do want to give up in the stretch zone. This is why I also show my class a brilliant clip from the BBC's *Frozen Planet* series, available here: www.bbc.co.uk/programmes/p00l4qkz. The clip shows a gentoo penguin trying to escape from a sea lion. The sea lion is faster and stronger than the penguin on land and it manages to capture it in its jaws twice. But both times the penguin keeps fighting and struggles free. It's a very dramatic clip. I first showed this clip to a Year 2 class and their response was amazing – they whooped, cheered and clapped when the penguin finally escaped back into the sea. The phrase 'Be like the penguin' was born and I use it as a symbol for resilience and perseverance.

Whenever we find something hard and feel like giving up, we remember the penguin, we dig a bit deeper and we keep going.

Figure 5.4: *A focused table gets the penguin toy*

The penguin is a great metaphor for the children because it is the underdog but it triumphs due to its grit and tenacity. I have two stuffed penguin toys in my class (which former pupils bought me as end-of-term presents) and I place them on the tables where I can see children working in the stretch zone and trying their best (see Figure 5.4). I even have a penguin stamp that I use in books where I can see that pupils have really tried to stretch themselves and put in extra effort.

This is one way of giving 'process praise'. By recognising where children have stepped outside of their comfort zone, made mistakes, tried hard, persevered and bounced back, it encourages them to spend more time in the stretch zone. There is an interesting paradox with working in the stretch zone and it is this: the more that you step outside of your comfort zone and become familiar with the uncomfortable feelings that often accompany working there, the more comfortable you become with those feelings and so your comfort zone grows! The stretch zone becomes a less scary place to work, it becomes more exciting to be there and so children continue to stretch themselves and grow.

Youcubed.org

Another excellent resource is the **Youcubed.org** content created by Dr Jo Boaler at Stanford University. Although this website contains videos that are designed to change children's mindsets about maths, they perfectly sum up the latest neuroscience in easily digestible ways for children and are relevant to *all* subjects that children learn. I often show these videos in class because they reinforce key messages such as:

- There is no such thing as a 'maths brain' (or an English or science or anything brain).
- Mistakes grow our brains.
- Struggling with tricky problems helps to grow our brains more (stretch zone!).
- Speed is not important in maths (or any subject) but thinking deeply is.
- Our brains are plastic and grow with practice, persistence and effort.
- Believing in yourself helps your brain to grow more than doubting yourself.

I have found that teaching children about the stretch zone works on many levels. This is not just about helping them to do better at their schoolwork. The stretch zone teaches children about how to deal with the inevitable anxiety and stress that come from modern life. It teaches them that in order to grow and fulfil your potential, you will often have to encounter uncomfortable feelings, face your fears and make mistakes – and that's OK. It works in the classroom, it works on the sports field and it works in any area of their lives where they have some difficult thing to do (e.g. visiting a sick relative, dealing with friendship issues or sticking up for themselves if they face bullying). The stretch zone really does help children to develop self-confidence, resilience and perseverance.

Key points

- When learning anything new, children need the right level of challenge, stress and stimulation to engage them.
- The stretch zone provides this sweet spot of challenge but it can feel unnerving for children to leave their comfort zones.
- You may need to change children's mindsets from fixed ones (where they believe that talent and intelligence are innate) to growth ones (where they believe that intelligence and talent are grown and worked at).
- Share with children the different zones of learning and get them to reflect on where they spend most of their time.
- Encourage children to be brave and work more inside the stretch zone by celebrating mistakes, providing a supportive classroom environment and making it exciting to work there.
- Get to know your children well and tailor your feedback to nudge them into their stretch zone, and know when you need to back off and release the pressure as well.
- If children start to panic, encourage and support them, go back to basics to build confidence, be positive and normalise the fact that everyone goes into the panic zone at times (even Olympians!).
- Give 'process praise' when you can see them working hard and attempting challenges, and develop their determination and resilience by encouraging them to 'be like the penguin' and by sharing stories of their role models' successes and failures.

Chapter 6
Flow and strengths

May what I do flow from me like a river, no forcing and no holding back, the way it is with children.

— Rainer Maria Rilke

Chapter overview

In this chapter, we'll explore exactly what flow is and why it is vital for our creativity and wellbeing. We will understand how we can cultivate more flow experiences in the classroom and how, by nurturing and tapping into children's strengths, we can help to foster a love of learning.

In theory	In action
• What is flow?	• Show me your flow
• Benefits of flow	• Differentiation
• The anti-flow classroom	• Making learning meaningful
• Strengths	• Flow-rich activities
• Strengths in the classroom	• Strength spotting

In theory

What is flow?

Think back to a time in the classroom when you were working at your best. The children were focused and engaged, you were enjoying what you were doing and you were in your element. You would have naturally incorporated your innate strengths into the lesson, maybe utilising your creativity, sharing your love of learning and using timely humour. Time rushed by and you didn't think about anything else other than what you were doing. In moments like these, you would have been experiencing 'flow' – a state of pure concentration and deep satisfaction.

Psychologist Mihaly Csikszentmihalyi (pronounced cheeks-sent-me-high) has extensively researched the concept of flow – a state of mind he discovered whilst researching creativity and productivity. He describes flow as: 'Being completely involved in an activity for its own sake. The ego falls away. Time flies. Every action, movement, and thought follows inevitably from the previous one… Your whole being is involved, and you're using your skills to the utmost.' (Geirland, 1996) Flow experiences are times when we are operating at our highest levels and reaching our full potential. Flow occurs when we are deeply absorbed and engaged in something. People often describe it as 'being in the zone', which is why it is so closely related to working in the stretch zone (see Chapter 5, p. 101). You cannot experience flow if you are either bored or anxious. Similar to the Yerkes-Dodson graph in Chapter 5 (p. 104), Figure 6.1 shows when flow is most likely to be experienced.

Csikszentmihalyi (2002) notes that there are certain conditions that need to be in place for us to experience flow:

1. We must engage in a challenging task where the level of challenge matches our level of skill.
2. The challenge must be clear and have obvious goals.
3. We must get immediate feedback from the task so that we know how well we are doing.
4. We must be able to really focus on the task in hand.
5. We should have a sense of autonomy over our actions in relation to the task.

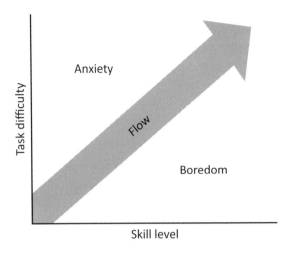

Figure 6.1: *A graph showing when flow is experienced*

Although experiencing flow mainly happens when working in the stretch zone, they are not the same thing. Let me illustrate the difference with a personal example. Writing a book definitely puts me in the stretch zone. I am a relative novice at book writing, so I'm out of my comfort zone, I'm making mistakes and I'm learning lots. Very often, I experience flow whilst writing. There are times when I'm so absorbed in writing that, before I know it, the afternoon has arrived and I haven't eaten lunch, had a drink or gone to the loo since the morning! After being in flow, I feel great. I look back and realise how much I enjoyed writing, and I feel satisfied and can't wait to start again. However, there are also times when I have been stuck for ideas or received some critical feedback, or I've read back my work and disliked it. At these times, I'm not in flow but I am still in the stretch zone. I have to dig deep, keep going and push through the difficult feelings until I can find my rhythm again. As Ken Robinson writes in his book *The Element*, 'Doing the thing you love is no guarantee you'll be in the zone every time. Sometimes the mood isn't right, the time is wrong, and the ideas just don't flow.' (Robinson, 2010, pp. 88–89).

There are also different levels of flow that we might experience. We might enjoy the 'micro-flow' of an engrossing conversation with a friend or getting lost in a good book. But we can also experience really deep flow when all of our strengths, talents and faculties are being tested to their limits. This description by world-famous cellist Yo-Yo Ma gives us an insight into how deep flow feels: 'I… turn off that part of the mind that judges everything. I'm not thinking or worrying… It's when I'm least conscious of what I'm doing, when I'm lost in the emotion of the music, that I'm performing at my best.' (Quoted in Lehrer, 2012, p. 89)

Benefits of flow

Flow doesn't just feel good; it does us good too. Studies show that being in flow is strongly associated with happiness and wellbeing. When he tracked 500 teenagers in one study, Csikszentmihalyi found that the 'high-flow' teenagers (those who experienced flow on a regular basis) had more hobbies, were involved in more sports and did more homework than the 'low-flow' children (those who rarely experienced flow). Interestingly, the high-flow teenagers didn't always report that their higher levels of engagement were fun or enjoyable at the time, but their experience of flow paid off later down the line. It turned out that the high-flow teenagers scored more highly on measures of psychological wellbeing, were more likely to go to university, had stronger social ties and were ultimately happier and more successful (Csikszentmihalyi, 2002).

Pupil engagement and experiences of flow in school are also strongly correlated with academic performance. Additional research by Csikszentmihalyi and colleagues shows that flow deepens learning and encourages long-term interest in a subject. This stands to reason. Every teacher knows that children who are engaged in lessons learn better than those who aren't.

Flow experiences in the classroom really help children to develop a love of learning, which is surely one of the key aims of any primary school teacher. When children are turned onto learning, they can really start to reach their full potential, both academically and emotionally.

The anti-flow classroom

One of the challenges that teachers face, however, is that schools are often set up in such a way that make flow experiences hard to achieve. American psychologist Jill Suttie (2012) claims that 'The learning conditions in classrooms have been practically antithetical to the conditions people need to achieve flow and all the benefits that come with it.' She points the finger at high-stakes testing and over-regimentation in classrooms, saying that it is 'making it harder for students to get deeply engaged with topics that interest them.' When you have an education system that values academic achievement over pupil engagement, Suttie claims that children start to disengage and burn out, as they don't see the point in what they are learning. Alarmingly, when researchers at Harvard and Villanova universities studied high-achieving pupils at secondary schools in America, they found that the feeling of needing to achieve, in the absence of true pupil engagement in learning, was associated with 'cheating, sleepless nights, depression, and drug abuse.' (Suttie, 2012)

Educational expert Sir Ken Robinson agrees that schools often stifle creativity, and the experience of flow in the process. He believes that creativity in schools should be given equal status to core subjects like English. But he realises that many schools do the complete opposite of this. Robinson argues: 'We're now running national education systems where mistakes are the worst thing you can make. And the result is that we are educating people out of their creative capacities.'

(Robinson, 2006) Csikszentmihalyi also thinks that a lot of schools generally make learning dull and uninteresting. He believes that 'Schools generally fail to teach how exciting, how mesmerizingly beautiful science or mathematics can be; they teach the routine of literature or history rather than the adventure.' (Csikszentmihalyi, 1998)

Teachers need to be mindful of the constraints of the system within which they are working, but there is still lots that they can do to create more flow-rich experiences in the classroom, and one way is to focus on children's strengths.

Strengths

Our strengths are core parts of ourselves and they shape our personalities. They are what drive our thoughts, feelings and behaviours and, ultimately, they are what motivate us. Vanessa King, a leading expert in positive psychology, says that 'When we're using our strengths, we tend to enjoy what we're doing more, learn easily and do better.' (King, 2016, p. 191) When we use our strengths, we feel energised rather than burnt out. According to strengths expert Martin Seligman, using your strengths is essential in experiencing flow. He states: 'There are no shortcuts to flow… you need to deploy your highest strengths and talents to meet the world in flow.' (Seligman, 2011, p. 11) Therefore, tapping into children's strengths in the classroom can be a key tool in motivating them and engaging them in learning.

But what are the different types of strengths? Seligman and psychologist Christopher Peterson have identified 24 universal character strengths and virtues, summarised in Figure 6.2.

They have been grouped under the six virtues: courage, wisdom and knowledge, humanity, justice, temperance, and transcendence. Seligman argues that each of us have several 'signature strengths', which we will use more than others, and when we use them in our work and play, we are often at our happiest (Seligman, 2002). Indeed, when participants in one study

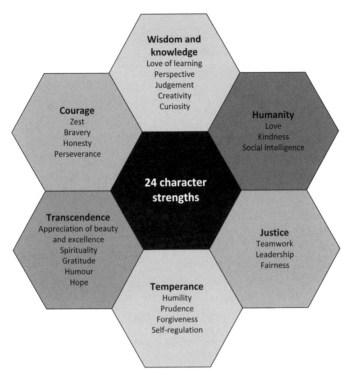

Figure 6.2: *The 24 character strengths identified by Seligman and Peterson (Seligman et al., 2005)*

were asked to identify their top five strengths and actively use one of them in a new way for a week, they were significantly happier up to six months later (Seligman et al., 2005).

Strengths in the classroom

One of the challenges with strengths is identifying them in ourselves. Because they are innate to us, we can easily overlook them or take them for granted. Therefore, teachers are key in helping children to identify their character strengths and making them explicit. Praising a child for their 'persistence' or 'teamwork' helps them to acknowledge that strength in themselves, which in turn builds self-confidence. This has the knock-on effect of encouraging that child to take risks and step into their stretch zone. Teachers can create a classroom culture of identifying strengths, where the children also start to identify strengths in each other.

Children have the capacity to develop all 24 strengths and virtues, but some are more prevalent in childhood than others. For instance, very young children tend to display the strengths of love, kindness, creativity, curiosity and humour (Park and Peterson, 2006). Other strengths, such as perspective, prudence and appreciation of beauty, tend to be more common in adults. The ICEP warns against teaching children the strengths that adults value over their innate values, and they state, 'We need to be careful to nurture the strengths they already possess, otherwise they may lose them as they mature.' (Institute of Child Education and Psychology, Module 3, p. 21) The aim is not to limit children to their core signature strengths but to allow them to develop, practise and cultivate the full spectrum of their strengths.

An important point to note is that many studies show that strengths of the 'heart', such as love and gratitude, are more strongly associated with wellbeing than strengths of the 'head', like critical thinking or leadership (Park and Peterson, 2009). There is a strong case for focusing more on the former if we truly want to teach children the skills of happiness. In Chapter 7, we'll look at some great ways in which to develop strengths of the heart like kindness, empathy and compassion (p. 145).

In action

By giving children more experiences of flow in the classroom, and by helping them develop their strengths, teachers can really start to help pupils to reach their full potential. When pupils are fully engaged in their learning and using the best parts of themselves to work, you really start to see them flourish. Schoolwork no longer becomes a chore or tiresome, it becomes a joy – a source of both pleasure and purpose.

Show me your flow

A simple activity to get children to think about flow, what it feels like and when they experience it, is to get them to share with the class their favourite flow activities. Ask your class:

- What are the things that they love to do at home or school where they experience flow? (I.e. what activities do they get lost in, where time rushes by and they lose a sense of themselves?)
- Get them to discuss as a class what it feels like to be in flow.
- Individually, they could create a poster, drawing and writing about their top five flow activities, and present these to the class. Identify whether there are any common themes (are they mainly sports-related, arts and crafts based, inside or outside school?) and notice whether their flow activities tend to be ones that they do on their own, in a group or a mixture of both.

When we experience flow, we are often using some of our signature strengths.

- Can the children identify what signature strengths they might be using when they are performing their flow activities? Maybe 'focus' when playing an instrument, 'love of learning' when reading a book or 'joy' when playing games with their friends.

The key is to get children more familiar with the concept of flow and to notice when they experience it the most, as well as to identify what strengths they might be using. This helps them to realise that by choosing to do an activity where they experience flow, they have the ability to boost their wellbeing.

Differentiation

One of the key preconditions for children experiencing flow is that the challenge of the task must match the skill of the child. This is normally done through differentiation in the classroom, and requires teachers knowing their children really well. Here are three of the ways in which you could differentiate work in your classroom:

- **By task:** In this scenario, you provide different tasks that the children could complete depending on their skill level. Some schools use a 'chilli' system, where work is rated as 'mild', 'medium' or 'hot' chilli. By allowing the pupil to select the work that they feel matches their skill level, it affords them autonomy in getting to exercise choice (another key ingredient in experiencing flow). If they start on the 'mild' task, they can always move up to the 'medium' and 'hot' tasks later, increasing the challenge as they go. Be mindful of those children who choose to remain in their comfort zones by selecting work that they know they can do, and make sure that you challenge them to move on to trickier tasks.

- **By support:** Teachers can give every child the same task or challenge but may give more assistance, feedback and support to children depending on their needs. By giving support and using scaffolds, you can guide and encourage pupils, whilst also creating a safe space so that they can cope with the struggle they'll experience on the task. You're also on hand to praise their effort and persistence, which helps them to identify strengths and fosters a growth mindset. The key is not to always assist the same children or they may become overly reliant on adult support, so mix up who you work with. Your aim is to stretch the children and to grow their independence.

- **By outcome:** Here you set the same task but every child will produce different outcomes depending on their skill level.

One really good way in which to do this is to provide them with 'low floor, high ceiling' tasks. These are tasks where each pupil can access it at their level. So, the 'low floor' allows pupils new to the subject to find the right level of challenge for them, and those pupils who are more experienced can go much deeper with their thinking and aim for the 'high ceiling'. These tasks are often open-ended investigations and with more than one 'right answer'. In fact, sometimes there are no 'right answers' at all, just the opportunity for children to discuss, debate, experiment and explore.

Remember, the key with any differentiation or adaptive teaching is to make sure that children are regularly in the sweet spot of challenge that is inherent to the stretch zone.

Making learning meaningful

Another key facet of flow-rich classrooms is that the challenge or task must have clear and obvious goals. Now I'm certainly not a teacher who recommends having a learning objective for every single lesson, along with very prescriptive success criteria. I believe that this can sometimes hinder creativity and hamper flow. However, children do need to know what the point of the task is that you are asking them to complete. When children know what the challenge involves and what the goals are, they are then able to lose themselves in the task and are more likely to experience flow. So, when any challenge or task is set, make sure that you set clear and understandable goals (one to three at a maximum) towards which that the class can work.

Furthermore, to engage pupils in their schoolwork even more, it really helps if they know how the work is relevant to their lives. You can either:

- Make it clear during a lesson how the learning is relevant to them (e.g. improving mental addition can help you when you're out shopping and need to know whether you can afford some items, or to check that you've been given the correct change).

- Alternatively, you can get the children to work out how the learning is relevant to them. A study that got low-performing science students to write about how a lesson was relevant to their lives found that they showed more interest in the subject and got higher grades than those students who didn't do the writing task (Hulleman and Harackiewicz, 2009).

- Finally, if you are teaching something that neither you nor the children can see the point of, maybe you could use your time more wisely to teach something more relevant and valuable.

Flow-rich activities

Here are three activities to try with your class to help you and them to experience more flow in the learning:

1. Debates

I love a good philosophy debate in class and they are often a great way in which to experience flow. They are inclusive, everyone can join in and they can take many twists and turns. They also help to develop children's reasoning and oracy skills. Here is how you can do it:

- Start by having a stimulus to generate open questions that the children would like to debate. The stimulus could be an object, a short film clip or a picture book.

- In groups, the children then come up with an open question that they'd like to discuss based on the stimulus (examples of previous questions my classes have debated are: Why do we have to go to school? Why do we need money? Is it ever OK to break the law?). Each group chooses their favourite question and the teacher scribes these on the board.

- Once you have about five or six questions on the board, everyone in the class then votes for the question that they'd like to debate. The question with the most votes wins. In doing so, you've also introduced your class to democracy – its benefits ('Yay, I got to debate my question!') and its pitfalls ('Boo, I didn't want that!').

- Once the debate gets going, your role as teacher is not to get involved too much. Encourage the quieter children to have their say. See whether children can take the role of devil's advocate (intentionally finding faults in others' arguments). Definitely encourage respectful arguing – 'I disagree with David's point because…' rather than 'Err, that's a rubbish point, Dave!'

- If a question runs its course, simply move on to debate the next most popular question. If your first debate doesn't go so well, don't be disheartened – it can take a few attempts before your class get into the flow of debating, as it is likely to be a new skill that they are learning.

Tales from the classroom

It was Mental Health Week and we decided to begin it with some wellbeing challenges. The children were assigned two different tables: one was the 'nine-dot challenge' (children had to connect a square grid of nine dots using only four straight lines) whilst the other was the 'one-minute portrait challenge' (you draw a portrait of a classmate in one minute but can't look down at the paper once you've started). The children listened to the instructions and eagerly began to work on their challenges.

Fifteen minutes after the challenges had started, I walked around the class and could sense an atmosphere full of fun, laughter and giggles. As I continued to walk around and observe the children, I noticed that it wasn't just them enjoying participating in the challenges – the teaching assistants were too!

'I look so funny, let's try this again and this time you try to draw my face,' said Vashnavi to her friend. 'I am almost there, just one dot to go,' said Mo, excitedly.

Twenty-five minutes went by and not one of them had moved from their tables. This is a rare feat!

I rang the bell and announced that it was time for the English lesson.

'Just five more minutes, Miss Sara, I want to do just one more portrait,' Eda pleaded.

'I need two more minutes, Miss Sara. I want to try the nine-dot challenge one more time!'

And then Rafi spoke up: 'One second, are we all in the flow? Remember what Miss Sara told us? That's why we don't want to stop!'

My heart began beating faster; I could feel a sense of satisfaction along with joy, and couldn't help but smile back. And our English lesson may even have started a little later that day than normal.

Sara Mekhari, teacher, international school in Bahrain

2. The beauty of maths

Maths professor Jo Boaler has worked closely with Carol Dweck to try to change the way in which teachers, children and parents view maths. Rather than it being viewed as a dry subject, mainly about calculations with right and wrong answers, Boaler has created a three-week course for primary school children to show them the creativity, beauty and imagination of maths. The lessons have useful plans, resources and extension tasks, which means that for three whole weeks you don't need to plan a maths lesson, as Jo Boaler and her team have done it for you!

I have taught the 'Inspirational Maths' lessons to several classes and they really do help to turn all children on to maths and help them to realise that maths is not just about numbers! In these lessons, the children and I really do experience flow, as we get stuck into interesting investigations. The focus is on group work and children working collaboratively in teams to help to prove points and argue their case (very similar to the skills used in debating). Go to **youcubed.org/week-of-inspirational-math** to sign up to the free resources and get your children exploring maths in a new and engaging way.

3. Design and technology

From my experience, children often experience flow when drawing, designing and making things. The James Dyson Foundation has created some excellent free 'challenges' for primary schools to help children to understand and experience the design and engineering process. Why not try the 'spaghetti bridge challenge'? Here is how you do it:

- Give the children their 'brief', which is to design and build a bridge to support the weight of a 250 g bag of sugar.

- Hand out the raw materials of spaghetti, masking tape and sticky tack.

- The resource card from Dyson gives the children some design ideas but, really, it's over to them to design and test their bridges.

- Don't overteach this. Let the children explore the brittleness of their raw materials. Let them experiment with how to stick it all together. Let them fail, then redesign, fail again and redesign again!

- Finally, test the bridges and get the children to evaluate each other's designs.

This is a great lesson. It is easy to show the relevance of the learning because what the children are doing is basically the design process that any object in the classroom or their house would have gone through before being manufactured. Be prepared for lots of spaghetti to clear up at the end, though! Go to **www.james dysonfoundation.co.uk/resources/other-engineering-resources/challenge-cards.html** for more ideas and to download your free pack of 'Challenge cards'.

Strength spotting

It is likely that your children will be unfamiliar with some of the 24 character strengths. Therefore, you will need to teach children what strengths are and what they look like in action, and give them opportunities to spot their own and their classmates' strengths. Here are some ways in which to bring strengths to life in the classroom:

- A great video to show to your class, which explains what character strengths are and how we can grow them, is called The Science of Character (**letitripple.org/films/science-of-character**).

- It can also help to have a display in your classroom listing the 24 character strengths so that your children become more familiar with them. One of the best online resources is the VIA Character Strengths website (**viacharacter.org/Character-Strengths**), which gives a short description of each strength. They also have great visual character strengths icons, which you could enlarge, print out and have on display: **https://viacharacter.org/resources/activities/via-youth-twenty-four-character-strengths-with-descriptions**

- Children in Years 5 and 6 could even take the VIA Character Strengths Youth Survey online (aimed at ten- to 17-year-olds: **viacharacter.org/survey/account/register**). It is free and takes about 15 minutes to complete. The survey will identify their top five signature strengths.

- At the start of some lessons, you could identify three strengths that you would like the class to use during the task. If they're working in groups on a problem-solving challenge, for example, you might select 'teamwork', 'perseverance' and 'creativity'. When you notice children displaying those strengths, you simply acknowledge it and praise them. If you see anyone using other strengths, notice and praise those too. By getting into the habit of noticing and praising strengths in your pupils, not only is it another way in which to counteract their natural 'negativity bias' but it also models to the class that we all have things that we are good at, and it's great to point those things out.

- A lovely activity to help children to spot strengths in each other is to give each child a class list of everyone's names and an empty box next to each name. They have to take each name and think of one strength that that child has displayed, with an example, and then write it down in a sentence in the box. For example: 'Mo – shows kindness when he lets other children join in with his games' or 'Sinita – showed bravery when she stuck up for me at netball club'. The teacher collects these in and cuts up the names and sentences into strips. All of the sentences that are about Mo get collected and stuck onto his sheet, and the same for Sinita and every other child. Laminate the sheets and then present each child with their strengths sheet. It can be an extremely positive experience for a child to be shown the strengths that others have spotted in them. I bet that some of them they never knew they had!

Flow and strengths

Superhero in you

As well as others spotting strengths in us, it is important that we develop the skill of identifying strengths in ourselves. A fun way in which to do this is to carry out the following 'superhero in you' exercise:

- Give each child a blank superhero template with their own headshot photo stuck on (see Figure 6.3). You can download the superhero template using this link: **www.teachappy. co.uk/resources-and-downloads**.

- Tell children that strengths are like superpowers that we have inside of ourselves. If you haven't done so already, show them the 'Science of Character' video (see p. 138).

- Get them to think of their top three strengths (if they struggle with this, they could choose the three that they'd most like to have or a friend could spot strengths in them) and write these next to their superhero figure. They can then give their superhero a name and design a colourful outfit.

- The next part is to create a comic strip called 'At My Best' (you can download the comic strip template here: **www. teachappy.co.uk/resources-and-downloads**). Using their superhero figure, they create a short-story comic strip about how they have used their superpower strengths to good effect (see Figure 6.4). The comic strip can be fiction or they could write about a real-life situation when they used their strengths.

- The children can then present their 'At My Best' comic strip story to the class. This is a fun and engaging way for children to think about their own strengths and how they can apply them in the real world. It teaches children that when we use our strengths, we often perform at our best, and doing so helps us to experience flow, as well as making us feel happier.

Figure 6.3: *A superhero figure, 'Captain Cakes', whose strengths are humour, determination and kindness*

Role models

Sometimes, children (and adults!) have a hard time recognising their strengths. For whatever reason, they simply aren't able to identify what they're good at or what strengths of character they have. Some people argue that the role models to whom we choose

Figure 6.4: *The comic strip showing 'Captain Cakes' putting his strengths into action*

to aspire actually have the character strengths and qualities that we possess but which we are too humble or short-sighted to recognise. Therefore, using this role model activity in class can be a good way in which to develop their strengths:

- Ask the children to choose one role model whom they admire from books, TV or films. It can be a fictional character, like Matilda from the Roald Dahl book, or someone from real life like Raheem Sterling. Maybe they could print off a photo of their role model.

- They then think of what their role model's top three character strengths are and list these next to their picture.

- Ask the children to think about how their role model uses their strengths and what they can learn from this. Do their strengths benefit society at all and, if so, how?

- Children could end the task by thinking about how they can develop the strengths that their role model has. For example, if their role model shows kindness, maybe they could choose to do more acts of kindness in school by helping to tidy up in class or inviting children to join their games at playtime.

Even if they've chosen someone famous for their looks or (heaven forbid) a reality-TV star, shifting the focus onto that person's character strengths avoids focusing on superficial qualities such as having nice hair, a pretty face or simply 'being famous'.

Key points

- Flow is a state of mind when we are completely absorbed in an activity. We lose a sense of ourselves, time rushes by and we use our skills and strengths to meet the challenges of the task. Flow is associated with higher levels of happiness and an improved ability to learn.

- We often experience flow when we use our strengths. Our strengths are the core parts of ourselves that shape our personalities and drive us. People report higher levels of wellbeing when they use their strengths in daily life.

- Teachers can actively create the classroom conditions that are conducive to flow, such as:
  - differentiating work so that the challenge of the task matches the skill of the child
  - giving children choice in the work that they are completing
  - setting clear goals and making work relevant to the children
  - allowing children to focus on work completely and lose themselves in the task
  - ensuring that pupils get feedback from the task, each other or the teacher.

- Provide fun and engaging lessons where children get to debate big ideas, discover the beauty in maths, and design, build and create.
- Create a classroom culture of spotting children's strengths. Praise children when they use different strengths and encourage them to spot strengths in each other.
- Encourage children to identify their own 'superhero' strengths and when they have used them to be 'at their best'. Use role models to spot strengths and identify how we can cultivate those strengths too.

Chapter 7
It's cool to be kind

You can always, always give something even if it's a simple act of kindness.

– Anne Frank

Chapter overview

In this chapter, we'll delve into the science of kindness. We'll look at why we are hardwired to be kind, and how kindness positively affects our health and levels of happiness. Finally, we will learn novel ways in which to develop the strength of kindness in children.

In theory	In action
• Hardwired to be kind	• It's cool to be kind week
• Benefits of kindness	• Class acts of kindness
• The virtuous circle	• Good deed feed
• Cultivating kindness	• Fundraising
	• Befriending meditation

In theory

Hardwired to be kind

In this chapter, I will refer to empathy, kindness, altruism and compassion. They are similar but all slightly different. Let me explain.

Empathy is the ability to sense other people's emotions and to think about what others may be thinking or feeling. Kindness is a general term that means being friendly, helpful and generous towards others (psychologists often call it 'prosocial' behaviour). Altruism is when we act to promote someone else's welfare, even at a risk or cost to ourselves. Compassion is the ability to sense another's suffering and then feeling compelled to try to relieve their suffering.

There is growing evidence that compassion and kindness are hardwired into our DNA because it was essential to our survival as a species. We learned in Chapter 1 (p. 15) that Charles Darwin's theory of human evolution noted that communities that were the most kind and sympathetic to one another flourished the best and raised the most children. Similarly, our 'social brain' means that we need to connect and cooperate with others to help our development. Other studies show that mothers' brains are wired to experience positive emotions when bonding with their children (Nitschke et al., 2004). When a mother is kind, loving and caring towards her baby, it feels good because it does her and her baby good.

Cozolino also notes that in the early twentieth century, doctors couldn't work out why children in orphanages had such high mortality rates. Believing that infections were to blame, doctors separated children from one another and kept handling by adults to a minimum to reduce infections spreading. Despite these rules, mortality rates remained alarmingly high. It was only when attachment researchers suggested that children be held and played with by consistent caregivers and allowed to interact with one another that their survival rates improved (Blum, 2002, cited in Cozolino, 2013). To be loved and cared for actually helps to keep us alive.

But humans' hardwiring for kindness goes beyond the parent–child relationship and extends to others too. When people help unrelated others, neurons in the reward and pleasure centres of the brain are firing away (Rilling et al., 2002). When our brain's reward centres are active, it is nature's way of saying to us, 'This feels good. Do this again.' Even babies' brains are wired to be attracted to kind others. In his book *A Force For Good,* emotional intelligence expert Dan Goleman relays a novel experiment in which babies were shown a cartoon of three shapes: a circle, a square and a triangle, each with large cute eyes. In the cartoon, the circle struggles to move up a hill and the kind triangle comes along and gives the circle a helpful push to get to the top. Next, the circle struggles up the hill again, but this time the mean square jumps on it, knocking the circle back down the hill. In the final part of the experiment, the babies, given the choice of toys in the shape of the kind triangle or mean square, invariably choose the kind one (Goleman, 2015).

Cynics may argue that kindness, although hardwired, is still ultimately a selfish act (either by promoting our genes or by making us feel good). But there is evidence that shows that when we are focused on being kind to others, and the reward centres of our brains are firing away, the areas of the brain that are concerned with ourselves and our problems actually quieten down (Lutz et al., 2008). So, by thinking about and helping others, we actually think less about ourselves.

Benefits of kindness

Emerson (1965) once said, 'It is one of the most beautiful compensations of this life that no man can sincerely try to help another without helping himself.' Science now backs this up, as numerous studies on kindness and compassion show that they benefit our happiness levels and our health. Let's take a look at these areas:

1. Happiness

As mentioned above, when we partake in kind acts towards others, our brain's reward centres are firing and our bodies release happy hormones like dopamine. These make us feel good and boost our levels of happiness. Vanessa King cites one study of 1,700 female volunteers, where the researchers found that many of the women experienced a 'helpers' high'. This was characterised by a feeling of euphoria after helping others, resulting from a release of endorphins, followed by a longer period of feeling calm, peaceful and serene (King, 2016, p. 17). Similarly, Sonja Lyubomirsky has found that people told to complete five acts of kindness over the course of a day report feeling much happier than the control group, and that the feeling lasts for many days after the exercise is over (Lyubomirsky, 2007).

It appears that we also get more happiness from spending money on others rather than on ourselves. In an experiment carried out by Professor Elizabeth Dunn, volunteers were given envelopes with either $5 or $20 inside, accompanied by a note. The note instructed the volunteers either to spend the money on themselves or to spend it on someone else (either by buying a gift or donating it to charity). The experiment concluded that 'Individuals who spent money on others were measurably happier than those who spent money on themselves – even though there were no differences between the two groups at the beginning of the day.' Interestingly, it made no difference whether $5 or $20 was spent – just the act of spending on others boosted happiness levels (Dunn and Norton, 2013).

And the link between prosocial spending and happiness is replicated throughout the world. Between 2006 and 2008, more than 200,000 people responded to a Gallup World Poll survey. Some of the questions asked whether they had donated to charity in the last month and how satisfied they were with their lives. In 120 out of 136 countries, people who donated to charity in the last month reported greater life satisfaction (Aknin et al., 2013a). These studies prove that doing good feels good.

2. Health

In his book *The Happiness Advantage,* Shawn Achor explains that a long line of empirical data shows that people who are altruistic towards loved ones and strangers have lower levels of stress and improved mental health (Achor, 2011). This may be because when we show kindness towards others, our bodies release the happy hormone oxytocin (Barraza and Zak, 2009). This powerful hormone can counteract the negative effects of the stress hormone cortisol, and even improve the health of our hearts (Szeto et al., 2008). Dr David Hamilton, in *The Five Side Effects of Kindness*, states that oxytocin causes the release of nitric oxide, which helps to lower blood pressure, as well as reducing the volume of free radicals in our system (which are responsible for ageing and tissue damage) and reducing inflammation of our cardiovascular system (Hamilton, 2017). All of this from simply being kind!

Being more kind and giving towards others also appears to help us to live longer. Studies of older people show that those who give support to a variety of people (such as emotional support to a spouse or by helping friends, relatives and neighbours) live longer than those who choose not to (Brown et al., 2009). Just the act of caring for something else (even if it isn't a person) seems to have amazing health benefits. In an experiment in an elderly nursing home, researchers gave a potted plant to two groups of residents (Langer and Rodin, 1976). One group was told that the nurses would take care of the plant for them, whilst the other group was instructed to care for the plant themselves. On average, the residents who cared for the plant themselves showed improved levels of health and wellbeing and actually lived longer than those who didn't care for their plant. These studies show that doing good does us good.

The virtuous circle

We hear lots about *vicious* circles in life (the fact that one bad event can lead to another and another, and we can get stuck in a rut of bad news and negativity) but we hear very little about *virtuous* circles. But it appears that carrying out acts of kindness creates a virtuous circle of positivity. When we help others, it makes us happier, and when we are happier, we tend to help others more (Aknin et al., 2011). And so it continues.

More than that, studies show that kindness is contagious. When people benefit from the kindness of others, they often 'pay it forward' by helping others in return. The ripple effect of kindness means that one small act can spread far and wide to people whom we don't know or haven't even met (Fowler and Christakis, 2010). Fascinatingly, each act of kindness helps to promote the release of oxytocin in those who carry it out, those who receive it or even those who just *witness* it happening. As well as the health benefits that we receive from oxytocin listed above, it also helps to foster trust and connection between people.

Even just being reminded of kind things that we have done in the past allows us to experience 'moral elevation' (the positive feeling of knowing that you have done a good deed), which in turn increases our motivation to be kind and increases the likelihood that we will partake in altruistic acts in the future (Schnall and Roper, 2011).

Cultivating kindness

Although humans may be hardwired to be kind and altruistic, we will all vary in how kind we are to others. Some people will naturally give a lot of their time and support to others, whereas other people will appear to be a lot stingier. Various researchers have looked to see which factors affect people's levels of empathy, kindness and compassion, and to learn how we can cultivate more of these important skills. This is what they have discovered:

- **Secure attachment:** It has been found that children who are securely attached to their parents are more likely to be sympathetic and kind towards their peers from as early as three and a half years old, compared to those children who are insecurely attached (Waters et al., 1979). We saw in Chapter 1 that teachers leading tribal classrooms can help to foster secure attachment in children (pp. 20–21). Tribal classrooms, where all children feel safe, protected and cared for, may be key in providing a secure base for children to show more kind and prosocial behaviour towards others.

- **Empathy:** Another study looked at how parents responded to their children when they had caused harm (Eisenberg and Fabes, 1990). Some parents reasoned with their children, prompting them to consider the consequences of their actions and how their actions might have harmed others. They encouraged empathy in their children by getting them to put themselves in another's shoes. Other parents used 'power assertion' in response to harmful behaviour, simply declaring what was right and wrong, and often using anger and physical punishment. The children raised to be more empathic were shown to be better adjusted and more likely to help their peers. Therefore, getting children to reflect on their harmful behaviour at school and helping them to understand how their behaviour affects others can help to increase their empathy and prosocial behaviour.

- **Modelling:** One of the most likely ways in which children learn kindness is from witnessing their parents being kind. In a landmark study, psychologists Pearl and Samuel Oliner looked at Germans who had helped to rescue Jews during the Nazi Holocaust. One of the strongest predictors of this courageous and extremely altruistic behaviour was the individual's memory of growing up in a family that prioritised kindness and compassion (Oliner, 2002). This is why schools that prioritise kindness and care for others provide the best example for their pupils to follow.

- **Loving-kindness meditation:** Brain research shows that a part of the brain known as the 'insula' is activated when we feel genuine empathy for another person. But studies also show that the insula is activated when we partake in mindfulness meditation, and regular practice even helps the insula to grow and expand (Williams and Penman, 2011). It appears that mindfulness training may increase our ability to show empathy towards others, a prerequisite for being more compassionate and kind. But a meditation practice often referred to as 'loving-kindness' has been shown to really help to cultivate compassion in people (Weng et al., 2013). In a 'loving-kindness' practice, you would typically start by cultivating feelings of kindness towards yourself, then extending these feelings to a loved one, then to a neutral stranger, then to someone whom you find difficult and then finally to all living beings. Research by Professor Barbara Fredrickson and colleagues showed that loving-kindness meditations boosted positive emotions in participants, increased their zest for life and increased their sense of purpose, whilst reducing feelings of isolation (Fredrickson et al., 2008).

In action

Given that we know that humans are hardwired to be kind, I believe that the following activities are less about *teaching* children to be kinder and more about giving them opportunities to be kind and to experience the kindness of others. When you try some of the following practices, be prepared to be amazed at how far the ripples of small acts of kindness can travel and how powerful those ripples can be when they sometimes turn into waves.

It's cool to be kind week

Having got fed up with the negative message of 'anti-bullying week' in a former school, one year I decided to rebrand it. Knowing that bullying behaviour often comes from feelings of isolation and insecurity, I wanted all the children to experience what it feels like to be kind to others and to be on the receiving end of kindness too. I wanted to create a virtuous circle of kindness, and so 'It's cool to be kind week' was born. In practice, this is how it worked:

- Every child in our school, from Nursery up to Year 6, was set a home-learning challenge – to carry out a random act of kindness.

- They could choose whatever they wanted to do (from helping their grown-ups tidy the house to baking treats for family) but they had to capture it in a photo, video or poster.

- Importantly, they had to reflect on how it made them feel to carry out the act of kindness and, if possible, how it made the person feel who received the act of kindness.

The first year was overwhelming. The whole school enthusiastically carried out their acts of kindness and the home-learning projects started flying in. The children showed their creativity in the acts of kindness that they chose to carry out. One child helped their mum to do the shopping for an elderly neighbour, whilst another decided to bake cupcakes and go with their dad to the local train station to greet commuters returning from work.

There was a real buzz in our school that week, and even the staff started to carry out acts of kindness for each other by making rounds of tea and buying chocolates (no one offered to do my marking, though, which was a shame). In fact, we received the dreaded Ofsted call that week and even they enjoyed it, writing in their report, 'Pupils responded particularly well to "It's cool to be kind week"… they show great care and consideration for each other.'

Class acts of kindness

The following year, we wanted to build on the fabulous response that we'd had to our first 'It's cool to be kind week'. So, as well as every child receiving the challenge of carrying out an individual random act of kindness (encouraging them to be creative and do something different to last year), we challenged every class to go out into the local community and carry out a whole-class act of kindness. Maybe you could take some inspiration from some of the things that the classes got up to and encourage your own class to carry out an act of kindness this school year:

- **Year 1:** They made delicious cookies in school and then went to Brockley High Street to give them out to members of the public.

- **Year 2:** They were on a school trip to the Cutty Sark in Greenwich, London. They'd made a massive banner with 'Laugh more, worry less!' written on it for commuters, tourists and the general public to enjoy.

- **Year 3:** They wrote kindness notes (see Figure 7.1) and attached them to the front of *Metro* newspapers and then handed them out to commuters at Brockley Station. The school started to receive emails from people all over the London Underground network who had found a copy of the *Metro* with one of their notes, thanking the children for spreading some positivity.

- **Year 4:** They wrote beautiful inspiring quotes, such as 'To thine own self be true' and 'That smile looks good on you!' and gave them out to the public or left them on benches for people to find.

- **Year 5:** They got to Brockley Station early one morning to see off commuters with renditions of 'Don't Stop Believing' by Journey. You have never seen so many commuters smiling, singing and clapping before!

- **Year 6:** They made tea and cakes so that the builders working on the school extension could have a well-deserved break.

What we found was that once the week was over, the children had got into the habit of being kind, so acts of kindness continued to happen randomly throughout the year. The best way in which to

Figure 7.1: *An example of a kindness note*

continue the kindness after 'It's cool to be kind week', though, is for all of the staff to model it – smiling at children and colleagues, holding doors open, saying 'Hello' and asking how people are, and being kind with your feedback. All of these actions will make kindness part of the 'DNA' of the school and will become infectious for the children.

Tales from the classroom

It is always so special and humbling when members of the public get in touch during 'It's cool to be kind week' to say how the children's acts of kindness have touched them. Below is just one of the many responses that we have had over the years, and it shows how children's small acts of kindness can be just what someone needs in their time of difficulty:

> *Dear Headteacher,*
>
> *I have been meaning to send a note for several weeks and apologise for the delay. I wanted to say a heartfelt thank you to you and your staff for encouraging the children in your care to think about others in their random acts of kindness.*
>
> *I received a delicious cookie and lovely poinsettia. I have been widowed this year and I cannot say how much I appreciated this act of kindness.*
>
> > *Thank you very much indeed.*

Good deed feed

If you have any blank wall spaces in your playground or communal areas, why not liven them up with a 'good deed feed'? The idea is really simple: if children or members of staff witness someone else being kind, they can write about it on the good deed feed. This helps to promote the idea that it is good to acknowledge other people's acts of kindness and to savour them. Remember, just witnessing acts of kindness can release the bonding, stress-relieving happy hormone, oxytocin!

To do this, all you need is:

- an area of wall in the playground or a display board inside the school
- laminated sheets of paper to write on, stapled to the board
- permanent marker pens to write with
- a member of staff or some responsible Year 6 pupils in charge of the pens and supervising children as they write their messages on the board.

Our school was undergoing major building work, and a large section of the playground was blocked off by a plain-looking

Figure 7.2: *A 'good deed feed'*

hoarding. We decided to turn the hoarding into a 'good deed feed'. At playtimes, lunchtimes and after school, children would be filling the board up (see Figure 7.2). Parents and carers would often be stood reading the feed before and after school. The good deed feed contained things like:

> 'When I was feeling sad, Shane came and made me laugh. By Shalom'

> 'I saw four Year 3 children helping a child in Reception who had fallen over. This made me smile. Mr Casey'

> 'I saw a man help a woman down the stairs with her buggy at the station. Kerry'

This is a simple but effective way of getting children and staff to notice all of the everyday acts of kindness that we often overlook.

Fundraising

Most primary schools that I know do some kind of fundraising. But for fundraising to make a real impact on the children, it really helps if it is more engaging than simply donating £1 for wearing your own clothes on a certain day of the year. The research on prosocial spending shows that for it to have the biggest impact on our wellbeing, we need to do the following:

1. **Make a connection:** People generally derive more happiness from spending money on people with whom they have a connection (Aknin et al., 2011). So, when doing a fundraising project at school, either choose a charity that has strong social ties to the school and local community, or choose a cause that means something to a member of the school community.

    One year, at a previous school, a member of staff had tragically lost her husband to a sudden heart attack. The following year, and with her permission, the school decided to take part in the British Heart Foundation's Three Peak Challenge. We didn't have mountains nearby to climb, so we hired in a five-metre climbing wall with qualified instructors. Children learned to do rock climbing over two days and were sponsored to see how high they could climb. Parents and carers could pay to climb the wall after school. It was one of the biggest fundraisers of the year.

2. **Make an impact:** When people donate money to a cause, they don't usually get to see how the money was spent. But you get a bigger boost to your happiness levels when you know that your donation has had an impact (Aknin et al., 2013b). Certain charities are very good at letting you know how they have spent your money.

    Charities like Toilet Twinning, for example, build toilet blocks in countries with poor sanitation. The idea is that schools can 'twin' their toilets with another country – i.e. if your school has four separate toilet blocks, you try to raise enough money to build four toilet blocks in your chosen country. For each toilet block you build, they send you a framed photo of the new flushing toilet block. Or, if you choose to support local charities, often their representatives will come to the school to host an assembly and show how the money has been spent. So, when choosing your charity fundraising events, make sure that you can show the children the impact that their donations have had.

3. **Make it fun:** If you want your children to get into the habit of giving to charities, try to make it fun! The happy hormones that they will release when involved in a fun charity fundraiser will make them want to do it again and again.

I worked in a school with a high number of male staff (primary school teaching is still about 85 per cent female to 15 per cent male) and we decided to take part in Movember. This is an annual event in which men grow moustaches during November to raise awareness of men's health issues, such as prostate cancer, testicular cancer and men's suicide. Not only did the male staff look pretty foolish for a whole month (especially when doing parents' evening with a dodgy tash!) but on the last day of November, all of the children and female staff got to wear fake moustaches for the day (see Figure 7.3)!

Figure 7.3: *Children wearing their fake moustaches to raise money for Movember*

Befriending meditation

A type of loving-kindness practice that you could try with your class is called the 'befriending' meditation. This meditation helps children to cultivate kind and friendly feelings towards themselves and others. This is a practice inspired by *Mindfulness* by Mark Williams and Danny Penman (2011). Ensure a strong, confident, seated posture before beginning and allow the children time to say the phrases to themselves, silently in their heads:

> *Start by taking three deep breaths – in through your nose and out through your mouth. Become aware of your body, sitting here, breathing. Then, with an attitude of friendliness and kindness, silently say to yourself:*
> *'May I be healthy, may I be happy, may I be peaceful.'*
> *Allow the phrases to sink down deep within you, as if you were dropping pebbles into a deep lake. Enjoy this feeling of showing kindness to yourself.*
> *Then bring to mind someone you love and care for very much. Imagine them sitting in front of you smiling. Now, silently say to them:*
> *'May you be healthy, may you be happy, may you be peaceful.'*
> *Enjoy seeing this person looking relaxed, calm and happy.*
> *Now bring to mind someone you know but not that well. It might be someone at school, or someone who works in a shop near where you live. You recognise them but you don't know them that well. Imagine them sitting in front of you, smiling and say to them:*
> *'May you be healthy, may you be happy, may you be peaceful.'*
> *Enjoy the feeling of sending kindness out to them and seeing them happy.*
> *Finally, bring to mind all living beings who, just like you, wish to be happy. Extend friendly, loving feelings to everyone on the planet, including yourself, saying:*
> *'May we all be healthy, may we all be happy, may we all be peaceful.'*
> *Enjoy this feeling of sending love and kindness out into the world.*

In summary, being kind and compassionate towards others is all about connection. When we put ourselves in another's shoes and think about how our actions affect others, we are more likely to act for the benefit of others, rather than just for ourselves. The great

Albert Einstein once said that to view ourselves as separate from one another and the universe was a kind of 'prison'. He went on to say that 'Our task must be to free ourselves from this prison by widening our circle of compassion to embrace all living creatures and the whole of nature in its beauty.' (Einstein, writing to Norman Salit on 4 March 1950.) Maybe teaching children the skills of kindness is one way of setting them free.

Key points

- Humans are hardwired to be kind to others. Kindness fosters social connection and cohesion, which were essential for survival in our tribal past.

- When we show kindness and compassion towards others, our bodies release happy hormones like endorphins and oxytocin, which not only make us feel happier but improve our health too.

- A virtuous circle can begin, as being kind makes us happier and when we're happier, we're more likely to be kind.

- Schools can host 'kindness weeks' in which children are encouraged to carry out random acts of kindness. Even whole classes can go out into the local community to carry out class acts of kindness.

- Get children to notice everyday acts of kindness by creating a 'good deed feed' in your school.

- When fundraising in school, ensure that children make a connection with the good cause; allow them to see the impact that their fundraising has had and make it fun for them!

- Children can cultivate kind feelings towards themselves and others by trying a 'befriending' meditation.

It's cool to be kind

Chapter 8
Digital wellbeing

Men have become the tools of their tools.

– Henry David Thoreau

Chapter overview

In this chapter, we will unpick the impact that digital technologies have on children's wellbeing and explore ways in which they can take greater control of their online lives to make their use of technology a more positive experience.

In theory	In action
• Digital natives	• E-safety
• Digital technology and physical health	• Digital boundaries (detox)
• Social media and mental health	• Digital citizenship
• Cyberbullying and social comparison	• Coping when things go wrong online
• Benefits of being online	• Parent and carer support
	• Being mindful online

In theory

Digital natives

Digital technologies are an integral part of children's lives in the twenty-first century. Children spend more time online than ever before and at younger ages. This is why children today are often referred to as 'digital natives', because they have grown up in the presence of digital technologies. But phrases like 'being online', 'using tech' or even 'social media' are so general and vague that it's useful to look at *how* primary-aged children are actually engaging with technology. Table 8.1 breaks down trends in British children's

Table 8.1: *British children's use of digital technologies by age (adapted from Ofcom, 2022)*

3–4-year-olds	5–7-year-olds	8–11-year-olds
• 17 per cent have their own smartphone • 24 per cent have their own social media profile • 89 per cent use video sharing platforms • 50 per cent use messaging sites/apps • 18 per cent play games online	• 28 per cent have their own smartphone • 33 per cent have their own social media profile • 93 per cent use video sharing platforms • 59 per cent use messaging sites/apps • 38 per cent play games online	• 60 per cent have their own smartphone • 60 per cent have their own social media profile • 95 per cent use video sharing platforms • 84 per cent use messaging sites/apps • 69 per cent play games online • 32 per cent have seen something worrying or nasty online

use of digital technologies by age, and it's clear how usage increases as children get older (Ofcom, 2022).

There is a growing concern amongst parents, teachers and society at large that children spending more time online is a bad thing about which we need to be very worried. But what does the research show about digital technology and children's wellbeing?

Digital technology and physical health

Of course, using technology and devices doesn't just affect children's mental health but also affects their physical health. Is there any research that points to more time spent using digital technologies being bad for children's bodies?

Sleep

Most devices emit blue light, which has an impact on natural sleep and wake cycles (circadian rhythms). Using devices with bright screens in the evening has been associated with reduced melatonin, a hormone that helps signal sleep to the body (OECD, 2019). A systematic review of the literature examining sleep patterns amongst school-aged children and adolescents found that the vast majority of the studies showed negative associations between screen time and sleep outcomes, such as delayed timing and shortened duration of sleep (Hale and Guan, 2015). Even if children use devices that block the blue light, this is also about stimulation. Good sleep hygiene is about preparing your mind and body for sleep, which often means relaxing. If children are on devices near their bedtimes, gaming, chatting or watching clips, their brains are unlikely to be getting the best preparation for sleep.

Sedentary behaviour

If children are sat or lying down whilst on their devices, then surely that is contributing to their sedentary behaviour? It's a compelling argument. It adds to this notion of a 'displacement effect' of technology – that time spent online is time not spent on other more 'valuable' activities, such as on sports, socialising or being outside in nature. However, a review of the literature suggests that reducing screen time may not motivate adolescents and children to engage more in physical activity (Kardefelt Winther, 2017). Moreover, other research has shown that screen-based, sedentary behaviour and leisure-time physical activity are independent of one another (Gebremariam et al., 2013). In other words, if children are going to be physically active, screen time won't stop them.

Eye problems

I remember my mum regularly telling me and my brother as children that if we sat too close to the television we'd need glasses. I now wear glasses but my brother doesn't, so make of that what you will. But cases of myopia (short sightedness, where objects nearby are clear but objects further away look blurry) have increased significantly in Europe and America over the last 50 years. A systematic review published in *The Lancet* (Foreman et al., 2021) found that smart device use and computer use were significantly associated with myopia. It's thought that the increased strain on the eyes to focus on our devices might be the reason. However, it may be linked to actually spending more time indoors (where most screen use happens), because other studies show that simply getting children to spend one to two hours more outside each day can reduce the incidences of myopia by up to 50 per cent (Wu et al., 2020) – even more reason to take learning outdoors!

Social media and mental health

First, let's take a look at children's use of social media and the impact that it has on their mental health. At the time of writing, a quick Google search of 'social media causes' brings up these top suggested searches:

- depression

- anxiety

- ADHD

- eating disorders

- cyberbullying

- loneliness

- low self-esteem

- body image issues.

It's no surprise that many people worry about children's use of social media! In Dr Lucy Foulke's book *What Mental Illness Really Is... (and What It Isn't)* (2022), she explores this topic in great detail, looking at the empirical evidence. Foulkes explains that a landmark paper in 2018 stated that 'There is compelling evidence that the devices we've placed in young people's hands are having profound effects on their lives – and making them seriously unhappy.' (Foulkes, 2021, p. 128) However, she goes on to show how this study was seriously flawed. It showed correlational links between social media usage and children's depressive symptoms, rather than a causal relationship. In other words, it wasn't possible to prove in this study whether social media was the *cause* of children's unhappiness. It could well be that unhappier children spent more time online because they were more withdrawn, they didn't socialise as much, played fewer sports, etc. Or perhaps these children were more likely to suffer with insomnia, and when they couldn't sleep, they spent more time online. Rather than social media *causing* their mental health difficulties, it could have been the lack of sleep. In short, there were too many variables that this study didn't account for, and so it was not possible to say without doubt that social media causes mental health issues.

Instead, Foulkes points to other more robust studies that show that social media doesn't have the strong negative impact that we often *think* it does. One study, looking at 12,000 ten- to 15-year-olds, showed that although there was a link between increased social media use and decreased life satisfaction, the relationship was tiny (Orben et al., 2019). Another longitudinal study looked at levels of anxiety and depression in 13- to 20-year-olds, linked to their use of social media (Coyne et al., 2020). It found that when a teenager spent more time online compared to their normal use, they didn't experience an increase in anxiety or depression (and when they spent less time online, they didn't experience a drop in these symptoms either).

Therefore, our strong fears around children's use of social media may be unwarranted. That isn't to say that spending time online cannot be harmful for some children, but the real issue is what children are actually doing online. As Dr Lucy Foulkes explains, 'If we want to understand how social media affects mental health, then we need to look… at *how* people are spending their time on apps, rather than simply measuring the number of hours they are on them.' (Foulkes, 2022, p. 131) We'll explore this a bit later in this chapter.

Cyberbullying and social comparison

Two things that we do know are inherently bad for wellbeing are being bullied and comparing ourselves to others (with the view that our lives don't quite match up).

Cyberbullying

ONS research in 2020 showed that:

- Around one in five children aged ten to 15 years in England and Wales (19 per cent) experienced at least one type of online bullying behaviour in the year ending March 2020, equivalent to 764,000 children.

- One in four (26 per cent) did not report their experiences to anyone.

- Being called names, sworn at or insulted and having nasty messages about them sent to them were the most common online bullying behaviour types, experienced by 10 per cent of all children aged 10 to 15 years.

It's important to bear in mind that most victims of cyberbullying are also being bullied in person too. The ONS study above showed that almost three-quarters of those who experienced cyberbullying experienced bullying in school as well. One study of teenagers by bullying expert Professor Dieter Wolke found that just one per cent of cyberbullying victims were 'only' bullied online (Wolke et al., 2017). As Wolke states in the report, 'Cyberbullying creates few new victims, but is mainly a new tool to harm victims already bullied by traditional means.' It strongly suggests that solving any issues of bullying starts inside the school gates.

Social comparison

Some fascinating research into Olympic medal winners shines a light on the impact of social comparison on our levels of happiness (Hedgcock et al., 2021). In short, bronze medal winners are happier than silver medal winners. Why? Well, it has to do with social comparison. The silver medal winners tend to compare upwards and they feel less satisfied about missing out on the gold medal. In contrast, bronze medallists compare downwards and feel happy and grateful that they made it onto the podium.

What's this got to do with social media? Well, many platforms encourage users to share snapshots of their lives, and because we care so much about what others think (we are a hyper-social animal, after all), we're more likely to only share the stuff that makes us look good. It can mean that there becomes this endless arms race to only post the most preened and edited snippets of our lives, and when we compare our lives to those of others, we can end up feeling unhappy. Let's use selfies as an example. A 2018 study asked one group of female students to take selfies of themselves and post them online and the other group of female students were simply asked to read a news article online (Mills et al., 2018). The study found that the selfie group experienced more anxious feelings and they felt less confident and less physically attractive after the task, but the group reading the news did not. Another study by the Happiness Research Institute in Denmark got one group of people to stop using Facebook for a week, and compared them to a group who used Facebook as normal (Wiking, 2019). The group that ditched Facebook were significantly happier after the week was over; they reported feeling less lonely, had increased their social activity and were more satisfied with their social life.

Benefits of being online

I wanted to end this section by shining a light on the good things that digital technologies can bring to children's lives. In fact, when researchers at the Children's Society actually asked children how they feel about their lives online, they were generally very positive (Moore and Raws, 2021). As Figure 8.1 shows, the 2,000 children surveyed rated their happiness with the things that they do online as 8 out of 10, their happiness with safety online as 7.8 out of 10 and their happiness with their online lives as 7.7 out of 10. These

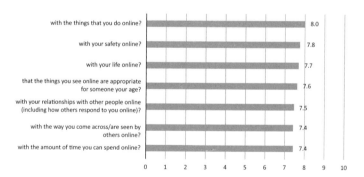

Figure 8.1: *Children's (aged 10 to 17) mean scores (on a scale of 0 to 10) when asked 'How happy are you…' (reproduced with kind permission from The Children's Society, Moore and Raws, 2021)*

are pretty healthy scores and most children are happy with their online lives which should reassure us adults (although, of course, we do need to ensure we protect those children at greater risk of harm online).

Being online offers the chance for children to communicate and connect with their friends, which is fundamental to wellbeing. Dr Lucy Foulkes shares research in her book indicating that the four pillars of friendship (validation, self-disclosure, instrumental support and companionship) are all as present online as they are in the offline world (Foulkes, 2022). Older children often go online to discuss things that are stressing them out, and this make them feel better, whilst others find it easier to discuss more personal matters online than face to face. Some children can support one another with homework or give advice about what to wear when going out. And, of course, social media provides the opportunity to have a laugh. As Foulkes explains, 'I think a key reason for their [social media apps] popularity might be far less sinister: it's a way of having fun with our friends.' (Foulkes, 2022, p. 142)

In action

Technology is here to stay, which means that a guiding principle for promoting wellbeing has to be about teaching children how to stay in control of it and make it work for them. The following ideas will help you to start the conversation with children and their parents about how to enhance their 'digital wellbeing'.

E-safety

Since I became a teacher in 2010, every school that I've worked in has taught children about e-safety, so there isn't anything ground-breaking or revolutionary about what I am sharing here. The fact of the matter is that when it comes to wellbeing, feeling safe is of paramount importance, whether that is in person or online. Some key principles to teach to children about staying safe online are:

- **Talk to a trusted adult:** If anything online makes you feel unsafe or scared, this is the most important thing to do. Seek support from someone whom you trust and who can help you.

- **Show respect and be kind:** Speak and interact with people online in the same way that you would face to face. If people are not kind or respectful to you or others, report it and speak to a trusted adult.

- **Keep it private:** Keep your private information private. Don't share passwords, your home address, date of birth, location or revealing photos.

- **Think before you share:** Before you post or share anything, pause and ask yourself, 'Will this help me and others or might it harm me or others?' If in doubt, don't share it out.

- **Check that it's for real:** Not everything you read or see online is real. Be curious and sceptical and if you're unsure, check in with a trusted adult.

Some useful sites to use in class are Google's Be Internet Awesome (**https://beinternetawesome.withgoogle.com/en_uk**), Childnet (**www.childnet.com**), Digital Matters (**www.internetmatters.org/digital-matters**) and BBC Bitesize Digital Literacy (**www.bbc.co.uk/bitesize/topics/zymykqt/articles/zym3b9q**).

Digital boundaries (detox)

As with most things in life, there is always a balance to be struck so that we experience a sweet spot of enjoyment. We see it with happiness itself – a balance of pleasure and purpose. We see it with learning, growth and the stretch zone – not too little or too much stress. The same is true of using digital technologies – too little and we can feel disconnected and too much and we may feel overwhelmed. Therefore, it's crucial that children learn how to regulate their own use of technology (with the help of the adults around them). Try these ideas for helping your class to learn how to get the balance right in their lives:

- Ask your class to discuss what things they enjoy doing online (e.g. gaming, chatting with friends, watching movies, etc.) and how technology helps them (e.g. staying connected with others, having a laugh to reduce stress, researching homework and learning new things, etc.). Highlight the fact that technology can help us to experience both pleasure and purpose.

- Now ask your class to reflect on and discuss some of the ways in which being online might not be so helpful for them (e.g. spending too much time online, being less active, not doing other hobbies they enjoy, not interacting with people at home, viewing content that makes them feel sad or unsafe, etc.).

- Discuss ways in which they could put boundaries in place so that they experience the 'Goldilocks zone' of online usage (not too much and not too little), and write these ideas on a flipchart, such as:
  - setting aside specific times to be online
  - logging off an hour before their bedtime
  - edit notifications so that they're not notified every time someone likes or comments on a post
  - taking a 'digital detox' where all tech is turned off
  - putting aside time to do non-digital activities like playing outside, drawing and reading.

- Children could make a poster about digital boundaries but, most importantly, they should start to **try them out** at home. So, why not set a home learning challenge to put some of these digital boundaries in place and then report back to the class with how they got on?

Adapted from a case study in the book *The Key To Happiness* by Meik Wiking (2019, p. 65).

A boarding school in Denmark were concerned that their children were spending so much time on their devices that they weren't forming important bonds with their classmates and fellow boarders. They took the fairly drastic decision to experiment for a term with only allowing pupils access to their devices and social media for one hour a day.

After the first term, the new system was put to a student vote. Should they stick with the limited access to phones and gadgets or give them back and allow them to be used as much as the children wanted? Amazingly, 80 per cent voted for the first option! The staff and the children recognised that spending less time on devices and more time connecting with the people around them made them happier.

Digital citizenship

Being a good digital citizen is not really any different to being a good citizen in real life. The values and habits that you're trying to foster in your tribal classrooms are the values and habits that you want children to exhibit in their online worlds as well. Reminding children of the following principles can help them to set a good example online for others to follow:

- **Don't forget the team flag:** The values that we try to live and breathe in class are just as important online. Be supportive, show respect and be a good team member.

- **Always be kind:** Remind children that the science of kindness works online as well and that kindness is contagious, it makes us feel happier and it does our bodies and minds good too.

- **Apologise:** We are human beings and we make mistakes. Sometimes we will say or do things online that we regret, and it's important to own those mistakes and apologise to anyone whom we may have hurt or upset (and commit to not making the same mistake again).

- **Stand up for others:** If you see other people being unkind or disrespectful to others, it's important to make a stand. Report it on the platform if you know how, let the victim know that you're there for them and talk to a trusted adult.

Coping when things go wrong online

Despite our best efforts, we may end up in situations online where we've got into a spot of bother and things seem to be spiralling out of control. I have learned the hard way myself on platforms like Twitter, where I've been embroiled in a few spats and my notifications have gone through the roof. I remember feeling quite anxious and I found it very hard to take my mind elsewhere, as I knew that when I logged back on there would be even more comments! In a way, these situations need to happen so that we can learn from them and understand when to respond to something and when to walk away. My top tips for children (and adults) coping when things go wrong online are as follows:

- **Talk to a trusted adult:** I know that this is the third time I've mentioned this, but it's because it is by far the most important rule to teach children in navigating their online lives. When we speak to people we trust, we get things off our chest and they can help us to resolve the issue with their support and a fresh perspective. This is especially true if we feel that we're being bullied.

- **Block and mute:** These functions appear on most social media platforms. If there are accounts that are particularly harmful and upsetting, block them immediately – you do not need their toxicity to pollute your mind. If you are included on a thread or chat that is stressing you out, you can mute it and you'll no longer be notified of updates.

- **Edit notifications:** Even though we can get a positive 'buzz' when we receive a like or message, constantly receiving them can be stressful and leave us unable to focus on the present moment. Tuning notifications off means that we get to choose when we log on and check our apps.

- **Take a digital detox:** If things are really getting you down, turning all tech off and having a complete break can be the ideal tonic. Instead, you can do something to bring you pleasure, like spending time in nature, playing with a pet, hanging out with your family or losing yourself in your favourite book.

- **Do something active:** Whether it's our online or offline world that's stressing us out, physical activity is probably the best remedy for using up the extra cortisol and adrenaline that's built up in our bodies. Being active, outside and with people you like is a triple-whammy of goodness.

Parent and carer support

Children pick up a lot of their digital habits from their parents and carers, and they will imitate what is modelled at home. Although teachers shouldn't be responsible for children's use of technology outside of school, we can certainly provide resources for parents and carers to influence what goes on at home and help children and their families to develop healthy habits with tech. These pointers can be helpful to share with families in handouts, newsletters and in workshops hosted at school:

- **Plan in tech-free time:** Dedicate parts of the evening and weekend when tech is put away and families engage in activities together.

- **Understand what tech your children use:** Parents and carers should know what apps, games and websites children spend time on. Talk to your children about their tech.

- **Use tech together:** Spend time online with your children. Play their favourite games with them, watch their favourite YouTube clips and use it as a chance to bond.

- **Set tech time limits:** It helps if families have clear boundaries for when tech can be accessed and for how long. Be consistent so that everyone is clear on those boundaries.

- **Design a family media plan:** The American Academy of Pediatrics has designed a really useful tool (**www.healthy children.org/English/fmp/Pages/MediaPlan.aspx**) to allow families to create their own media and tech plan. It helps families to communicate effectively about technology with their children, set boundaries and find the right balance for them.

- **Educate yourself:** The website KidsnClicks (**https://kids nclicks.com/resources**) was set up by parents for parents. It has useful tips for balancing screen time, being a good tech role model, using tech to encourage physical activity and understanding what apps are age-appropriate (and lots more!). Share this with your parents and carers so that they can educate themselves.

- **Be a good role model:** Be mindful of your use of technology and how long you spend on your phone and other devices. When your children speak with you, put devices down and give them your full attention.

Being mindful online

Mindfulness is about awareness and learning to be more in tune with our thoughts, our feelings, our behaviours and the people and world around us. When we're more mindful online, it means that we're more likely to notice when we might need a break from our screens or when our behaviour is tipping into an unhealthy pattern. Try these ideas for encouraging your children to be more mindful online:

- **How do you feel?** Encourage children to regularly check in with how they feel when online. If they notice that being online at that time does not feel good or it starts to feel uncomfortable, those are good signs to take a break.

- **When do you use technology?** It can help to become aware of when we feel the urge to reach for our devices. Do we often feel stressed or low when we use technology? If so, we may be using tech to dull or avoid our more uncomfortable emotions.

- **Manage emotions effectively:** If children experience uncomfortable emotions, discuss with them the different ways in which they could soothe themselves that don't involve technology. Talking to someone they trust, doing some exercise, carrying out short mindfulness practices, being creative, listening to music or reading can be great alternatives. Get children to reflect on what works for them.

- **Are you being kind to yourself and others?** Mindfulness is about being aware, with kindness, care and curiosity. Get children in the habit of asking themselves whether being online is the best thing for them in that moment, and also reflecting on whether their interactions with others are kind and caring.

Key points

- Children are spending increasing amounts of time online, and there is a fear that this is inherently bad for their wellbeing. However, research shows that these fears may be unwarranted and that most children are happy with their lives online.

- Using technology can be harmful to children's wellbeing, especially if they are being bullied or are regularly comparing themselves to others online in a negative way.

- There are many benefits to children spending time online, such as connecting with others, learning, playing games and having fun.

- It is important to teach children how to be safe online by talking to trusted adults if something doesn't feel right, thinking before they share online, keeping private information private, being kind and respectful, and checking that things are real and not fake.

- Digital technologies can be addictive, so having boundaries in place helps us to find the right balance.

- Children should learn to be good citizens in person and online by staying true to their values, being kind, apologising if they make mistakes and standing up for others who may need support.

- Things do go wrong online at times, and when they do children can learn to seek adult support, use block and mute functions, take some time offline and do some physical activity to cope with stress.

- Support parents and carers with useful ideas and resources to help them to maintain digital boundaries at home and to find the right balance.

- Help children to be more mindful online by tuning in to how they're feeling when they are online and noticing whether they're using devices to avoid negative emotions.

Chapter 9
How our thoughts shape our world

It is not what happens to you but how you react that matters.
                                                    – Epictetus

---

Chapter overview

In this chapter, we'll look at why it pays to be more optimistic, in terms of health and happiness. We'll understand how children's mental chatter affects their levels of optimism, and look at what we can do to nudge our pupils to look on the brighter side of life.

In theory	In action
• Optimism and its benefits	• Thoughts for the day
• Explanatory style	• Influencing explanatory style
• ABC model	• Conscience alley
• Reframing	• Music
• Priming	

In theory

Optimism and its benefits

Everyone knows the old saying that an optimist sees a half-drunk glass as being 'half-full', whereas a pessimist sees it as being 'half-empty'. But what's the big deal? Why does it matter that we all see the world differently? Well, increasing evidence shows that being more optimistic can have a wide range of positive implications for our happiness and wellbeing. For example, studies have shown that optimistic people tend to:

1. report higher levels of subjective wellbeing and happiness (Ferguson and Goodwin, 2010)

2. show higher levels of positive emotion (Chang and Sanna, 2001)

3. have better overall health and be less prone to disease (Seligman, 2011)

4. have less chance of suffering from clinical depression (Kahneman, 2011).

Psychologists describe optimism as the expectation that the future will be socially desirable, good and pleasurable and, although genetics and upbringing play a large part in affecting our levels of optimism, it is still a skill that we can learn. Moreover, Martin Seligman believes that it is a skill that could be taught in schools as an antidote to depression, a way of increasing life satisfaction and an aid to better learning and creativity (Seligman et al., 2009).

Blind optimism vs. realistic optimism

Although it is clear that having a more optimistic outlook is beneficial to us, it is important to note that there are downsides to being overly optimistic as well. Studies show that people who are *too* optimistic:

1. are often unable to delay gratification and so want everything immediately

2. have difficulty sizing up situations realistically and ignore important pitfalls

3. can make unwise decisions (e.g. making highly risky investments) (Davidson and Begley, 2012)

4. can suffer from 'false-hope syndrome', where they stick with ridiculous expectations way past the point at which they should have given up or changed tactics (Dolan, 2015).

This is often known as 'blind optimism', where people continue to feel that the future will turn out brilliantly, despite glaringly obvious obstacles or problems. Instead, positive psychologists argue that it is better to be aiming for 'realistic optimism'. According to Paul Dolan, this is where 'We should expect the best but have a contingency plan for the worst.' (Dolan, 2015, p. 97) Realistic optimism is also where you don't filter out the risks involved in a given situation, but you do filter out unhelpful negative thoughts that might be holding you back.

Explanatory style

Where we fall on the spectrum of optimism and pessimism is largely affected by our 'explanatory style', which is the mental conversations or chatter that we have with ourselves when good and bad things happen to and around us. When something happens to us, we can explain it as being temporary (a one-off) or permanent (it will last forever), local (specific to that situation) or global (it affects other areas of our lives too), and personal (we are the cause of the event) or impersonal (the event has nothing to do with us).

Table 9.1 shows the explanatory styles of an optimist and a pessimist, in response to a *negative* event. But look in Table 9.2 at what happens to the explanatory style of an optimist and a pessimist in response to a *positive* event.

The way in which optimists and pessimists view events, both good and bad, are completely opposite to each other. Whereas optimists can take credit for good events happening and see them

Table 9.1: *Explanatory styles of an optimist and a pessimist in response to a negative event*

Optimist	Pessimist
Temporary: 'This isn't what I had planned, but it won't last forever.'	**Permanent:** 'It is always going to be like this, no matter what I try.'
Local: 'This isn't great but at least other things in my life are going well.'	**Global:** 'This means that everything is ruined now.'
Impersonal: 'I tried my best, but this was out of my control.'	**Personal:** 'This is all my fault.'

Table 9.2: *Explanatory styles of an optimist and a pessimist in response to a positive event*

Optimist	Pessimist
Permanent: 'If I keep doing what I'm doing, I can expect positive outcomes like this.'	**Temporary:** 'This won't last forever.'
Global: 'This will positively affect other areas of my life too.'	**Local:** 'Just because this went well doesn't mean that anything else will.'
Personal: 'I worked hard and made this happen.'	**Impersonal:** 'I got lucky; this didn't have much to do with me.'

positively affecting other areas of their lives, pessimists see these as flukes and that life will go back to being rubbish as normal.

According to Seligman (2002), two of the main ways in which we develop our explanatory styles in childhood are by:

1. **Imitating our parents:** How our parents, especially our mothers, explain good and bad events to us directly impacts our own explanatory style. We will imitate the optimism or pessimism of our parents.

2. **Adult feedback or criticism:** When we are praised or scolded by adults, we internalise the messages. For example, if a parent or teacher tells us 'You *never* listen properly!', we may believe that, in any given situation, we find it hard to listen to what's going on. In turn, this affects our behaviour, so we're more likely to switch off because we believe that we lack the ability to pay attention. (Seligman, 2002)

This shows how important teachers are in helping to shape children's explanatory styles. By giving your pupils a realistic and optimistic example to imitate and by choosing your words carefully when feeding back to them, you can help to positively influence their explanatory style. We'll look at how we can do this in more detail in the 'In action' section (p. 189).

ABC model

The good news is that our explanatory styles and levels of optimism can be trained just like any other skill. Positive psychologist Ed Diener explains that we can teach people to get better at 'recognising unhelpful thinking strategies and replacing them with positive ones' (Diener and Biswas-Diener, 2008, p. 193). One way in which to do this is to teach the ABC model derived from the work of psychologist Albert Ellis (1962). The A stands for an adversity; B stands for your beliefs about the event; and C stands for your consequent feelings and actions (see Figure 9.1). One of the main ideas behind the ABC model is that our emotions do not follow inevitably from external events, but rather from our *beliefs* and *thoughts* about those events. A major insight is that we can actually exercise some *choice* over what we think about an event. The aim is to not let unhelpful and negative thinking run away with itself unchecked (remember from Chapter 3 (p. 59) how strong our negativity bias can be?), but instead to challenge these thoughts and be more flexible

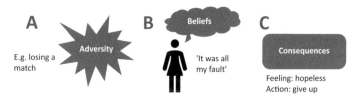

Figure 9.1: *The ABC model illustrated*

and accurate with our thinking, which in turn changes what we feel and how we behave.

For example, imagine that you're about to teach a lesson that is to be observed by a senior member of staff (A – an adversity). You start to worry that the lesson won't go so well and that you will get poor feedback (B – your beliefs). You end up feeling anxious and stressed, and this may lead to you teaching a poor-quality lesson (C – consequences). Because we have some choice over our thoughts and beliefs, we can challenge the thought that the lesson won't go well. We could bring to mind numerous other times when we've been observed and had positive feedback. We could simply notice the thought and let it go (using our mindfulness practice from Chapter 2, p. 37) and take some deep, calming breaths. Or we could remind ourselves that the person observing us is an amenable colleague and will give fair and honest feedback from which we can learn. Rather than letting an unhelpful and negative thought escalate and start to deplete us, we catch it early, challenge it and choose a more helpful response.

The ability to choose one's response to any given situation is perfectly embodied by Victor Frankl in his book *Man's Search For Meaning*. Frankl, a Jewish psychiatrist, was incarcerated in Auschwitz concentration camp during the Second World War, but was one of the few who survived. In his book, he writes these powerful words: 'Everything can be taken from a man but one thing: the last of human freedoms – to choose one's attitude in any given set of circumstances.' (Frankl, 1946, p.66)

Reframing

Shakespeare once wrote in *Hamlet*, 'There is nothing neither good nor bad, but thinking makes it so.' It turns out that this underlies another technique that we could use when faced with challenging situations, which is called 'reframing'. This is a process where we 'reframe' a negative situation into a positive one by changing our perspective. So, the 'problem' of the impending lesson observation becomes the 'opportunity' to show how much our teaching practice has improved. Or your 'weakness' of spending too much money on others at Christmas is viewed as your 'strength' of being generous and kind. Reframing is about acknowledging the fact that there is always a different perspective from which to view 'negative' events. As the Dalai Lama writes in *The Art of Happiness*, 'One must realise that every phenomena, every event, has different aspects. Everything is of a relative nature.' (His Holiness the Dalai Lama and Cutler, 1999, p. 173)

Harvard Business School psychologist Alison Wood Brooks has carried out a number of experiments to look at a type of reframing that she calls 'anxiety reappraisal'. In one study, Brooks asked her participants to do various scary things, from public speaking to sitting a maths exam. She found that when the participants reframed their nerves as 'excitement' rather than 'anxiety', their performance improved (Brooks, 2014). Teachers can employ this technique to help to manage their pupils' levels of anxiety and stress, as well as their own. As we learned in Chapter 5 (p. 101), just the right level of arousal and stress in the classroom leads to the greatest performance.

Priming

Psychologists have discovered that we can influence people to think and behave in certain desirable ways, and this is known as 'priming'. For example, experiments have shown that using a citrus air freshener makes it far more likely that people will clear up after themselves and that medical students will comply with hand hygiene regulations (Dolan, 2015). The smell of citrus in the air mentally prepares the mind (on a completely subconscious level) for cleanliness, and so people think and behave in more hygienic ways – something to bear in mind for the school toilets!

It transpires that, through priming, we can nudge people to feel more optimistic, hopeful and even kinder towards others. University of California psychologists Philip Shave and Mario Mikulincer were looking for ways in which to shift people who were insecurely attached towards feeling more secure. By showing people words like 'love' or having them recall happy memories of being with loved ones, they were able to induce that shift, at least temporarily. Shaver explains: 'Attachment words trigger a kind of comfort that makes tolerance for others more available mentally, even in insecure people, whose natural inclination is intolerance and lack of compassion.' (Cited in Goleman, 2015, p. 35)

Schools are often filled with quotes and aphorisms to try to motivate their pupils, which is another form of priming. One thing to bear in mind is that we tend to be drawn to aphorisms that rhyme and roll off the tongue nicely. A study by cognitive scientists found that pithy sayings that rhymed were found to be more believable by participants than sayings that had the same meaning but didn't rhyme (McGlone and Tofighbakhsh, 2000). For example, we would believe the 'truth' of Napoleon Hill's statement 'Whatever the mind of man can conceive and believe, it can achieve' more than if it was changed to 'Whatever the mind of man can conceive and believe, it can do'. Therefore, the words, posters, phrases and messages that appear around schools are important. They are mentally priming your pupils and staff, affecting how they think and behave.

Other primes to consider for schools are children and staff members' exposure to nature and music. Numerous studies show the amazing wellbeing benefits of immersing people in natural surroundings, and this is explored in detail in Chapter 11 (p. 221). Simply having plants in a room can lower levels of stress (Dolan,

2015) and, as we saw in Chapter 7 (p. 145), you'll really boost wellbeing if you actively take care of the plants yourself. Similarly, playing music can boost our mood and levels of optimism. Dolan explains: 'It most strongly affects the brain region associated with positive emotion and memory in a way that no other input to our happiness production process can.' (Dolan, 2015, p. 150)

In action

Teachers can be hugely influential in their pupils' lives. It is very common for children to go home and challenge their parents based on what their teachers have said at school. When children say to their parents 'Well, actually, Miss Davis said that…' or 'Mr Bond says that…', it shows that our pupils are actually listening to what we are saying and, more importantly, we are having an effect on what they think and how they behave. With this great power comes great responsibility! The following ideas will guide you in helping to shape your pupils' thoughts so that they feel inspired and empowered.

Thoughts for the day

To mentally prime your pupils to think more optimistically, you could start your morning with a 'thought for the day'. These are simply thoughts, sayings, quotes or aphorisms to get your children thinking and maybe to provoke a positive emotional response. The charity Action for Happiness regularly posts beautifully illustrated quotes on social media, and I often use these in my class. Here is how you could do it too:

- Choose an inspiring quote or saying to display on your board (see Figure 9.2 for an example). You could use the 'Inspiring words' Pinterest board by Action for Happiness for inspiration (www.pinterest.co.uk/actionhappiness/inspiring-words).

Figure 9.2: *A 'thought for the day' poster (credit: Julia_Henze, iStockphoto)*

- As the children come into class, ask them to silently read the 'thought for the day' to themselves and think about what it means.

- After all of the children have had a chance to read and digest the thought, ask a child to read it out loud and host a short discussion about what it could mean.

- You could then print the poster off and add it to a 'thoughts for the day' display (see Figure 9.3 as an example).

A lovely thing that grew out of 'thought for the day' in my class was that during the register one morning, when I said 'Good morning, Andy', rather than replying 'Good morning, Mr Bethune', as had happened every other day up until then, Andy decided

Figure 9.3: *'Thoughts for the day' display*

to reply with a thought for the day. 'One kind word can change someone's entire day, Mr Bethune,' came Andy's reply. I smiled, the other children giggled and it started a new way of replying during the register: 'Just be nice, Mr Bethune', 'A good laugh recharges your batteries, Mr Bethune', 'If plan A doesn't work, there are 25 other letters in the alphabet. Stay cool, Mr Bethune.' Now, instead of saying a thought for the day back to me, they pass it on to the next person on the register. Some children have even started to make up their own thoughts for the day or have said thoughts that they have read outside of school. In terms of starting your day on a positive and optimistic note, it doesn't get much better than this!

I hasten to add that this is not about brainwashing children to believe certain things, which is why discussion is a key part of this idea. Children are free to debate and challenge the thought for the day. I would also recommend that you are quite selective with the thoughts that you choose. Lots of quotes and sayings around happiness can be unhelpful and problematic. For example, a saying like 'If it doesn't make you happy, don't do it' is complete nonsense, as there are many important and meaningful things that might not bring immediate positive emotions (like working hard on a difficult project or looking after a friend who is upset). However, as your children get more familiar with discussing the thoughts for the day, and their thinking becomes more creative and flexible, you could choose to put a more controversial thought up, like 'Always be happy', and see what they think about it. My bet is that they'll easily find the flaws in sayings like these.

Tales from the classroom

A thought, image or quote of the day has been a feature of my morning board for three years now. I love to see how children's responses to them vary. Some read it as soon as they come in, before removing their coat; many record them in their wellbeing journals to return to during tricky moments; and others email me their own and beam proudly when I share them with the class. At times, they spark class discussions and become a favourite for a few days or a week. Occasionally, it seems that they have gone unnoticed, and then they pop up again when I least expect it. Beautifully illustrated quotes in cards, letters and even on clay have been shared with me, between peers and with family members.

It's the unexpected conversations that I enjoy most. A colleague covered a Year 2 class and stumbled over a few difficult names. Having asked children to help her to pronounce them correctly, a child said, 'Don't worry, Miss, mistakes are welcome here,' which was a quote that had become a class favourite.

And then one busy morning, I had forgotten to put a quote or image up, and one of my Year 6 students stood in front of the board looking disappointed. Having realised my oversight, we found one together. He stepped back, read it and said, 'That's better. They always give me that warm feeling in my stomach. I was missing that.' From a child who rarely managed to express how he felt, that was a golden moment for me (plus a reminder to always find the time for those quotes!).

Rhiannon Phillips-Bianco, teacher and wellbeing leader, international school in Rome

Influencing explanatory style

The children in your class will have a whole range of explanatory styles, but there is a lot that you can do as their teacher to influence them to be more optimistic. Many of the ideas that we have explored in the book already are designed to prime your children to think optimistically about certain things:

- **Tribal classroom:** This signals to children that they matter, they are part of something bigger than themselves and that people care about them (Chapter 1, p. 15).

- **Mindfulness:** This teaches children that their thoughts aren't facts and they don't have to believe them. They can choose to let them go and take their attention elsewhere (Chapter 2, p. 37).

- **What went well:** This helps children to realise that there is always something to be grateful for and to appreciate, and that the little things matter (Chapter 3, p. 59).

- **Neuroplasticity:** This lets children know that they have the capacity and potential to learn new things and master new skills (Chapter 4, p. 79).

- **Stretch zone:** This shows children that hard work is necessary to improve, that mistakes can be good, that they learn the most when they are challenged and that feeling a bit nervous when stretching yourself is normal (Chapter 5, p. 101).

- **Flow and strengths:** This teaches children that hard work can be fun, that challenging themselves can make them feel good and that we all have strengths that we can grow (Chapter 6, p. 123).

- **It's cool to be kind:** This allows children to experience the joy of giving and receiving kindness. It shows them that there is goodness in the world and that they have the power to spread that goodness themselves (Chapter 7, p. 145).

- **Digital wellbeing:** This shows children how to make technology work for them and that it's possible to have fulfilling experiences online (Chapter 8, p. 163).

It is also helpful to be mindful about the praise and feedback that we give, as the children will internalise it and it will become part of their explanatory style. This requires teachers being aware of their own explanatory styles and where they fall on the optimism and pessimism scale. So, when giving feedback to children consider the following:

- **Keep it positive:** A ratio of five positive comments to every negative one is found in most positive relationships (Gottman, 1994). As we saw in Chapter 1 (p. 15), the ratio may need to be higher when working with children.

- **Model an optimistic explanatory style:** When things go wrong in class or you deal with challenging behaviour, explain it to pupils in a way that shows it's temporary ('It won't be like this forever'), local ('This has gone wrong here but other areas are going well') and impersonal ('That was a bad choice but you are not a bad person').

- **Challenge and reframe:** When pupils show pessimistic and inaccurate thinking in class, don't let the thoughts go unchallenged. For example, if Jennifer is struggling on a maths problem and says 'I'm rubbish at maths!', you could ask whether that statement is *always* true. You could help her to recall lessons and areas of maths at which she has succeeded. You could reframe the situation by telling her that if she's struggling, that means the work is challenging and so she's working in the stretch zone and her brain is growing lots by working on this tricky problem.

Conscience alley

A fun and interactive way in which to get the children to reflect on explanatory styles (you could describe these to your class as the conversations or chatter that we all have in our heads when good and bad things happen) is to use a drama activity called 'conscience alley'. Here is how it could work:

- Get the children to generate a list of negative scenarios that they might experience in their lives (e.g. getting a low score on a test, losing a sports match or falling out with a friend).

- Explain that when we experience these negative events, we can often have negative thoughts about what has just happened. Sometimes these thoughts exaggerate how bad the situation is.

- Select a scenario to explore (e.g. losing a football match) and choose one child to walk down the conscience alley. The other children form two equal lines standing opposite each other, creating the alleyway for the first child to walk down.

- Now, as the first child takes one step forward, each child in the alley takes it in turns to say out loud a *negative* thought that they might be having: 'I'm rubbish at football!', 'No one wants me on their team!', 'My team is so bad!' or 'My team will never win anything!'

- Get the children to reflect on the feelings that they might experience if those are the thoughts that they're having when something goes wrong in their life. What might the person be feeling when having these thoughts? How might they behave as a result? Were the thoughts kind? Were they accurate? Are they likely to help the person to deal with the problem?

- Do the activity again but, this time, ask the children to *reframe* the situation and choose more *realistically optimistic* thoughts as their classmate walks down conscience alley: 'Never mind, it wasn't my fault', 'I can work on my mistakes in training', 'We played our best, the other team were just better today', 'It still felt good to run around and play footy with my friends!'

- Ask the children to reflect again. How did these thoughts affect what the person might be feeling? Were the thoughts kinder? Were they more accurate? Are they more likely to help the person to deal with the problem?

- It might be helpful to end by showing the ABC model image (Figure 9.1, p. 186) and to explain that in any situation we have the power to choose what thoughts we have, which in turn affects what we may feel and how we might behave. If our thoughts are particularly negative, we can practise swapping them with more positive ones.

Music

It may be because I worked in the music industry for several years before retraining to become a teacher, but I play a lot of music in my classroom. I love to start my day with music, especially when setting up my classroom, but I also like to play it during the day, when the children enter the classroom in the morning, for example, or during some lessons. Why not experiment with the following ideas?

- Play an uplifting piece of music when your class come in first thing in the morning. I love *The Lark Ascending* by Ralph Vaughan Williams.

- Have your 'thought of the day' on the board whilst the music is playing, so that children have something to contemplate as they sit down.

- Have calm and peaceful music playing in the communal areas of your school, like the reception area and hall.

- During lessons, when you want to encourage 'silent' working (or at least no talking), play some classical or instrumental music in the background to enable children to focus better. (Avoid having the music on too loud or it becoming a distraction to pupils.)

- Intersperse your day with music. Share with your class some of your favourite tracks and music videos at the end of the day. Expose them to styles and genres that they might not have heard before. (Be sure to check that lyric and video content is age-appropriate!)

- Get your children moving to music. It's instinctive to want to move your body when you hear a good beat and rhythm, so use music to get your class out of their seats.

Key points

- Having a realistic optimistic outlook on life has many health and wellbeing benefits.

- Our levels of optimism are heavily influenced by our explanatory styles, which are shaped by our parents and the feedback and criticism that we receive and internalise.

- We can become more optimistic by changing how we think about the good and bad events in our lives. Our thoughts and beliefs are also 'primed' by the things that we read and by our environment.

- Start your day in class with a positive thought for the day. Get the children to discuss what it means and how it relates to happiness.

- Positively influence your pupils' explanatory styles by setting a good example and by helping them to challenge and reframe their inaccurate negative beliefs.

- Use the drama activity 'conscience alley' to explore how optimistic and pessimistic thinking can affect what we feel and how we behave. Get children to practise 'reframing' negative situations into positive ones.

- Play more music during the day. It can lift mood, get children moving and help them to concentrate.

Chapter 10
Exercise makes me happy

If you are in a bad mood, go for a walk. If you are still in a bad mood, go for another walk.

– Hippocrates

Chapter overview

In this chapter, we'll discover why exercise might be one of the most underrated ways in which we can improve our happiness and wellbeing. We'll look at exactly what happens in our children's brains and bodies when they get moving and how we can incorporate more exercise into the school day.

In theory	In action
• The problem	• The Daily Mile
• Parental influence	• Parent/carer engagement
• Exercise as medicine	• Hindu squats
• Dosage	• Go Noodle
	• Yoga
	• Dance

In theory

The problem

There is a growing epidemic in the UK and it is the increasing inactivity of our children. According to government statistics, nearly a third of children aged two to 15 are obese, and younger generations are becoming obese at earlier ages and staying obese for longer (UK Government, 2017). The government set out to tackle this by introducing a 'sugar tax' on fizzy drinks and increasing the sports funding that primary schools receive. Although increasing obesity levels are an obvious sign that our children are exercising less, the fact is that inactivity is bad for you whether you're overweight or stick thin. In his book *Flourish*, Martin Seligman shares evidence from one study that showed that 'the fit, but fat, individual has almost half the risk of death of the unfit, fat individual'. Other data he explores shows that if you are unfit, 'normal and obese people both have a high risk for death, and it does not seem to matter if you are fat or thin' (Seligman, 2011, pp. 216–217).

The good news is that more children are physically active now than when I wrote the first edition of this book, but much more still needs to be done. The Chief Medical Officer in the UK says that children between the ages of five and 18 should be taking part in *at least* 60 minutes of moderate to vigorous activity every day (Department of Health and Social Care (DHSC), 2019). The latest Sport England Active Lives Children and Young People Survey shows that about 45 per cent of children and young people meet this target (2022). Previously, it was about 15 to 20 per cent of children. That still means that over half of children in the UK are not moving enough. But it really isn't surprising when you consider where it is that children spend a disproportionate amount of their time sitting down and being sedentary – that's right, at schools (DHSC, 2019)! This is a big problem because sedentary behaviour has been linked in adulthood to increased chances of heart

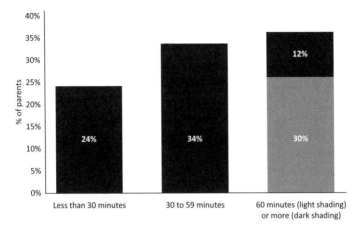

Figure 10.1: *The amount of daily physical activity that parents think that five- to 18-year-old children should be doing (reproduced with kind permission from YouGov Plc and Youth Sport Trust)*

disease, diabetes, some types of cancer and depression (DHSC, 2019). In short, schools need to do more to get their children out of their seats and moving.

Parental influence

We definitely cannot lay all of the responsibility for children's lack of physical activity at the feet of schools, as the children's parents and carers play a big role. In fact, if a child has two active parents/carers, they are almost six times more likely to be active compared to children of inactive parents (Moore et al., 1991). But it's not just how active children's parents are that matters; their knowledge of necessary physical activity levels matters too. As Figure 10.1 shows, most parents do not know the amount of physical activity that their children need to stay healthy (Youth Sport Trust, 2022).[1]

[1]Figures from YouGov Plc. Total sample size: 2184 adults, of whom 533 were parents of children aged 18 and under. Online fieldwork was undertaken between 28 and 29 March 2022. The figures have been weighted and are representative of all UK adults

Only 30 per cent understand that one hour of moderate to vigorous activity is the minimum requirement, and 58 per cent believe that children need less than an hour a day of physical activity. As parents play such a crucial role in how active their children are, some education for parents seems like a vital part of the solution.

Exercise as medicine

According to Public Health England, the direct cost of obesity to the NHS is estimated to be over six billion pounds a year (Public Health England, 2017). But there is a medicine that schools can administer to its children, not only to prevent the rise of obesity but also to help to reverse its negative effects. This medicine costs nothing to give out, it starts working immediately, it is easy and fun to take and one of its side effects is chronic smiling and happiness. This medicine is exercise! Let's have a look at how this medicine can positively affect our body and mind.

Health

Not only does exercise promote stronger muscles and bones, but it boosts the immune system too, meaning that you'll get ill less and recover more quickly from illnesses if you're fit. When we're inactive, mitochondria (which are like battery cells in our bodies) start to charge up, ready to be used. When we're inactive for too long, mitochondria can cause inflammation in the body, which can lead to all types of diseases. However, according to the NHS, regular exercise reduces your risk of major illnesses such as heart disease, stroke, type 2 diabetes and cancer by up to 50 per cent, as well as lowering your risk of early death by up to 30 per cent (NHS Choices, 2015).

This is partly because physical activity releases myokines in the body, which dampen activity in mitochondria and thereby reduce inflammation in the body. Sitting down for prolonged periods of time is linked with shortening your lifespan; conversely, there is compelling evidence that the more physically fit you are, the longer that you can expect to live (King, 2016).

Happiness

Exercise can have profound positive effects on our moods. When we do strenuous physical activity, our bodies release endorphins. Endorphins are nature's way of dulling pain (in case we are fighting or running away from a lion on the savannah) and calming the mind, so that we can focus on the task in hand. In his book *Spark!*, John Ratey explains that endorphins work like the powerful painkiller morphine and 'produce euphoria in the mind' (Ratey and Hagerman, 2010, p. 117). This is why people often report a 'runner's high' after completing a marathon. But we don't have to run 26.2 miles to get this high (even just thinking about it makes me tired). Studies also show that simply going for a walk can lift our mood. Psychologist Paul Taylor says that 'Walking works like a drug, and it starts working even after a few steps.' (Cited in Montgomery, 2015, p. 188)

Regular exercise also boosts our body image and self-esteem. People who take part in regular exercise feel better about themselves generally. Vanessa King believes that this is important because 'Poor body image and low self-esteem, experienced by both men and women, is linked with depression, anxiety and with the likelihood of detrimental health behaviours such as smoking, excessive alcohol consumption and extreme dieting.' (King, 2016, p. 83)

Overall, regular exercise appears to make children feel better about their lives. The report by PISA on student wellbeing (OECD, 2017) showed not only that active children are less likely to skip school, feel anxious about schoolwork or be bullied, but the report goes on to state that 'physically active students report higher levels of life satisfaction… and psychological wellbeing' (p. 5). Life appears to feel better when we get moving.

Stress, anxiety and depression

As we have read in earlier chapters (Chapter 2, p. 37 and Chapter 3, p. 59), when we perceive a threat, our amygdala kicks in and our bodies prepare for fight or flight. Stress hormones like adrenaline and cortisol flood our body, giving us extra energy, so that we can defend ourselves or run away. The problem in this day and age is that, rather than escaping or fighting, we sit there getting more stressed, worried and anxious, not knowing what to do. But we are meant to move when the stress response kicks in! John Ratey explains that 'when we exercise in response to stress, we're doing what human beings have evolved to do over the past several million years' (Ratey and Hagerman, 2010, p. 64). By moving our bodies after stressful events, we actually use up all of the biochemicals and extra energy that have flooded our system (which can cause us harm if left unattended). It is no surprise, then, that people who are more physically active report fewer incidences of emotional distress and feelings of anxiousness, as well as reacting less when things go awry and recovering more quickly when they do (King, 2016). Exercise, therefore, helps to boost our levels of resilience by allowing us to manage our levels of stress and anxiety.

There is even evidence showing that exercise can help people suffering from clinical depression. One study split participants suffering with depression into three groups to try out different interventions. The first group were given anti-depressants, the second group had to exercise for 45 minutes three times a week and the third group did a combination of the two (Babyak et al., 2000). After four months, all three groups experienced similar improvements in their happiness levels, proving that exercise can be as effective as the most potent anti-depressants. However, the most remarkable finding from the study came six months later, when the participants were assessed to see who had relapsed into depression. Of the medication group, 38 per cent had relapsed into depression. The combination group fared slightly better, with 31 per cent suffering a relapse. Astonishingly, the exercise group's relapse rate was only nine per cent! So, not only is exercise a fast-working medicine at lifting your mood, but it appears to be a long-lasting one too. More recently, a meta-analysis of physical activity interventions with children and teenagers showed that they are associated with significant reductions in depressive symptoms. (Recchia et al., 2023)

The brain

If you think of your brain like a plant, then exercise produces a fertiliser to help your brain to grow. There is something that our brains produce called brain-derived neurotrophic factor (BDNF), which helps to build and maintain the brain circuitry. Ratey explains that BDNF 'improves the functions of neurons, encourages their growth, and strengthens and protects them against the natural process of cell death' (Ratey and Hagerman, 2010, p. 40). He describes BDNF as Miracle-Gro® for the brain. It turns out that when we exercise, our bodies produce more BDNF, which means that exercise directly helps our brains to grow new neurons and protect the ones that are already there. This may explain why physically active adults are less likely to experience dementia or Alzheimer's in later life (King, 2016). Furthermore, in a 2007 study cited by Ratey, researchers found that when learning new vocabulary words, participants learned them 20 per cent faster after they did some exercise, and that the rate of learning correlated with the increased levels of BDNF (Ratey and Hagerman, 2010, p. 45).

It seems that exercise perfectly primes the brain for learning. Straight after exercise, with our heart rates increased, our heart pumps more blood, oxygen and glucose up to our brains. This wakes our brains up and helps them to be alert to new information and to be able to pay attention. The happy hormones that are released after exercise, like endorphins and dopamine, put us in a good mood, help us to be more creative and flexible in our thinking, and motivate us to want to learn. Numerous studies show that fitter children tend to perform better academically. A 2013 report by the American Institute of Medicine stated that fitter children 'show greater attention, have faster cognitive processing speed and perform better on standardized academic tests than children who are less active.' (Institute of Medicine, 2013) Ratey explains that when children's brain activity was measured, there was 'more activity in fit kids' brains, indicating that more neurons involved in attention were being recruited for a given task' (Ratey and Hagerman, 2010, p. 25). A meta-analysis by UCL in 2019 looked at 42 studies from around the world where basic physical exercise (e.g. star jumps or running on the spot) was incorporated into academic lessons. The conclusion was clear – compared to sedentary lessons, children in active lessons showed a large and significant improvement in their educational outcomes (Norris et al., 2019).

Dosage

So, if exercise is the medicine, what dosage do we need to take in order to gain from all of the benefits listed above? Let's look at some various forms of exercise:

Walking

In his brilliant visual lecture called *23 and 1/2 hours* (**ed.ted.com/ featured/Mot8KdLT**), Dr Mike Evans makes the case that we can benefit hugely from spending 30 minutes a day walking, and limiting our sitting and sleeping to the remaining 23 and a half hours in the day. It's an excellent and compelling video, and reassuring that all we need to do is go for a brisk walk!

Running

When Elaine Wyllie was headteacher of St Ninian's Primary School in Scotland, she became concerned when the school's sports coach told her that the children were shattered after the warm-ups in PE lessons. They were simply unfit. She decided to do something about it and created the 'Daily Mile', where the children had to jog or run for 15 minutes every day (children can roughly cover a mile in this amount of time). Due to the success of the scheme at Elaine's school, where obesity levels at the school are shown to be about 45 per cent less than the national average (The Daily Mile, 2018), the Daily Mile has been rolled out nationally.

In 2016, a study was conducted at Coppermill Primary School in London to evaluate the impact of the Daily Mile (London Playing Fields Foundation, 2016). Two Year 5 and one Year 6 class took part in the Daily Mile three times a week, over an eight-week period. Not only did pupils register big improvements in fitness levels, but they also showed increases in self-esteem, and the Year 6 class, who also completed the Daily Mile every morning before sitting their SATs exams, scored significantly higher than the national average on their reading, writing, grammar and maths tests. See more about how you can incorporate the Daily Mile into your school routine in the 'In action' section (p. 208).

Yoga and dance

What Works Centre for Wellbeing carried out a large review of published reports on sport and wellbeing, called Sport, Dance and Young People. The review found that yoga-type activities 'can improve feelings of anxiety, depression, anger, attention and overall subjective wellbeing.' (What Works Centre for Wellbeing, 2017, p. 3) Yoga is also a great way in which to experience flow, so much so that Csikszentmihalyi notes, 'it makes sense to think of yoga as a very thoroughly planned flow activity.' (Csikszentmihalyi, 2002, p. 105) It seems that yoga is a really good workout for the body and the mind.

Similarly, the review also showed that taking part in aerobic and hip-hop dance can boost our mood, and dance training is shown to be effective in lowering self-reported depression (What Works Centre for Wellbeing, 2017). Ratey also believes that learning irregular rhythms and dance patterns can help to improve brain plasticity (Ratey and Hagerman, 2010).

See more on how to use yoga and dance in your class in the 'In action' section (p. 216).

Group movement

If we can combine physical activity with helping children to feel part of a team (or tribe!), then that can be really positive for their wellbeing. The Sport, Dance and Young People review cited above demonstrated that, 'On average, across all activities including sport, those who were alone demonstrated lower happiness, higher anxiety and lower sense of purpose.' (What Works Centre for Wellbeing, 2017, p. 3) Chapter 1 of this book has already illustrated the power of feeling part of a team (p. 15), so it's no surprise that when we take part in sports as a group or team, we tend to be happier. The review also confirmed that playing sports outdoors is better for young people's wellbeing than playing inside, so get outside in nature whenever you can.

In action

The key thing to remember with this chapter is that it is all about *movement*. We need to get our children sitting down less and moving more, and the following activities will allow you to do this in a way that not only supports their learning but also develops long-term healthy habits.

The Daily Mile

One of the best things about introducing the Daily Mile into your school is that it costs absolutely no money! It also only takes 15 minutes out of your day. As a result of the Daily Mile, your class are more likely to be alert in lessons, feel better about themselves and be fitter and healthier too. Here are some of the key things to bear in mind to get your children running the Daily Mile:

- **Keep it simple:** Do not overcomplicate what is a very straightforward intervention. The children simply need to have a safe, open space to be able to run laps for 15 minutes.

- **Start off small:** We introduced the Daily Mile incrementally at my school. The children ran for five minutes daily in the first week, then ten minutes in the second, and then built up to 15 minutes by the third week.

- **Make it fun:** Allow the children to talk and chat as they run around, as this is as much a social exercise as it is a fitness one.

- **Join in:** Teachers and teaching assistants can join in too. I love running with the children. Not only do I benefit from the fresh air and endorphins, but I also get to chat to my class and check in with my more vulnerable pupils in an informal way.

- **Make it inclusive:** The Daily Mile is not a competition or a race. Everyone is encouraged to jog or run for the full 15 minutes at his or her own pace. If children have mobility issues, adapt to suit their needs.

- **Go with the flow:** It's best if the Daily Mile is fitted into your timetable in a flexible way. My class normally complete it at the same time every morning but, if weather or changes to the timetable mean that we can't, we'll fit it in elsewhere that day.

- **Do it daily:** Unless it is really tipping it down or there are gale-force winds, get outside. At a minimum, complete the Daily Mile three times a week. The Daily Mile is also meant to be in *addition* to your weekly PE lessons (not as a warm-up for PE).

- **Don't change kit:** Children can run the mile in their normal uniform. Ensure that children have appropriate footwear to run in (a quick change into trainers works or make black trainers part of your school uniform).

- For more information, go to: **https://thedailymile.co.uk/faq**

Figure 10.2: *Team Nevelson running the Daily Mile*

My school has been doing the Daily Mile for several years now, and the children really love taking part (see Figure 10.2). If you ever forget to do it, your class will be sure to remind you!

To help to keep the children at my previous school engaged with the Daily Mile, we used the following ways to keep it fresh and interesting:

- In our weekly wellbeing assembly, using an interactive online map (**freemaptools.com/radius-around-point.htm**), we worked out how far our children had run around the world. If every child in every class from Year 1 to Year 6 ran a mile, that would be 180 miles a day or 900 miles in a week (which was enough to reach Berlin, but not quite far enough to make it to Barcelona!). The children really enjoyed seeing how far they had collectively travelled around the globe each week.

- We introduced Daily Mile marathon wristbands. For every 26 Daily Miles the children complete (which should take just over a half-term), they receive a rubber wristband.

- To encourage older residents to keep physically active, Hertfordshire Council asked their Daily Mile schools to invite the children's grandparents in to complete the mile with them. With the council's help, my previous school hosted a Daily Mile grandparent morning.

- Our school became the proud owners of a school dog, Milo. Milo often joined classes on their mile run and he was probably the best motivator that we've seen for getting the children moving.

Tales from the classroom

At Kensington Primary School, physical health is at the centre of our learning and a core part of our trailblazing Curriculum K. We introduced 30-minute daily exercise sessions, including anything from high-intensity interval training to fun games such as rob the nest, tag, and cups and saucers. To fit these into our timetable, it did mean that we had to shorten our English and maths lessons (yes, you did read that correctly!). We also incorporate movement breaks during classroom learning, and use 'active lessons' using TeachActive (where movement is a core part of the lesson itself), meaning that our children are never sedentary for long periods. The children love to move and there is a real excitement about the lessons.

The results have been staggering. We conducted age-appropriate 'fitness tests' to check children's stamina and ability at the start and end of term. The results show that our children are a lot fitter, stronger and have much higher levels of stamina. Our wellbeing surveys show that our children are also healthier, happier and much more ready to learn, with optimal levels of concentration.

The fitness culture throughout the school has not only had a positive impact on children, but staff are also benefitting. Since introducing the new curriculum, I have had fewer days off sick. Introducing the new fitness curriculum at Kensington Primary School has proven to be an all-round success!

Ben Levinson, headteacher,
primary school in East London

Sit down less, move more

As studies referenced previously have shown, when children are more active in their lessons, they tend to pay more attention, learn more and make better progress. More than that, they will be reducing inflammation in their bodies, boosting their immune system and making themselves stronger, healthier and happier. What's not to like?

We really shouldn't have primary children sat down for an hour at a time without moving. Take inspiration from Ben Levinson at Kensington Primary School (see Tales from the Classroom, p. 211), who gets their children moving every 30 minutes. Or try to bring more movement into lessons by:

- breaking sedentary periods up with short bursts of physical activity like 20 star jumps, a few laps of the playground or ten Hindu squats (see p. 213)
- bringing movement into lessons where appropriate – for example, at the start of a maths lesson, where you might get children to chant a times table, get them out of their seats and jumping up and down in time with the chanting.

Parent and carer engagement

I do think that it is imperative that schools work with children's parents and carers to help to increase everyone's physical activity.

Wellbeing in the Primary Classroom

We have hosted parent coffee mornings and afternoon workshops at my current school, with a focus on ways in which to develop children's wellbeing and physical activity. The key is to keep the format simple, offer refreshments and schedule the workshops for times that are accessible for parents and carers (straight after drop-off or just before pick-up seems to work well, as you have a captive audience; alternatively, online workshops in the evening can work well too). At the workshops, it is beneficial to share the following information:

- Children should be getting a minimum amount of one hour of physical activity every day.

- Over half of all children in the UK are not getting that level of exercise.

- Parents have a big influence on children's levels of physical activity, and if parents are active, children are six times more likely to be too.

- Physical activity makes children healthier, happier and smarter.

- There are lots of ways in which families can be more physically active, such as travelling to and from school on foot, bikes or scooters, signing up to sports clubs, going for family walks and bike rides in nature and breaking up sedentary periods at home with some movement.

I have created several guides for how families can foster children's wellbeing at home, which can be shared with parents and carers at workshops and on the school website. They can be downloaded for free using this link: **https://fdslive.oup.com/www.oup.com/oxed/Wellbeing/Primary_Wellbeing_Parent_Toolkit.pdf**

Hindu squats

I was watching a TED Talk by Dr John Ratey and was fascinated when he started by getting the audience to perform some 'Hindu squats'. Then, as they sat down, smiling and breathless, Ratey announced, 'Now you're ready to learn.' (Ratey, 2012) Ever since watching that talk, I have used Hindu squats in the classroom to give my class a break and a reboot for their brain. Here is how they work:

- Before they begin, ask the children to place one hand in the middle of their chest and notice their resting heart rate and their normal breathing. Do this for a few breaths.

- Then, ensure that the children stand, tuck their chairs under their desks and have enough space to perform the Hindu squats.

- They start by standing straight, with their arms outstretched in front of them (see Figure 10.3 opposite).

- As the teacher calls out 'One!', the children pull their arms and elbows back towards their bodies whilst calling out 'Boom!' (Figure 10.4). Saying 'Boom!' is just a bit of fun.

- They then squat down, touch the floor (Figure 10.5) and stand back up, with their arms stretched out, ready for the next Hindu squat.

- Repeat these steps ten times.

- After ten Hindu squats have been completed, ask the children to place one hand in the middle of their chest again to notice how hard their hearts are beating and how quick their breathing is. Just this short burst of exercise is enough to get their brains turned on and the happy hormones flowing.

Go Noodle

A newly qualified teacher called Rachel introduced me to the resource Go Noodle (ECTs often have some of the freshest ideas!). I was walking past her classroom and noticed her class on their feet and moving their bodies to the instructions of Maximo, Go Noodle's on-screen animated monkey. The children were all

Figure 10.3: *Hindu squats step 1*

Figure 10.4: *Hindu squats step 2 (shout 'Boom!')*

engaged and having a 'brain-break' in the middle of a lesson. Go Noodle describes itself as 'Movement for the classroom – hundreds of videos to activate kids' bodies and brain' (**gonoodle.com**). Here is what I like about Go Noodle:

Figure 10.5: *Hindu squats step 3*

- It is free to sign up to and use.

- Lots of the videos are educational (raps about the water cycle, anyone?).

- Videos are fun and engaging (I challenge you not to join in with the 'How to dab!' dance video).

- They get children moving.

- They're short and, at only two to four minutes in length, they are perfect for mini-breaks during your day.

Visit **gonoodle.com** to sign up for free and explore the vast array of videos that they have available.

Yoga

If you want your children to experience and practise yoga, the best way in which to do this effectively is to get a qualified yoga instructor in to teach the children. A good place to start is to search for a local teacher on the British Wheel of Yoga website (**www.bwy. org.uk/find-a-yoga-class/**). Here are some things to bear in mind:

- Decide how you will fund hiring a private yoga instructor. You can use the Sports Premium funding to hire external providers, but these classes will need to be in addition to your normal PE lessons (i.e. before school, at lunchtime or after school). Some schools use pupil premium funding too, and parents could be asked to make a small contribution if necessary.

- Find a local teacher who is experienced at working with children, has current DBS paperwork in place (the Disclosure Barring Service makes checks to ensure that adults are safe to work with children) and full public liability insurance.

- Meet with any instructor before you hire them and interview them. Ask them to teach a lesson as part of their interview and observe how they interact with the children. Ensure that they are the right fit for your school.

As well as hiring qualified yoga instructors to teach the children in your school, there are some things that teachers can do in class. Go Noodle has a range of 'stretch' videos based on some basic yoga moves (**www.gonoodle.com/tags/6Yl682/stretch**). The children simply follow the instructions and movements shown on the video, and you can join in as well.

If you're interested in training to teach yoga in school, then **yogaatschool.org.uk** offers training for teachers with their own yoga practice.

Dance

Dancing is as instinctive to humans as storytelling. Who can hear an infectious rhythm or beat and not start tapping their foot or nodding their head? Teaching children how to dance is a whole other ball game, though! Once again, Go Noodle comes up trumps, as they have a dedicated guided dance section (**www.gonoodle.com/tags/0YZ0G2/guided-dance**). These are short videos that involve a song to learn and some simple dance moves to copy. My personal favourites are the videos by Blazer Fresh – a young hip-hop trio who remind me of De La Soul.

Another excellent resource is the BBC School Radio primary dance website (**bbc.co.uk/schoolradio/subjects/dance**). Teachers can play the audio files, which guide the children through the dance moves and routines. Many of the lessons are cross-curricular, so children can learn about the Great Fire of London, World War I, the Tudors or even computer coding, via the medium of dance!

Key points

- Children are taking part in less physical activity and are becoming more sedentary and obese. This lifestyle behaviour can lead to adult health problems, such as type 2 diabetes, heart disease and even premature death.

- Increasing physical activity and fitness in young people has been proven not only to prevent and reverse the health problems noted in this chapter, but also to boost levels of mental wellbeing, increase happiness levels and longevity, and help to improve pupils' academic attainment.

- Schools can introduce the Daily Mile at little or no cost at all, to get children moving on a daily basis. Children have the opportunity to improve their fitness, socialise with their friends and prepare their brains for learning.

- Teachers can easily incorporate more movement into their lessons by using Hindu squats or other short-burst exercises to break up the day. Go Noodle has some great interactive videos to get your class moving.

- Yoga has been shown to really help young people's mental wellbeing, so why not find a local teacher to give lessons in your school? Teachers can use simple stretching techniques in class as well.

- Use dance and choreographed movement to help children to learn about other areas of the curriculum. Not only will the children get their heart rates up, but the learning of coordinated moves will also increase brain plasticity.

Chapter 11
The nature fix

Nature does not hurry, yet everything is accomplished.

— Lao Tzu

Chapter overview

In this chapter, we will understand the power that nature has to heal our bodies and minds and to help us to learn better too. When we get back in touch with nature, our stresses melt away and our brains are better able to focus and think.

In theory	In action
• Our natural habitat	• Outdoor learning
• Nature disconnect and climate anxiety	• Playing outside
• Forest bathing	• Rewild your outside areas
• Stress, sleep and the immune system	• Bringing nature inside
• Cognition, learning and behaviour	• Natural art
• Happiness	• Nature bathing
	• School farm

In theory

Our natural habitat

It is impossible to talk about our deep connection with nature without delving back into our tribal past. Our species is roughly 300,000 years old. For most of our existence, we hunted, gathered and foraged out on the savannah. We were deeply connected to and in tune with the natural world because our entire survival depended on it. Early humans needed to be in rhythm with the seasons, they needed to know which plants and fruits would be edible or which would be harmful, and they learned how to extract goodness from the natural defences of food sources (such as shells and bitter toxins). All of this was done outside in nature.

It is only very recently that humans have become more of an urban-dwelling species. Some of the oldest cities that exist are only about 6,000 years old. What this means is that for the overwhelming majority of our existence, we humans have been a nature-dwelling species. Nature is our natural habitat – where we feel safest, healthiest and happiest. The biologist Edward Wilson wrote his book *Biophilia* (1984) about this topic. He argued that humans' brains have been shaped by their natural environment so that they are primed to respond positively to cues that would have enhanced our survival (trees, lakes, rivers and grassland, etc.). This is why nature makes us feel good, he argues, because we're at home in nature and it gives us everything that we need to live. Biophilia is about our innate affinity with nature. As Dr Rangan Chatterjee says, 'Nature is profoundly good for us for a simple but easily forgettable reason: we're part of it.' (Chatterjee, 2018, p. 216)

Nature disconnect and climate anxiety

Even though humans are an integral part of nature, we are living in ways that are making us less and less connected to it. By 2050, it's projected that around 70 per cent of the world's population will live in cities (United Nations, 2018). This means that more of us will be spending time indoors rather than outside, and many of us will be stuck to our screens and devices. An Ofcom report in 2021 showed that seven- to eight-year-olds spent an average of almost three hours online a day in September 2020. The report confirmed that the pandemic increased people's dependence on devices. At a time when we need to be in touch with nature more than ever, we may be steadily moving further away from it.

And it is probably because we are genetically determined to love the natural world that it pains us acutely to see it slowly but surely decimated due to human industry and activity. The 2022 United in Science report by the World Meteorological Organization made it clear that we are heading in the wrong direction in terms of climate change. The past seven years have been the warmest on record and, despite the biggest single drop in CO_2 emissions during the pandemic lockdowns, CO_2 levels are now *higher* than they were pre-pandemic. The report does not sugar-coat the fact that without much more ambitious action, the physical and socioeconomic impacts of climate change will be increasingly devastating.

This dire situation has an inevitable toll on children's mental health and wellbeing. A global survey into climate anxiety in children and young people, and their beliefs about government responses to climate change (Hickman et al., 2021), highlighted the fact that 84 per cent of children were at least 'moderately worried' about climate change (59 per cent were 'extremely worried'). Over half of the 10,000 children and young people reported feeling negative emotions such as sad, anxious, angry, powerless, helpless and guilty. Seventy five per cent said that they think the future is frightening and 83 per cent felt that people have failed to take care of the planet. These statistics are very alarming and they should be a wake-up call to us all. Not only do they show that, as adults, we need to model the fact that we care about the world and are doing our part to protect it, but they also show that we need to give children hope that they can, along with our support, positively impact the planet.

Forest bathing

In Japan, an interesting concept called *shinrin-yoku* developed in the 1980s to help people to reconnect with nature and rebalance their lives. *Shinrin* in Japanese means 'forest' and *yoku* means 'bath'. So, *shinrin-yoku* means bathing in the forest atmosphere or taking in the forest through our senses (Li, 2019). It was developed as part of a national health programme to help Japanese citizens to manage increasing levels of stress, anxiety, depression and ill health. In his fascinating book *Into the Forest* (2019), Dr Qing Li, professor at Nipon Medical School in Tokyo, shares the ever-increasing research into the powerful effects that nature has on our minds and bodies. He explains that there is now a wealth of data to show that spending two hours forest bathing, where you connect to nature using all of your senses, can:

- reduce blood pressure
- lower stress
- lift depression
- increase energy levels
- boost the immune system
- strengthen the cardiovascular system
- improve concentration and memory (Li, 2019).

Suffice to say, spending time outdoors in a mindful way, soaking up the natural atmosphere, does us good in every cell and fibre of our bodies.

Stress, sleep and the immune system

Let's have a look in a bit more detail about what actually happens in our minds and bodies when we reconnect with and dwell in nature.

Stress

As we learned in Chapter 5 (p. 101), we need stress in order to learn, and it's an inherent by-product of being in our 'stretch zone'. However, too much stress means that our cortisol levels sky-rocket and we enter the panic zone. Being stressed for prolonged periods of time without giving our bodies the chance to rest and recover is very bad for our wellbeing. But studies show that nature lowers our stress levels. Dr Li (Li, 2019) explains that his studies, and those of fellow researchers, have proven that spending time in natural settings can lower the levels of cortisol and adrenaline in our bodies, supress the sympathetic or 'fight or flight' system, enhance the parasympathetic or 'rest and recover' system and lower blood pressure and improve heart health. In fact, simply having plants in your room can lower your stress levels, which is good news if you live in built-up, urban areas (Dolan, 2015).

Sleep

We have already looked at how crucial sleep is for wellbeing and learning in Chapter 4 (p. 79). As diet and exercise affect the quality of our sleep, so too does our exposure to nature. We know that stress negatively affects the quality of our sleep, so if having greater access to nature means that our stress levels decrease, we are much more likely to sleep better too. One study by Morita et al. (2011) looked into the impact of forest bathing on people who suffered with a variety of sleep complaints (such as insomnia, struggling to fall asleep at night or waking very early). The results were clear that spending time in nature improved the length of the participants' sleep by as much as 15 per cent (they slept for almost an extra hour on average). Not only that, but the quality of their sleep improved and they felt significantly less anxious. Interestingly, an afternoon walk in nature had a bigger impact on sleep than a morning one (something to bear in mind when you see your class become sluggish after lunch – get them outside!).

Immune system

One of the ways in which scientists test the strength of our immune system is by measuring levels of natural killer cells. Natural killer cells are a type of white blood cell that attack and kill unwanted cells in our bodies that might cause us harm, such as those infected with a virus or cancerous cells. Generally speaking, people with higher levels of natural killer cells show a lower incidence of diseases such as cancer. One study showed that spending time in nature (specifically three days and two nights in a forest) increased natural killer cell activity by over 50 per cent, and the presence of an anti-cancer protein increased by 48 per cent (Li, 2019). If this boost to the immune system comes from spending a short amount of time in nature, what if people were surrounded by it all the time? Well, Dr Li investigated this and found that 'people who live in areas with fewer trees not only have significantly higher levels of stress, they also have higher mortality rates than people who live where there is a good density of trees' (Li, 2019, p. 87).

It is thought that trees boost our immune system through providing cleaner air via higher levels of oxygen, but also through their natural oils, known as phytoncides. Simply breathing in the natural aroma of a forest, which is full of phytoncides, has been shown to boost our levels of natural killer cells (Li, 2019). Even if you can't get outside, a famous study into the healing effects of nature showed that patients recovering from surgery recovered more quickly if their beds overlooked a natural setting rather than another building (Ulrich, 1984).

Nature also positively affects our gut microbiome (the trillions of microorganisms in our gut, such as bacteria and fungi). The more diverse our gut microbiome, the better for our health and wellbeing. When we're outside in nature and coming into contact with soil and breathing in the air, we inhale and ingest more good bacteria such as Mycobacterium vaccae, and this has a positive effect on our immune system (Li, 2019). Our gut microbiome varies depending on whether we live in urban or green spaces, with those who live in green spaces tending to have a more diverse microbiome (Bowyer et al., 2022). One experiment attempted to enrich the biodiversity in urban day-care centres by covering the floor with soil, turf and forest floor for a month (Roslund et al., 2020). The researchers noted a change in children's gut microbiomes, making their profiles more similar to children who attend day-care in forest settings. Getting down with nature is good for our health!

Cognition, learning and behaviour

If nature can have such a profound effect on our bodies, it is no surprise that it positively affects our minds too. A study by the University of Michigan looked into the effects of nature on memory and cognition. It found that people can remember 20 per cent more after they have been for a walk in nature, compared to a walk through a busy street (Berman et al., 2008). This study supports an earlier theory called Attention Restoration Theory (Kaplan, 1995), which proposed that exposure to nature allows our brains and bodies the chance to rest and reset and, in turn, improves our ability to pay attention and concentrate.

There is increasing evidence that nature can benefit children's attainment in schools. Studies in Canada (Sivarajah et al., 2018) and America (Tallis et al., 2018) show a strong relationship between school sites with a greater proportion of tree coverage and improved performance on standardised tests. When four- and five-year-olds are taught in a natural environment, research shows that it has a positive effect on their speech and language development, and they use a richer variety of language, compared to traditional classroom environments (Richardson and Murray, 2016). Another American study (Kuo et al., 2018) looked at over 300 schools in Chicago and measured their 'green cover' (how much the students could view and have access to nature). The researchers found that increased green cover predicted statistically significantly better school performance on standardised tests of maths (the impact was largest when the students could look at trees rather than grass). One study in Taiwan (Han, 2009) brought nature into the classroom in the form of small plants and trees. Compared to the control classroom (which was business as usual), the green classroom had students who showed increases in pro-social and friendly behaviour, lower absence and a reduction in punishments issued by the teacher.

Happiness

All of the research shared so far suggests that nature will ultimately make us happier. If spending time in nature or simply looking at it can lower our stress, boost our immune system functioning, prevent us from getting ill, strengthen our hearts, improve our gut health, make us friendlier and help us to concentrate and do better in school, then it's inevitable that we will feel the quality of our lives improve.

Although the pandemic may have increased our reliance on devices and screen time, other research suggests that it positively changed our relationship with nature too. Professor Sohyun Park at the University of Connecticut looked at how people's perceptions of nature changed before, during and after the COVID-19 pandemic, by studying language use on social media and machine learning (Park et al., 2022). Park found that people showed an increased appreciation of nature, people sought out more natural settings and they reported heightened spiritual and emotional experiences when in nature.

In action

It is clear that we have taken nature for granted over the centuries, but I do believe that the pandemic and climate change are waking us up to its healing powers and our urgent need to reconnect with our natural habitat. The following ideas will help you and your children to get back in touch with nature so that they know how to appreciate and look after it now and long into the future.

Outdoor learning

This is a huge topic in itself, and multiple books have been written about outdoor learning (see 'Further reading and recommended resources'). This section is merely to help get you started and point you in the right direction.

Golden principles

In her book *Dirty Teaching* (2014), outdoor learning expert Juliet Robertson explains her four golden principles for learning outdoors:

1. **Take a sustainable approach:** We need to care for the environments in which we learn and play and we should ultimately leave them better places as a result of our care.

2. **Value free-play and playful learning:** Modern life and schooling are full of structured activities and directed time. When learning outside, adopt a playful approach to learning and allow children time and space to play for its own sake (that means all year groups, including Year 6!).

3. **Provide a natural, nurturing environment:** Schools need to provide outdoor environments that benefit children's health and wellbeing, which means plenty of access to green spaces and nature (the wilder, the better!).

4. **Develop children's creative capacities:** The outdoor environment should encourage positive risk-taking and provide opportunities for problem-solving, transferring skills to new areas and lateral thinking (looking at things in new ways).

It is worth reflecting on the outdoor spaces at your school and your approach to learning outdoors to see how you are currently embedding these golden principles. What small changes could you make to ensure that outdoor learning is upholding these principles?

Plan ahead

Some teachers are reluctant to teach outdoors because there are too many unpredictable variables (e.g. the weather, children's behaviour, accidents, etc.) and so prefer to stay in their comfort zones in the classroom. But, with a little forward planning, those fears can be addressed to make learning outdoors as smooth as possible. Bear in mind the following:

- **Establish ground rules:** Be clear about your expectations around behaviour outdoors. Get children to help establish these ground rules so that everyone accepts them.

- **Positively manage risk-taking:** If you're doing an activity like den building, always ask the children what the potential risks are and how they plan to manage those risks skilfully. Empower them by helping them to assess and manage potential risks.

- **Clothing:** If you're going outside in all weathers, make sure that parents/carers are informed well in advance so that they can provide things like wellies and waterproofs (but it's always useful for the school to have spares).

- **Be inclusive:** Who are the children in your class who have specific needs that must be taken into account when planning outdoor learning? Ensure that the right support is in place to make sure that all children can participate fully in outdoor learning.

- **Be prepared for the worst:** Make sure that you have a first aid kit to hand, children's medicine is easily accessible (inhalers, epi pens, etc.) and that you can easily contact adults in the school if you need additional help.

Can this be taught or completed outside?

Whatever you are teaching, always have the question in the back of your mind: 'Can this be taught or completed outside?' If the answer is 'Yes', then, with a bit of forward planning, outdoor learning can become second nature to you and your class.

If it's a maths lesson on measurement, is it possible for your class to work in teams and use the trundle wheels to measure the length of parts of the playground? If you're studying the life cycle of plants, as well as growing them from seeds indoors, can you get outside and study plants at different stages of their life cycle? If you end your day reading a class story, can this be done outside in nice weather? Can you break up sedentary periods of indoor lessons with some movement and exercise outdoors (Hindu squats outside, anyone?). In short, the more opportunities to get your class outside and learning, the better.

Do it weekly

Try to make a habit of getting your class outdoors for learning at least once a week (even in the winter months!). This makes it sustainable and manageable for you (i.e. when you plan for the week ahead, you're just thinking about how you can turn one lesson into an outdoor learning opportunity) and it also means that you're making it a habit. You and your children will then just get used to and expect to spend part of each week outside and learning.

Playing outside

As we learned in the previous chapter, playtime minutes have been reduced in primary schools over the last three decades, and this is not good for wellbeing or learning. For children, play is a serious business and schools must invest time, energy and resources in ensuring that children's outdoor play is as fruitful as can be. Here are some top tips to help you and your children to get the most from your outdoor play:

- Reintroduce the afternoon breaktime. Go on, I dare you!
- Ensure that children have access to natural spaces.

- Host regular play assemblies where you can introduce new equipment with which children can play, build and experiment (e.g. old tyres, crates, wooden blocks).

- Regularly check that the equipment is safe, and replace when it becomes too worn or damaged (ask parents and the local community for donations).

- Train 'play leaders' who can help to initiate games with other children and be responsible for helping to tidy equipment away at the end of play.

- Ensure that staff engage with children's play when on playground duty.

- Create a 'quiet zone' outside – somewhere for children to chill and relax away from the hustle and bustle – and see whether it can be filled with plants and nature!

Rewild your outside areas

When I taught at an inner-London primary school, we didn't have any immediate access to nature. We had a concrete playground and our 'grass' was artificial. Despite this, one of our green-fingered teaching assistants called Helen was a keen gardener, and she made sure that our playground was filled with lots of large pots containing shrubs and exotic-looking plants. It meant that our outside space was as green as it could be. Taking inspiration from this urban but green school in particular, why not try out the following ideas:

- Tap into the green strengths in your school – ask whether any staff or parents are keen gardeners and would be happy to volunteer to 'greenify' your outside areas.

- Use your newsletter to ask parents and carers for donations of outdoor shrubs, trees and plants to breathe new life into the grey and dull areas of your outdoor spaces.

- Set up an eco-team at your school so that children are a core part of making sure that your school is as green and eco-friendly as possible. Go to **www.eco-schools.org.uk** for more information.

- Set up an outside area as a dedicated 'allotment'. With the help of staff and parent volunteers, grow seasonal fruit and vegetables, and give children regular opportunities to plant, pick and eat the produce.

- If you're lucky enough to have lots of green space at your school, dedicate some spaces to be 'wild' areas that are not mown or cut, but which are allowed to grow wild and free to attract a diverse range of insects and bugs.

Tales from the classroom

I wanted to bring more plants into classrooms in my current school, but there was one major problem: I had zero budget to help. I tried to contact local garden centres and nurseries and just one replied with a kind donation of a £10 gift voucher. Enough to get me started but not enough to get plants into eight classrooms and our library!

But then I had an idea. I knew that many of my neighbours were keen gardeners and several had allotment patches nearby. So, I posted on my road's Facebook group:

'Hello lovely neighbours! We're trying to get indoor plants into our school and classrooms. There is research that shows that having plants in rooms and access to nature can lower stress levels, clean the air and improve wellbeing, behaviour and concentration. As always, budgets are non-existent and we can't buy any, so I'm appealing for any green-fingered neighbours to:

- donate a plant
- give us some cuttings of your plants that we can grow
- offer some seeds for plants.

If you can help please let me know!'

Immediately, several neighbours replied saying that they would drop off cuttings or that they'd be happy to donate some of their plants. Before long, I had about 15 plants from a variety of neighbours and, so far, our children have taken great care of them and they are all still alive! This was a year ago and even now I'll open my front door and there'll be a random plant on my doorstep.

Adrian Bethune

Bringing nature inside

In a passing conversation with Helen, the TA, I mentioned that I'd love to have plants inside my classroom. A few days later she came in with several cuttings from some of her house plants. She assured me that they were low-maintenance and that even I should be able to manage to keep them alive. My class and I ensured that we watered and took care of them each week, and the five cuttings that we had grew into healthy, established plants. Our classroom had a different feel with plants dotted around it and there was a distinct feeling of emptiness when we lent all of our plants to Team Year 3 for a couple of weeks when they were studying plants in science. I remember that the children's faces lit up when we finally got our plants back! They really did make our classroom feel more alive.

Bringing plants and nature inside is not only likely to induce a sense of calm and reduce stress, but they're also likely to improve air quality. Indoor air is two to five times more polluted than outdoor air, and plants are natural air purifiers (Li, 2019)!

To bring nature inside more, try these simple ideas:

- Tap into the strengths of your school community and ask staff, parents and carers whether they can donate any indoor plants or cuttings for classrooms.
- Reach out to local nurseries and garden centres and ask for donations of house plants for your classrooms.
- Host green fundraisers (e.g. sponsored nature walks, healthy bake sales) and the money raised can buy indoor plants for your school.
- Get as many low-maintenance indoor plants in classrooms and communal areas as possible, and, importantly, create plant monitors where children take ownership of taking care of them.
- According to NASA (cited in Li, 2019), some of the top air-purifying plants are peace lily, English ivy, chrysanthemum, bamboo palm and spider plants.

Natural art

Art lessons give you the perfect opportunity to take learning outdoors. Not only does nature provide inspiration for various artworks and exploration of colour, but you can also use nature in your art by using natural materials such as mud, clay and sticks. These ideas can help you to make the most of the outdoors in your art lessons:

- Study artists like Andrew Goldsworthy, who make sculptures using natural materials, and then have a go at working in teams to create your own nature-inspired sculptures and artworks (see Figure 11.1).
- Do at least one art lesson outside each half-term, focused on local landscapes to try to capture the changing seasons.
- Take your class outside with only sketch pads or paper and nothing else. Challenge them to create a painting or drawing using only natural materials that they can find outside.

Figure 11.1: *Andrew Goldsworthy-inspired art created by Team Year 3 at a local park in inner London*

Nature bathing

You may not have a forest on your doorstep, so this nature bathing is my take on 'forest bathing' – it's about bathing in whatever natural settings we have available to us. The key is to slow down and be mindful in these natural settings and to use all of our senses. The guide below can help you:

- Explain to your class what nature bathing is and share the many benefits that people report from spending time in nature.

- Take your class to a natural setting in the school grounds or one nearby.

- Remind the class that nature bathing is best done in silence, so that we can engage all of the senses.

- Sound: Listen and tune in to the birds singing and the breeze rustling in the leaves of trees.

- Sight: Really pay attention to the different shades of greens and browns around and the sunlight filtering through any branches.

- Smell: Are there any strong aromas coming from this natural setting?
- Taste: Really taste the fresh air as you take some deep breaths in and out.
- Touch: Place your hands on the bark of a tree, lie on the ground and scrunch some leaves in your hands.
- Allow yourself to fully relax and be in the moment in this natural setting. Close your eyes and drink it all in.

School farm

If space allows, it can be very therapeutic to have a school farm with farm animals in your school grounds. Having a school farm can help you to teach children about animal welfare, sustainability, food sources and healthy eating. My current school is based in Buckinghamshire and we have an abundance of green space. Our headteacher, Charlie, was keen on us having farm animals on site, so we are now the proud owners of several chickens and two goats (see Figure 11.2 for a photograph of Tilly the goat). The children have responded really well and are often found looking after our free-range chickens or watching the goats climbing in their paddock. Some things to bear in mind when considering a school farm:

- **Consider your outdoor space:** Look at what space you have and what animals will be best suited. Work out the cost of fencing or building shelters for your animals.
- **Consult with children and staff:** Give your school community a voice with regard to which animals you should get.
- **Engage the local community:** You'll need strong ties with a local vet and maybe some volunteers to help to look after the animals in the holidays, so make those connections.

Figure 11.2: *Tilly the goat*

- **Follow DEFRA guidelines:** Cloven-hoofed animals need to be registered, and your land needs to be registered as well. Find out more here: **www.gov.uk/guidance/animal-welfare**

- **Enjoy your school farm:** The benefits are not just for children but for staff, parents and carers too.

Key points

- Being outside in nature is our natural habitat. Biophilia is the term used to describe how humans feel at home in nature because we evolved for hundreds of thousands of years living outside. We are happiest in natural settings.

- More of us are living in urban areas, spending more time indoors and having less contact with nature. At the same time, children are increasingly worried about the future of the planet.

- Forest bathing is when we spend time in woods and forests, engaging our senses and soaking up the natural environment. It has been shown to be extremely beneficial for our wellbeing.

- Spending time in natural settings reduces our stress levels, improves the quality of our sleep and strengthens the functioning of our immune system. Our gut microbiome seems to improve the more time that we spend outdoors.

- Access and exposure to nature can also benefit our minds and help us to think and concentrate better. Children appear to do better in schools where there is more 'green cover', and their behaviour improves too.

- Embrace outdoor learning and seek every opportunity to get your class outside. But plan ahead for it and make it a weekly event so that you and the children get used to it.

- Increase the playtime minutes of your children and give children lots of opportunities to explore, take positive risks and be creative outside.

- Bring more nature inside your school and get as many plants as you can in classrooms, with the children taking ownership of them.

- Bathe in nature and use all of your senses to soak it up.

- If space allows, create a school farm and teach children about animal welfare, food sources, sustainability and healthy eating.

Chapter 12
Teacher wellbeing

Thousands of candles can be lit by a single candle and the life of the candle will not be shortened. Happiness never decreases by being shared.

– Buddha

Chapter overview

In this chapter, we'll learn why it is vital for teachers to prioritise their own wellbeing and how, in doing so, we can improve pupil wellbeing too. We'll look at what can get in the way of teacher wellbeing, and then discover the practical steps that we can take to thrive and not just survive in teaching.

In theory	In action
• Prioritising your wellbeing • Why teacher wellbeing is important • Good-enough teaching • Perfectionism • Shifting old habits	• Applying the lessons to your own life • Small changes, consistently applied • Simplify • Flex appeal • Nourishing or depleting? • When you feel swamped • Humour • Focus on what matters • Be courageous

In theory

Prioritising your wellbeing

There is no getting away from the fact that teaching is an inherently stressful job. In fact, figures published by the Health and Safety Executive show that teaching is one of the most stressful careers that there is (Health and Safety Executive, 2022). The most recent Teacher Wellbeing Index showed that 77 per cent of staff had experienced behavioural, psychological or physical symptoms due to their work, and 54 per cent had considered leaving the sector over the past two years due to pressures on their mental health and wellbeing (Scanlan and Savill-Smith, 2021). This means that teachers need to take *extra* care of themselves to protect them from the corrosive effects of chronic stress. And although schools play a large role in affecting a teacher's levels of happiness and wellbeing, I believe that your wellbeing is too important to be left in the hands of someone other than yourself. It's absolutely essential that teachers know how to prioritise their own wellbeing.

However, a survey by Teacher Tapp in 2022 suggested that, on the whole, teachers are not very good at being able to do this. Around 8,000 teachers were asked how often they were able to prioritise their own wellbeing in the last half-term in school (see Figure 12.1). Fourteen per cent said that they never prioritised their own wellbeing and 51 per cent said that they only managed to at the weekends. That means that almost two-thirds of respondents believed that they couldn't prioritise their wellbeing at all during the working week – their wellbeing had to wait either until the weekend or, presumably, until the holidays. I find this staggering. On reflection though, I wonder if many of the respondents didn't understand what it means to prioritise their wellbeing, assuming that it must be doing 'big' things. My definition of prioritising your wellbeing is as follows:

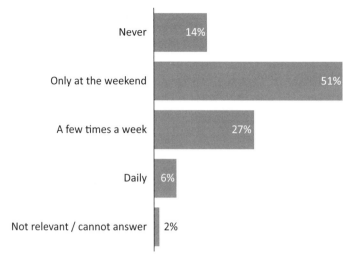

Figure 12.1: *How often were you able to prioritise your own wellbeing during the last half-term in school?*

You make it a priority to do small things each day that support your wellbeing.

This is, I believe, what the six per cent of Teacher Tapp respondents who say they prioritise their wellbeing daily do. They likely make sure that every day they do a few small things that they know will help them to cope with the pressures and challenges of daily life. This approach to our wellbeing is open to all of us, and not just six per cent of teaching staff. We can all manage this but it partly requires a shift in mindset (to believe that these small things are important and need time set aside to do) and also an awareness of the small things that nourish us.

Why teacher wellbeing is important

As discussed in the introduction to this book (p. 1), teacher wellbeing is at a crisis point in the UK. With record numbers seeking medical advice for stress and a third leaving teaching within five years of qualifying, it is vital that teachers and schools start to take the issue seriously. Here are three key reasons for why *teacher* wellbeing should be a priority for schools:

1. Role models

Any teacher who wishes to teach happiness and wellbeing to children must first be a role model for happiness and wellbeing. A report on mental health commissioned by the government in 2008 stated that 'Teachers who are stressed, or demoralised, make poor role models for young people.' (Foresight Mental Capital and Wellbeing Project, 2008) We learned in Chapter 1 (p. 15) from child psychologist Alison Gopnik (2016) that children learn more from caregivers' unconscious behaviours and how they act, rather than anything that they consciously teach them, so I believe that we have to behave and act in a way that models health and wellbeing to our pupils. This is not about teachers being perfect role models, feeling 'happy' the whole time, or always smiling and being positive in front of pupils. That would be inauthentic and unrealistic. Teachers are allowed to be human and experience the full range of emotions. I'm also not proposing that you need to eat organic salads, know all the asanas of yoga and live a completely Zen lifestyle. Being a role model for wellbeing simply means that teachers show that they take care *of* themselves and care *about* themselves, just as much as they care for their pupils.

2. Pupil success

There is evidence that when teachers look after themselves more, their pupils do better academically. A review of evidence carried out by Lancaster University and the Teacher Support Network, entitled *Healthy teachers, higher marks?*, makes a strong case for schools really looking after their key resource – teachers. The report notes that across many industries, employees with high wellbeing are more productive, their quality of work is better, they're more creative and they generally perform better too. The review cites evidence that shows a 'statistically significant positive relationship between staff wellbeing and student SAT outcomes' (Bajorek et al., 2014). However, when employee wellbeing is low, work performance drops and absences increase. In 2018–19, a staggering 2.13 million days were lost to teacher absences in the UK (Department for Education, 2022b). Another report, entitled *Staff wellbeing is key to school success*, suggests that a virtuous circle is likely to arise in schools when teachers are happy and healthy, and pupils are doing well. The report states, 'there is a two-way relationship between teacher wellbeing and pupil performance… increases in teacher wellbeing can lead to improvements in the performance of pupils, so increases in pupil performance may lead to increased wellbeing in teachers.' (Briner and Dewberry, 2007)

3. This is your life

Teachers' happiness matters because it is important in and of itself. Just as pupils' wellbeing is more important than their grades, so too is your wellbeing. When you start to view your happiness as 'the ultimate currency', then everything changes. It means that you naturally start to look for ways in which to make teaching more meaningful and pleasurable for you and your pupils. You start to do less of the stuff that saps the life out of you and more of the stuff that makes you come alive. Teaching then becomes a source of happiness and you are far more likely to enjoy a long and sustainable teaching career.

Good-enough teaching

Back in the 1950s, English paediatrician and psychoanalyst Donald Winnicott coined the term 'good-enough mothering' (Winnicott, 1962) to describe a mother who does a good-enough job in an extremely complex, difficult and constantly evolving arena. The 'good-enough' mother does her best to attend and attune to her baby's needs but will not always get it right. The 'misattunements' help her child to realise that they are a separate person from mum and also gives them opportunities to learn how to handle difficulties. Perfection is not an option because not only is it impossible to be a perfect mother, but it also denies the child important developmental processes (such as learning how to be an independent individual and cope with the trials and tribulations of life).

I believe that there is a need in education for the 'good-enough teacher', particularly in response to the tyranny of the 'outstanding teacher' (which is a form of perfectionism, in my opinion). The good-enough teacher does their best to care for and educate their class. They always try to make their lessons interesting and engaging. The good-enough teacher aims to develop a love of learning in their pupils and help them to reach their full potential. They aim to provide a safe and secure learning environment for their class, and respond to children's physical, emotional and spiritual needs. They want their children to be happy and enjoy coming to school. But sometimes they will get it wrong. Some lessons may be a bit dull. Tiredness may mean that the good-enough teacher can be grouchy at times, and not as warm and responsiveness as they normally are. Good-enough teachers may even, from time to time, yearn for an escape from the huge responsibility that they have. But, overall, they enjoy being a teacher, they believe in what they are doing and they do a good job. The blips and mistakes are all accepted as part of being a good-enough teacher and, ultimately, being human.

Perfectionism

One of the things that gets in the way of being 'good enough' is striving for perfection. On my graduation day from my teacher training course, a senior lecturer said to the audience of newly qualified teachers, 'If you are a perfectionist, either change yourself or you may need to change careers.' I remember the advice clearly but didn't quite heed it at first. I also remember thinking to myself, 'You could have told us this a year ago!' In the past, I have tried to be the perfect teacher. I spent ages planning my lessons, scouring the web for the best resources around. I would always be thinking about teaching outside of school and on the lookout for ideas to bring into class. I would tirelessly try to tick off everything from my to-do list each day (not realising that this is impossible!). In every observation or book scrutiny that I had, I aimed for 'outstanding'. I would also stay at school later than necessary, marking in detail to please management and parents. The problem was that this was unsustainable and unrealistic. Not only was I putting myself under massive unnecessary pressure and stress, but by aiming for extrinsic rewards and recognition, I also lost sight of the intrinsic joy of being a teacher.

Studies show that perfectionism can be a barrier to happiness. Psychologist Barry Schwartz and colleagues have carried out research into people who are either 'maximisers' or 'satisficers' (Schwartz et al., 2002). Maximisers are perfectionists who always try to seek the best, whereas satisficers are content with what is good enough. It turns out that maximisers are less happy than satisficers for two main reasons:

1. They tend to have more regrets about the *other* choices or decisions that they could have made ('That lesson was a bit flat! I wish I'd used those other resources now!').

2. They compare themselves to others more. When given the same task as a peer, their happiness is greatly affected by whether they did better or worse than their peer ('I can't believe that their lesson was graded "outstanding" and mine just "good"!').

Perfectionism may be one reason why teachers leave the profession. Louis Cozolino notes, 'Teachers with the highest levels of commitment and idealistic expectations when they enter the profession are more likely to burn out or leave the field.' (Cozolino,

2013, p. 127) Maybe it is time that more teachers aimed to be good enough and more like satisficers. This isn't about becoming complacent or being happy with mediocrity. The good-enough, satisfied teacher aims to do their best but is wise enough to not aim for perfection. Nor do they seek constant approval from others. Being good enough and satisfied means stripping away layers of unnecessary stresses and pressures that get in the way of the innate pleasure and purpose of teaching.

Shifting old habits

I once read that there is no such thing as getting rid of habits. You simply replace old ones with new ones. But establishing new habits isn't always easy because we often fall back on our default ways of behaving.

However, the Behavioural Insights Team UK have shown that if you want to encourage a new behaviour, you need to make it 'easy, attractive, social and timely' – they call it EAST (Service et al., 2015). They also note that only small changes and shifts are needed to have big results, so don't feel that you need to overhaul your entire life to improve your wellbeing. Small and manageable change is the key to success, and it normally takes around two months for a new habit to become set (Lally et al., 2010). Let's look at what EAST could mean if, say, a teacher wanted to increase the amount of physical exercise they were getting:

- **Easy:** Try to reduce the 'hassle factor' of the new behaviour. If you want to behave a certain way, pave out the path of least resistance for yourself. Also, harness the power of defaults. People have a strong tendency to go with the default option, so making an option the default makes it more likely to be adopted. Conversely, if you want to stop a certain behaviour, make it harder for yourself to do it. You could, for example, leave your gym kit by the front door the night before, take your running shoes to school and join in with the Daily Mile, or cancel your bus or train ticket and walk or cycle to school.

- **Attractive:** We are more likely to do something that attracts our attention, is novel or seems appealing and relevant to us. You could watch the '23 and 1/2 hours' visual lecture by Dr Mike Evans (**www.youtube.com/watch?v=aUaInS6H IGo**), which highlights the huge gains that you can expect from exercising more, and then go for a run. Alternatively, you could treat yourself to a shiny new bike or some fancy trainers to encourage you to exercise more – the newness of the equipment will make you want to use it, and if you keep it up for eight weeks, a new habit should have set in.

- **Social:** We are highly social creatures and often behave in ways that are similar to others. If we see other people do something, we're more likely to adopt that behaviour ourselves. We are also more likely to do something when we have made a promise to someone else to do it. If you wanted to start doing yoga, for example, you could join a yoga group in your local area – being part of a group will increase your chances of going each week. You could also tell a friend that you're starting yoga and this would make you more likely to turn up. Or you could see whether your colleagues are interested in doing this too and find a yoga teacher to run a class in your school.

- **Timely:** Our success at adopting a new behaviour varies greatly depending on *when* we choose to do it. Behaviour is easier to change when our habits are disrupted by big life events (such as moving house, changing jobs, getting married or having a child). It might be best to make changes at the start of a new school year. The six-week summer holiday will have broken you out of old habits, so you can start afresh with new intentions. Also, you could choose to exercise at the same time each day or week to establish a new routine, making it a default habit.

In action

Applying the lessons to your own life

Hopefully, as you have been reading about how you can teach children to be happier, you have also been reflecting on how the lessons and techniques in this book can be applied to your own life as well. Maybe reading about tribal classrooms (p. 15) has made you think about creating more of a sense of team in the staffroom. You might have thought about setting up a wellbeing team to focus on staff happiness (regular staff nights out, anyone?). Or, after reading about 'what went well?' (p. 59), you might have decided to treat yourself to a nice new journal to write down three good things each day before you go to bed. Reflection and thinking about the ideas is great, but if you want to work at boosting your levels of wellbeing, it is going to take *action*. When you start to prioritise happiness and wellbeing, you benefit and the children benefit. Your classroom starts to become a place of refuge rather than a drain. There are lots of ideas to experiment with but, remember to make any changes small and manageable. It would be self-defeating if you attempted all of the ideas in this book and then burned out trying to prioritise your wellbeing! A key thing to remember, though, is that you have a lot of control over your wellbeing – maybe more than you think. Below are some further ideas to bear in mind and act upon when focusing on your wellbeing.

Small changes, consistently applied

Tal Ben-Shahar was asked what the key to improving wellbeing was and he replied 'Making small changes, consistently' (Ben-Shahar, 2021). Improving our wellbeing as teachers, therefore, is not about making dramatic lifestyle changes – these are bound to fail. Instead, it's about making small tweaks and changes to how we teach and lead our lives, which, incrementally build up to positively change our lives in the long run. This is what prioritising our wellbeing is about – the small things that we do each day and each week that support our wellbeing.

When I think about how I prioritise my own wellbeing, these are some of my daily habits:

- meditate for five minutes every morning
- go for a lunchtime walk by myself when I'm in school
- try to get a minimum of 8,000 steps in per day
- play football on Thursday evenings with some friends
- eat a healthy, balanced diet
- watch 30 minutes less TV each night and go to bed earlier
- spend quality time with my wife and kids every day
- reduce the amount of time spent on my phone (still a work in progress!).

These are just a handful of some of the things that I do each day and week. But let's say that I don't do four of the above eight habits – that still means that I am doing three or four other things each day that support my wellbeing. Now, these are the things that work for me, but your list will probably be different. Have a go at the following activity to see how you can prioritise your wellbeing:

1. Make a list of the small daily and weekly things that you consistently do that you know are good for your wellbeing.

2. Can you add one or two other small things that you believe would benefit you?

3. Keep these activities going for a half-term and see whether it makes a difference.

Simplify

When I switched careers to become a teacher, I couldn't believe how busy and complicated a typical teaching day was. Not only was the school day crammed to the brim with lessons and activities, but also every other week there was an event, a school trip, an important visitor or a special occasion to plan for! Being a busy teacher isn't great for wellbeing. Recent brain scans show that people who spend their days rushing around mindlessly have an amygdala (the primitive part of the brain involved in the fight or flight response – see Chapters 2 and 3 pp. 37–59) that is on 'high alert' (Way et al., 2010). Being busy also means that we can feel 'time poor', where we feel that we don't have enough time to do all of our tasks. This can leave us feeling rushed, overworked and constantly playing catch-up. But it doesn't have to be this way.

In his book *Happier*, Tal Ben-Shahar strongly advises that everyone, teacher or otherwise, should simplify their lives. Shahar states that 'This means safeguarding our time, learning to say "no" more often – to people as well as opportunities… It means prioritising, choosing activities that we really, really want to do, while letting go of others.' (Ben-Shahar, 2008, p. 154) He also talks about reducing our list of 'have-tos' (things we do that are motivated by extrinsic factors like obligation, fear, status or a desire to please) and increasing more of our 'want-tos' (activities that are intrinsically rewarding and give us meaning and pleasure). Ultimately, simplifying your life is about taking control and using your autonomy to carve out a lifestyle that works for you.

I have fully embraced this philosophy. Wherever possible, I try to simplify what I do personally and professionally. At work, I have set clear boundaries for myself and make sure that the majority of my schoolwork is carried out at school and not at home. I arrive at school at around 8.00 am (I live locally) and leave no later than 5.00 pm. As a lot of my work now is outside of school, writing and speaking for a variety of schools and education organisations, I have to be super-organised. I prioritise all my work so that important stuff gets done each day, and if I am not able to do it, it can wait. I have sought out simpler ways of working at the schools in which I've worked and then suggested these to my headteachers. Not all of my ideas were taken on board but embracing simplicity at work has led to schools slimming down our planning requirements, halving the length of school report templates and reducing the number of morning briefing meetings we had from five down to one. All have resulted in staff feeling a lot more time-rich, with more time to do other things. I have also made personal choices like choosing to work part-time so that I can be around to look after my sons more. By simplifying my working life, I feel like my job works for me rather than the other way around.

Two important questions to ask yourself, then, are:

1. In what ways can I simplify my working life?

2. How can I engineer my life so I get to spend more time on the things that I really *want* to do, and less time on the things that I feel I *have* to do?

Flex appeal

One way in which to bring more balance to your life is to work flexibly. Flexible working is basically thinking differently about *how* you work, *when* you work and *where* you work. The four main ways in which you can work flexibly are:

1. part-time working (you work reduced hours and are paid pro-rata)

2. job share (one job is split between two or more people, who all work part-time)

3. compressed hours (you work full-time hours but do so in fewer but longer days)

4. working from home (you complete all or some of your work from home).

All employees in the UK now have the statutory right to request to work flexibly, and employers have to give the request due consideration. In fact, your school should have a flexible working policy by law. Now there are some obvious limitations to how flexibly you can work when you have a class to teach. It would be great to work from home and teach your class from the comfort of your sofa, but that isn't going to happen any time soon. However, some schools embrace flexible working by allowing staff to take their planning, preparation and assessment (PPA) time off-site, so this may be something that you could request at your school. Depending on when your PPA time is, it could mean coming into school late or leaving early one day a week, which could make a big difference. One school in which I worked would give staff a day off in lieu if they ran an after-school club for a term. It meant that you could earn up to three 'club days' a year. These came in handy for when teachers wanted long weekends or days off in the middle of term time. The fact is that schools and teachers do not need to be beholden to the outdated industrial structure of nine to five, five days a week, and can be more creative with how staff work.

When my wife and I were expecting our first child, his due date was right at the beginning of a school year. Plus, I was starting work at a brand new school. The thought of teaching full-time with a newborn baby at home terrified me, so I asked my new headteacher whether I could work part-time for the first term. She agreed, and so from September until January, I worked four days a week. That day off with my wife and new baby was a real lifesaver. Not only did it give me some respite in the busy autumn term, but I also got to spend some quality time with my new enlarged family. The following academic year, when my wife returned to work part-time, I requested to work three days a week so that I could share childcare with my wife (see Figure 12.2). Again, my headteacher was accommodating and granted me part-time working. My headteacher had the right to turn my request down, but the fact is that I asked. If you feel that flexible working is something that might help with your work–life balance, then ask your headteacher. You do not need to be a parent to request flexible working. It is worth reading this guidance from the Department for Education

Figure 12.2: *Me and my son enjoying some café culture on one of my 'days off'*

(2017) about flexible working, so that you know your rights and your school's responsibilities: **www.gov.uk/government/publi cations/flexible-working-in-schools**. Also, organisations like **www.timewise.co.uk** are on a mission to make flexible working the norm in all sectors, so check them out too.

Nourishing or depleting?

It can be really helpful to audit what we do on a daily basis and see which activities motivate us and which ones sap us of energy. Based on a practice from *Mindfulness-Based Cognitive Therapy for Depression* (Segal et al., 2002), a useful activity to do is called 'nourishing or depleting'. Here is how it works:

- First, bring to mind all the activities that you do on a typical day, starting from when you wake up to when you go to sleep.
- Next, write these down in a list.

Table 12.1: *Example of a 'nourishing or depleting' table*

Daily activities	Nourishing or depleting?
Alarm goes off	D
Shower	N
Get dressed	N
Eat breakfast and watch news	N/D
Drive to school	D
Set up classroom	N/D
Check emails	D

- Now, consider each activity and decide which ones give you energy, make you feel good or lift your mood. These are nourishing activities, so put an 'N' next to these ones.

- Then consider which activities drain you, leave you feeling stressed or frazzled, or pull you down. These are depleting ones, so put a 'D' next to these ones. If an activity is both, or you can't decide, you can put 'N/D' next to them. Table 12.1 gives an example of how a list may start.

It can be quite revealing to realise how many of our activities drain and deplete us. This isn't meant to upset you but to help you bring more awareness to how you live day to day. Your list does not even have to be in perfect balance, as one nourishing activity that really energises you can outweigh several smaller depleting ones. Once you have a good idea of how your daily activities affect you, ask yourself these two questions:

1. **How can I turn depleting or neutral activities into more nourishing ones?**

   It could be a simple thing, like changing your alarm tone from a harsh beep to a more melodic one, turning off the news whilst you eat breakfast or not checking your emails at the start of every day. Experiment with small, subtle changes and see what impact they have.

2. **How can I incorporate more nourishing activities into my day?**

   Maybe you choose to take part in an activity that gives you flow (see Chapter 6, p. 123), take up an old hobby, go for a nice meal or call a good friend for a chat. Try to have a bank of nourishing activities that you can dip into, and attempt to do at least one a day to add more balance to your life.

When you feel swamped

Often, when we are most stressed, busy or exhausted, we become paralysed and don't know what to do to ameliorate our suffering. It can start to feel like you're losing control over your life as the demands of teaching and your personal life take over. But there are some simple things that you can do to wrest back some control and regain your sense of agency:

- **Take some deep breaths:** Just pausing and focusing on your breathing for a few minutes can gradually take you out of fight or flight mode.

- **Do something that gives you pleasure:** You can use your bank of nourishing activities for inspiration. Go for a walk, listen to your favourite music, meet up with a friend, take a long bath, have a massage, eat your favourite food or watch a funny film. Doing something just for you can distract you from your worries and nourish you.

- **Complete a small task, any task:** Even just vacuuming a room in your house or renewing your car's MOT can give you a sense of control over your life.

- **Ask for help:** If you are swamped, ask someone for help. You may find that they too are swamped and at least you realise you're not on your own. Don't be afraid of saying to your leadership team that you are struggling with workload, or speaking to friends and family about your worries. The Education Support Partnership (**www.educationsupport partnership.org.uk**), who give mental health and wellbeing support to teaching staff, have a free helpline: 08000 562 561. Asking for help is a courageous act and not something to be ashamed of.

Humour

Laughing is one of the fastest ways to counteract tension and stress. Not only does your body flood with happy hormones when you're laughing, which reduces stress levels and makes you feel good, but it is also contagious. When you laugh with others, it is a shared and bonding experience. It is impossible to feel stressed or overwhelmed when you are laughing! Fortunately for you, primary school teaching gives you no end of humorous material in which to indulge. From the funny things that children say (like the boy with whom I spent an entire afternoon trying to help him say the word 'flamingo', but who kept on saying 'flamango') to the hilarious things that happen to you (such as the time I joined in with a kickabout in the playground and completely ripped my trousers), your week is full of opportunities to laugh. Make sure that you don't let them drift by unnoticed. Savour the funny moments that you share with your class and your colleagues, and try not to take yourself too seriously. In fact, right now, why not try the following activity?

- Bring to mind your all-time top three funniest moments of your teaching career. What happened, who was there and why was it so funny?
- Relive those funny moments by sharing them with a colleague or friend. Laugh until you're crying.
- Repeat often.

Focus on what matters

In my first two years of teaching, I had many doubts about whether I had made the right choice in changing careers. Teaching wasn't living up to my expectations and I didn't like the fact that the timetable was packed, I was churning through content and there didn't seem to be enough time to focus on children's emotional health and wellbeing. In just my second year of teaching, I decided that that would be my last year in the classroom and, at the end of the year, I would do something different. When I made that choice, I decided that I may as well focus on the things that I felt were important and do less of the stuff that I thought was a waste of time. My class and I began to meditate more, we had more breaks for physical activity and I started teaching mini-happiness lessons (sharing little nuggets from the science of wellbeing). I discovered that I started to enjoy teaching more and I woke up in the morning excited to go to work. By the end of the year, I reflected that maybe I'd been too rash and that I'd give it 'just one more year'. That was 12 years ago and I am still teaching.

I realised that by saying that I was only having one more year in the classroom, it helped to increase my perspective. I started to see what mattered and what didn't, and I adjusted my teaching accordingly. It made me realise that life is short and I won't be a teacher forever, so I may as well try to foster as much pleasure and purpose as I can whilst I'm still in the classroom.

Why not ask yourself, if this was your last year in teaching:

- What would you keep doing because you know that it's important?
- What would you ditch or do less of because you don't value it?
- What would you have the courage to do differently?

Be courageous

When it comes to happiness, many people delay their happy life until the future, falsely believing that they will be happy when some event or thing happens to make life better. A teacher might say, 'Oh, I'll be happier when Ofsted have been and gone, or when this term is over, or once I've completed this project.' But the time for happiness is now! Happiness comes from the day-to-day, the ordinary and even the mundane. As Ben-Shahar comments, 'A happy – or happier – life is rarely shaped by some extraordinary life-changing event; rather, it is shaped incrementally, experience by experience, moment by moment.' (Ben-Shahar, 2008, p. 168) And we *all* have the ability to be the designer and architect of our own happiness.

But to teach happiness and wellbeing at school, and to apply the lessons to your own life, may take courage and may require you to dare to be different. But my question to you is what have you got to lose? Therefore, I lay down a challenge before you. Start to mix things up at your school. Prioritise your wellbeing and the children's. Be bold, be brave and experiment. This is your life and your teaching career, so take back control and steer your own ship. Mary Oliver wrote in a poem called 'The Summer Day', 'Tell me, what is it you plan to do with your one wild and precious life?' (Oliver, 1992). So, what is it that you plan to do with yours?

Key points

- It is important for teachers to prioritise their wellbeing because they cannot give to their pupils if they are depleted. If we are good role models for our children, our wellbeing can impact pupil attainment, and our wellbeing matters in and of itself.
- Perfectionism gets in the way of our happiness. Aiming to be simply 'good enough' can help us to find pleasure and purpose in teaching.
- If we want to make changes to our behaviour, we should make them easy, attractive, social and timely.

- Teachers can apply all of the lessons in this book to their own lives.

- Small changes, consistently applied, build up to make the biggest difference to our wellbeing.

- We can simplify our working lives to free up more time, set boundaries for work and start to feel less pressured. You have the option of requesting to work flexibly to bring more balance to your life.

- Find opportunities to laugh. Humour is a great stress-reliever.

- If teachers feel really swamped, doing something pleasurable, completing a task or asking for help can alleviate those pressures.

- Regain perspective by imaging that this is your last year in teaching. Think about what you would keep doing because it really matters, what you'd ditch because it doesn't matter and what you'd try out because life is short.

- Be bold and brave with teaching happiness and wellbeing, and with making teaching work for you!

Glossary

Adrenaline A hormone released by the adrenal glands whose major function is to prepare the body for fight or flight by increasing blood flow to the muscles.

Altruism When we act to promote someone else's welfare, even at a risk or cost to ourselves.

Amygdala A primeval part of the brain central to emotion and motivation. Its major function is to act as an alarm bell to other areas of the brain and the body when it senses danger, by kick-starting the fight or flight response, otherwise known as the **stress response**.

Anxiety reappraisal When we 'reframe' our anxious feelings as 'excitement' during nerve-wracking activities. Studies show that this can help us to perform better.

Attachment The term that psychologists use to describe 'love'. Our levels of attachment are strongly influenced by the nurture and care that we received as infants. We can grow up with attachment styles that are 'secure', 'avoidant', 'anxious' or 'disorganised'.

Auto-pilot A state of mind where we do things automatically, without thinking about them. When our brain learns something well, it automates it, freeing up vital brain power and energy to focus on other things. When we operate on 'auto-pilot', we are not being mindful.

BDNF   Brain-derived neurotrophic factor (BDNF) helps to build and maintain brain circuitry. It improves the functions of neurons, encourages their growth and strengthens and protects them against the natural process of cell death.

Compassion   The ability to sense another's suffering and then feeling compelled to try to relieve their suffering.

Cortisol   A stress hormone that is released by the adrenal glands, along with adrenaline, during the stress response. In large doses, cortisol makes you hypervigilant, halts your immune system, stops your ability to learn and prevents you from relaxing.

Dopamine   A hormone and neurotransmitter that helps us to pay attention and is part of our 'reward system' – that is, when something good happens to us, we get a rush of dopamine that makes us feel good. It gets released when we achieve something, when we exercise and also when we laugh and find something amusing.

Empathy   The ability to sense other people's emotions and think about what others may be thinking or feeling.

Endorphins   Hormones and neurotransmitters that help to protect us against stress, reduce our experience of pain and produce pleasure. They are often released during exercise, hence the 'high' that runners feel after a run.

Flow   A state of mind that we experience when we are fully absorbed in an activity that challenges us. When we are in flow, we often lose a sense of ourselves and time feels like it rushes by. Experiencing flow benefits our wellbeing.

Happy hormones Hormones that positively contribute to our physical and mental health, which are released by the body when we partake in particular behaviours or have certain experiences (see also **dopamine**, **endorphins**, **oxytocin** and **serotonin**).

Hippocampus A part of the brain central to forming new memories (especially spatial memories). It is also involved with putting things in perspective and calming down the amygdala when necessary. New neurons are born in the hippocampus.

Kindness A general term that means being friendly, helpful and generous towards others (psychologists often call it 'prosocial' behaviour).

Metacognition The ability to be aware of your thinking and able to regulate it. It also involves knowledge of when and how to use particular strategies for learning and problem-solving.

Mindfulness Paying attention to what's happening in the present moment in the mind, body and external environment, with an attitude of kindness and curiosity.

Mirror neurons Discovered by neurophysiologist Giacomo Rizzolatti, mirror neurons fire when we carry out an action or witness someone else carry out an action, and they might move us to imitate what we observe. They are also thought to be partly responsible for our ability to empathise with other people and feel what they are feeling.

Negativity bias The default nature of our brains to look out for dangers and spot threats easily, so as to avoid them in the future. Our brains are better at storing and remembering negative events because of this.

Neural Darwinism Some neurons form connections that stay intact and become strong, whereas others do not and die off in a process that resembles natural selection. The strongest and most adaptable neurons and connections survive in a battle of survival of the fittest.

Neurons A cell in the brain that sends and receives signals to and from other neurons. Each neuron has one axon (axons are the main way by which neurons pass information on and *teach* other neurons) and up to 100,000 dendrites (which are the main way by which neurons get information and *learn* from other neurons).

Neuroplasticity The brain's ability to continually change and adapt in response to thoughts, actions and experiences.

Neurotransmitters Chemicals and hormones that allow neurons to send messages to one another. Happy hormones are a type of neurotransmitter that contributes to our sense of happiness and wellbeing (see **happy hormones**).

Optimism The expectation that the future will be socially desirable, good and pleasurable.

Oxytocin A hormone and neurotransmitter that promotes pro-social behaviour and bonding between people. It helps us to be kind and show empathy towards others. It causes the release of nitric oxide, which helps to lower blood pressure, as well as reducing the volume of free radicals in our system (responsible for ageing and tissue damage) and reducing inflammation of our cardiovascular system.

Pessimism	The expectation that the future will be socially undesirable, negative and uncomfortable.
Positive psychology	The study of how human beings flourish and what contributes to a happy and meaningful life.
Pre-frontal cortex	The part of the brain that sets goals, makes plans and directs action. It is also responsible for **metacognition**, regulating behaviour and abstract thinking.
Priming	Influencing people to think and behave in desirable ways by use of a stimulus (such as exposure to nature or a positive message).
Pro-social behaviour	See **kindness**.
Psychological wellbeing	A person's sense of meaning, purpose and engagement with life.
Reframing	When we take a negative situation and 'reframe' it by consciously adopting a positive perspective.
REM sleep	Rapid eye movement sleep is a period of sleep in which we typically dream. It is thought to be when our short-term memories get moved over to our long-term memory.
Sedentary behaviour	Any behaviour that involves sitting or lying down for extended periods of time.
Serotonin	A hormone and neurotransmitter that regulates our mood, sleep and digestion. When people suffer from depression, any antidepressants that

they are given aim to boost its effects. Our diet can affect our levels of serotonin, as can our exposure to natural light. Eating well and getting outdoors are two ways in which to help regulate our serotonin levels.

Signature strengths The character strengths (such as kindness, love of learning, humour, curiosity, bravery and honesty) that are most essential to who we are. They drive our thoughts, feelings and behaviours and they are what motivate us.

Stress response When we perceive a threat or sense danger, our bodies prepare for fight or flight. Our amygdala senses the threat and sends a message to the adrenal glands to release cortisol and adrenaline. Our heart rate increases and our pupils dilate as we prepare for action.

Stretch zone A state in which our skills, abilities and aptitudes are stretched to their limits and when we feel outside our comfort zone. We learn best when we are in our stretch zone, but if we are pushed too far, we enter the 'panic zone', where learning stops and we become overwhelmed.

Subjective wellbeing A person's own assessment of how well their life, or specific aspects of it, is going. Two commonly used measures of 'subjective wellbeing' are life satisfaction and the experience of positive and negative emotions.

Tribal classroom A classroom that taps into children's innate tribal instincts by creating a safe, secure learning environment and a sense of belonging to a team or family. Tribal classrooms are democratic and inclusive and they encourage laughter, exploration and play.

Further reading and recommended resources

Below I have suggested some further reading materials if you would like to further explore the topics and themes touched upon in each chapter. I also recommend websites and courses related to teaching happiness and wellbeing.

Chapter 1: Creating a tribal classroom

The Social Neuroscience of Education: Optimizing Attachment and Learning in the Classroom by Louis Cozolino – a fantastic book that I believe all teachers would benefit from reading. It is great at explaining the neuroscience behind learning and gives examples of teachers who have established tribal classrooms in their own unique way.

The Gardener and the Carpenter: What the New Science of Child Development Tells Us About the Relationship Between Parents and Children by Alison Gopnik – this book challenges how many of us teach, parent and raise our children today. It's a good book for teachers, as it shows how children develop, why play is so important and what children need most to help them to flourish.

Chapter 2: Mindfulness

Mindfulness: A Practical Guide to Finding Peace in a Frantic World by Mark Williams and Danny Penman – this is my go-to book for anything mindfulness-related. Really well-written and engaging, it clearly explains what mindfulness is and how it can help people to cope with the stresses of everyday life. It even has an eight-week mindfulness course that you can follow, along with a CD containing guided meditations.

Sitting Still Like a Frog: Mindfulness Exercises for Kids (and Their Parents) by Eline Snel – a lovely short book that explains mindfulness well for children to understand. Plus, it has some fun exercises to try, as well as a CD with guided meditations. I often play the 'A Safe Place' meditation because you get to lie down – a great one for a Friday in class!

Peaceful Piggy Meditation and *Moody Cow Meditates* by Kerry Lee MacLean – two picture books that show children how meditation can help us to cope with difficult feelings and emotions that come up in everyday life. They have guided meditations and activities at the back of the book.

100 Ideas for Primary Teachers: Mindfulness in the Classroom by Tammie Prince – this is a great little book packed with ideas for bringing mindfulness practices and activities to life in your classroom.

Chapter 3: What went well?

Hardwiring Happiness: How to Reshape Your Brain and Your Life by Rick Hanson – of the many books on happiness that I have read, this is one I keep coming back to. Hanson really gets to the route of how to make happy experiences become hardwired in our brains, and there are some great meditations and exercises to try to help you grow your happiness.

Thanks! How Practicing Gratitude Can Make You Happier by Robert Emmons – Emmons is the expert on gratitude, and this book explains the science behind why practising it makes you happier, as well as giving lots of practical ideas.

Chapter 4: Neuroplasticity – your elastic plastic brain

A User's Guide to the Brain by John Ratey – a must-read if you are interested in how our brains work. It is extremely comprehensive and is accessible for the neuroscience novice.

Buddha's Brain: The Practical Neuroscience of Happiness, Love and Wisdom by Rick Hanson – this book uses modern neuroscience to shine a light on ancient contemplative practices, to show how they actually change our brains and shape our thoughts. A very insightful book.

The Emotional Life of Your Brain: How its Unique Patterns Affect the Way You Think, Feel, and Live – and How You Can Change Them by Richard Davidson and Sharon Begley – this book explains how our brains give us our own unique 'emotional style' and that we can learn to change these to serve us better.

Your Fantastic Elastic Brain: Stretch it, Shape it by JoAnn Deak – a great picture book for children that really helps them to understand neuroplasticity and why mistakes are good for your brain.

What Goes On In My Head? How Your Brain Works and Why You Do What You Do by Robert Winston – a wonderful book to help children to understand how amazing their brains are. Packed with loads of facts and interesting insights.

Chapter 5: The stretch zone

Mindset: Changing the Way You Think to Fulfil Your Potential by Carol Dweck – apparently, growth mindset is one of the most talked-about topics in teaching at the moment, but very few people have actually read Carol Dweck's book. If you really want to know your stuff on growth mindset, this is your first port of call.

Happier: Can You Learn to be Happy? by Tal Ben-Shahar – this book has a whole chapter on education and will really help you to reflect on your teaching practice.

Chapter 6: Flow and strengths

Flow: The Psychology of Happiness by Mihaly Csikszentmihalyi – the undisputed expert on flow, Csikszentmihalyi explains what it is and how it could be an unsung yet key component of happiness.

Flourish: A New Understanding of Happiness and Wellbeing – and How to Achieve Them by Martin Seligman – Seligman started the positive psychology movement, and this book shares his research and wisdom but in a conversational and engaging way that isn't bogged down with science or data.

Chapter 7: It's cool to be kind

Do Nice, Be Kind, Spread Happy: Acts of Kindness for Kids by Bernadette Russell – some great ideas for children on what they could do for their random acts of kindness. They'll learn how to be a 'niceness ninja' and a 'happiness hero'.

A Force For Good: The Dalai Lama's Vision for Our World by Dan Goleman – Goleman shares the Dalai Lama's vision for humanity in this heart-warming and inspiring book. A good book to read to help restore your faith in humanity.

Humankind by Rutger Bregman – Bregman is a Dutch historian, and this book is brilliant at showing how human beings are essentially kind by nature. It shows how the instinct to cooperate rather than compete and to trust rather than distrust has an evolutionary basis that goes right back to the beginning of our species.

Chapter 8: Digital wellbeing

What Mental Illness Really Is (and what it isn't) by Dr Lucy Foulkes – although the book is about mental health in general, there is an excellent examination on the research around children's use of technology and their emotional wellbeing. It dispels a lot of the myths that exist around tech and mental health and offers a balanced and optimistic view.

Chapter 9: How our thoughts shape our world

Happiness by Design: Finding Pleasure and Purpose in Everyday Life by Professor Paul Dolan – happiness doesn't have to be hard work, according to Dolan. In this book, he promotes 'easy' proven ways to positively impact your wellbeing, and shares some of the research on 'priming'. A great read with lots of 'happiness hacks'.

Chapter 10: Exercise makes me happy

Spark! How Exercise Will Improve the Performance of Your Brain by Dr John Ratey – I thought that I knew a lot about how exercise affects our brains until I read this book. Ratey shares the latest research into just how powerful and crucial exercise is for our brains, health and happiness.

Chapter 11: The nature fix

Into The Forest by Dr Qing Li – an excellent book which shares the research behind the concept known as 'forest bathing'. Dr Li is one of the pioneers of this research and after you read this book I defy you not to want to fill your classroom and home with more plants!

Dirty Teaching by Juliet Robertson – if you are interested in outdoor learning but do not know where to start, then this is the book for you. It acts as an excellent guide to help primary teachers learn why outdoor learning is important, how to take more lessons outside and how to make outdoor learning enjoyable and successful for all children.

Chapter 12: Teacher wellbeing

A Little Guide for Teachers: Teacher Wellbeing and Self-Care by Adrian Bethune and Dr Emma Kell – Emma and I try to distil our wisdom from our collective 30 years in teaching to show how to find more pleasure and purpose in teaching. It's a short, practical book (you even get to scribble and jot ideas down inside it!) and one that you can keep dipping back in and out of.

General books on happiness

Happier: Can You Learn to be Happy? by Tal Ben-Shahar – so good that it gets a second mention. It is one of the best books that I have read on the subject of happiness. So much is packed into such a small book and it is all relevant and helpful.

10 Keys to Happier Living: A Practical Handbook for Happiness by Vanessa King – very practical, with lots of ideas to experiment with. It is so thorough and easy to dip in and out of.

Happiness: Lessons From a New Science by Lord Richard Layard – in terms of people trying to get wellbeing on the national agenda in relation to politics, economics and education, Layard is a pioneer in this country.

Websites

www.teachappy.co.uk – on my website, you'll find free resources, lots of interviews with wellbeing experts and psychologists, and my blog. You can follow me on Twitter @ AdrianBethune or Instagram @teachappyuk.

www.well-school.org – home of the Well Schools movement. Sign up for free and join thousands of other teachers and schools trying to put wellbeing at the heart of education. Lots of free resources and practical guides to download.

www.annafreud.org/schools-and-colleges/ – The Anna Freud National Centre for Children and Families have created 'Schools In Mind', which is a free network providing a trusted source of up-to-date and accessible information and resources that school leaders, teachers and support staff can use to support the mental health and wellbeing of the children and young people in their care.

www.mindfulnessinschools.org – a charity leading the way in terms of training educational professionals in delivering mindfulness curricula in schools.

www.greatergood.berkeley.edu – sign up to receive their articles on the latest research on the science of happiness.

www.foodafactoflife.org.uk/whole-school/ – a selection of lesson plans to teach your children more about the importance of food and diet.

Courses

Seeds of Happiness – together with positive psychology expert Yvonne Biggins (MAPP), I have created a six-week course in positive psychology for primary school children. It won a Teach Primary Award for wellbeing in 2021. Go to **www.teachappy.co.uk/seedsofhappiness** to find out more.

Staff Wellbeing and Self-Care in Schools – Emma Kell and I have created a self-paced online course to help staff to take care of their own wellbeing. It's evidence-based and practical and aimed at busy school staff. Find out more at: **www.teacha ppy.co.uk/staff-wellbeing-course**

Action for Happiness's *Keys to Happier Living: Toolkit for Schools* (by Peter Harper and Val Payne) – an engaging and accessible evidence-based programme to promote the emotional wellbeing and resilience of children aged seven to 11. Visit: **www.actionforhappiness.org/toolkit**

The Science of Wellbeing – Prof. Laurie Santos is a world-leading expert on wellbeing and teaches at Yale University. She's taken her popular university course and made it available online for free! Visit: **https://gb.coursera.org/learn/ the-science-of-well-being**

Measuring wellbeing

From my experience, most schools do not know where to begin when it comes to measuring staff and pupil wellbeing in a meaningful way. It can be a real headache if you don't do it well and, ironically, can end up increasing stress and dissatisfaction!

I worked with experts at the What Works Centre for Wellbeing and The Children's Society to create The Well Schools Guide to Measuring Wellbeing in Schools. The guide is completely free to download and covers:

- What is wellbeing?
- Getting started
- Administering a survey
- Analysing the data
- Sharing the results and creating an action plan
- Further reading, resources and references

You'll need to sign up to Well Schools first, but you can download the guide here: **www.well-school.org/t/well-schools-guide-to-measuring-wellbeing/1685**

Bibliography

Achor, S. (2011), *The Happiness Advantage: The Seven Principles of Positive Psychology that Fuel Success and Performance at Work.* London: Virgin Books.

Adler, A. (2016), 'Teaching well-being increases academic performance: Evidence from Bhutan, Mexico, and Peru'. Publicly Accessible Penn Dissertations. 1572.

Aknin, L. B., Barrington- Leigh, C. P., Dunn, E. W., Helliwell, J. F., Burns, J., Biswas-Diener, R., Kemeza, I., Nyende, P. and Ashton-James, C. E. (2013a), 'Prosocial spending and well-being: Cross-cultural evidence for a psychological universal', *Journal of Personality and Social Psychology*, 104, (4), 635–652.

Aknin, L. B., Dunn, E. W., Whillans, A. V., Grant, A. M. and Norton, M. I. (2013b), 'Making a difference matters: Impact unlocks the emotional benefits of prosocial spending', *Journal of Economic Behavior and Organization*, 88, 90–95.

Aknin, L. B., Sandstrom, G. M., Dunn, E. W. and Norton, M. I. (2011), 'It's the recipient that counts: Spending money on strong social ties leads to greater happiness than spending on weak social ties', *PLoS ONE*, 6, (2), e17018.

Amass, H. (2022), 'Why it matters whether your students like you', *TES*, www.tes.com/magazine/teaching-learning/general/attachment-theory-peter-fonagy-psychoanalyst-interview

American Psychological Association (2017), 'Secret to happiness may include more unpleasant emotions', www.apa.org/news/press/releases/2017/08/secret-happiness.aspx

Babyak, M., Blumenthal, J. A., Herman, S., Khatri, P., Doraiswamy, M., Moore, K., Craighead, W. E., Baldewicz, T. T. and Krishnan, K. R. (2000), 'Exercise treatment for major depression: Maintenance of therapeutic benefit at ten months', *Psychosomatic Medicine*, 62, (5), 633–638.

Bajorek, Z., Gulliford, J. and Taskila, T. (2014), 'Healthy teachers, higher marks? Establishing a link between teacher health and wellbeing, and student outcomes', The Work Foundation (Lancaster University), https://f.hubspotusercontent10.net/hubfs/7792519/healthy_teachers_higher_marks_report.pdf

Barraza, J. A. and Zak, P. J. (2009), 'Empathy toward strangers triggers oxytocin release and subsequent generosity', *Annals of the New York Academy of Sciences*, 116, 182–189.

Ben-Shahar, T. (2008), *Happier: Can You Learn to be Happy?* New York: McGraw Hill.

Ben-Shahar, T. (2021), 'Small changes consistently applied make a big difference', Facebook, https://m.facebook.com/DrTalBenShahar/videos/small-changes-make-a-big-difference/142545411042420

Berman, M. G., Jonides, J. and Kaplan, S. (2008), 'The cognitive benefits of interacting with nature', *Psychological Science*, 19, (12), 1207–1212.

Bethune, A. and Kell, E. (2020), *A Little Guide for Teachers: Teacher Wellbeing and Self-Care*. London: SAGE Publications.

Bethune, A. (2023), 'Seeds of Happiness Positively Impacts Pupil Wellbeing', Teachappy https://www.teachappy.co.uk/post/seeds-of-happiness-positively-impacts-pupil-wellbeing

Bjork, E. L. and Bjork, R. A. (2011), 'Making things hard on yourself, but in a good way: Creating desirable difficulties to enhance learning', in M. A. Gernsbacher, R. W. Pew, L. M. Hough and J. R. Pomerantz (eds), *Psychology and the Real World: Essays Illustrating Fundamental Contributions to Society*. New York: Worth Publishers, pp. 56–64.

Black, S. (2001), 'Morale matters: When teachers feel good about their work, research shows, student achievement rises', *American School Board Journal*, 188, (1), 40–43.

Blackwell, L. S., Trzesniewski, K. T. and Dweck, C. S. (2007), 'Implicit theories of intelligence predict achievement across an adolescent transition: A longitudinal study and an intervention', *Child Development*, 78, 246–263.

Bowyer, R. C. E., Twohig-Bennett, C., Coombes, E., Wells, P. M., Spector, T. D., Jones, A. P. and Steves, C. J. (2022), 'Microbiota composition is moderately associated with greenspace composition in a UK cohort of twins', *The Science of the Total Environment*, 813, 152321.

Bregman, R. (2021), *Humankind: A Hopeful History*. London: Bloomsbury.

Brickman, P., Coates, D. and Janoff-Bulman, R. (1978), 'Lottery winners and accident victims: Is happiness relative?', *Journal of Personality and Social Psychology*, 36, (8), 917–27.

Briffa, J. (2014), *A Great Day at the Office: Simple Strategies to Maximize Your Energy and Get More Done More Easily*. London: Fourth Estate.

Briner, R. and Dewberry, C. (2007), 'Staff wellbeing is key to school success: A research study into the links between staff wellbeing and school performance', Worklife Support, www.teachertoolkit.co.uk/wp-content/uploads/2014/07/5902birkbeckwbperfsummaryfinal.pdf

British Nutrition Foundation (2021), www.nutrition.org.uk/healthy-sustainable-diets/hydration/

Brockington, G., Gomes Moreira, A. P., Busoc, M. S., Gomes da Silvad, S., Altszylerg, E., Fischerh, R. and Mol, J. (2021), 'Storytelling increases oxytocin and positive emotions and decreases cortisol and pain in hospitalized children', *Proceedings of the National Academy of Sciences*, 118, (22), e2018409118.

Brooks, A.W. (2014), 'Get excited: Reappraising pre-performance anxiety as excitement', *Journal of Experimental Psychology: General*, 143, (3), 1144–1158.

Brown, S. L., Smith, D. M., Schulz, R., Kabeto, M. U., Ubel, P. A. Poulin, M., Yi, J., Kim, C. and Langa, K. M. (2009), 'Caregiving behavior is associated with decreased mortality risk', *Psychological Science*, 20, (4), 488–494.

Callard, S. (2022), Investigating the effectiveness of the Seeds of Happiness positive psychology programme for improving the wellbeing of primary school children in England, www.teachappy.co.uk/post/seeds-of-happiness-positively-impacts-pupil-wellbeing

Chang, E. C. and Sanna, L. J. (2001), 'Optimism, pessimism, and positive and negative affectivity in middle-aged adults: A test of a cognitive-affective model of psychological adjustment', *Psychology and Aging*, 16, (3), 524–531.

Chatterjee, R. (2018), *The Stress Solution*. London: Penguin Random House.

Clark, A., Flèche, S., Layard, R., Powdthavee, N. and Ward, G. (2018), *The Origins of Happiness: The Science of Well-Being Over the Life Course*. Princeton: Princeton University Press.

Coyle, D. (2018), *The Culture Code*. London: Penguin Random House.

Coyne, S. M., Rogers, A. A., Zurcher, J. D., Stockdale, L. and Booth, M. (2020), 'Does time spent using social media impact mental health? An eight year longitudinal study', *Computers in Human Behavior*, 104, 106160.

Cozolino, L. (2013), *The Social Neuroscience of Education: Optimizing Attachment and Learning in the Classroom*. New York: W. W. Norton & Co.

Cozolino, L. (2014), *Attachment-Based Teaching: Creating a Tribal Classroom*. New York: W. W. Norton & Company.

Csikszentmihalyi, M. (1998), *Finding Flow: The Psychology of Engagement With Everyday Life*. New York: Basic Books.

Csikszentmihalyi, M. (2002), *Flow: The Psychology of Happiness*. London: Rider.

Darwin, C. R. (1871), *The Descent of Man, and Selection in Relation to Sex* (Volume 1, 1st edn). London: John Murray.

Davidson, R. J. (2004), 'What does the prefrontal cortex "do" in affect: Perspectives on frontal EEG asymmetry research', *Biological Psychology*, 67, (1–2), 219–233.

Davidson, R. J. and Begley, S. (2012), *The Emotional Life of Your Brain: How Its Unique Patterns Affect the Way You Think, Feel, and Live – and How You Can Change Them*. London: Hodder and Stoughton.

Davidson, R. J., Kabat-Zinn, R., Schumacher, J., Rosenkranz, M., Muller, D., Santorelli, S. F., Urbanowski, F., Harrington, A., Bonus, K. and Sheridan, J. F. (2003), 'Alterations in brain and immune function produced by mindfulness meditation', *Psychosomatic Medicine*, 65, (4), 564–570.

Deak, J. (2011), *Your Fantastic Elastic Brain: Stretch it, Shape it*. San Francisco: Little Pickle Press.

Department for Education (DfE) (2017), 'Flexible working in schools', www.gov.uk/government/publications/flexible-working-in-schools

Department for Education (DfE) (2022a), 'School workforce in England: Reporting year 2021', https://explore-education-statistics.service.gov.uk/find-statistics/school-workforce-in-england

Department for Education (DfE) (2022b), '"Teacher sickness absence" from "School workforce in England"', https://explore-educat ion-statistics.service.gov.uk/data-tables/permalink/1f720 783-f8a2-4898-980c-d7adf2b2c0e9

Department for Health and Social Care (DHSC) (2019), 'Physical activity guidelines: UK Chief Medical Officers' report', www.gov.uk/gov ernment/publications/physical-activity-guidelines-uk-chief-medi cal-officers-report

Diener, E. and Biswas-Diener, R. (2008), *Happiness: Unlocking the Mysteries of Psychological Wealth*. Oxford: Wiley-Blackwell.

Dolan, P. (2015), *Happiness by Design: Finding Pleasure and Purpose in Everyday Life*. London: Penguin.

Dunbar, R. (1992), 'Neocortex size as a constraint on group size in primates', *Journal of Human Evolution*, 22, (6), 469–493.

Dunn, E. and Norton, M. (2013), *Happy Money: The New Science of Smarter Spending*. London: Oneworld Publications.

Dunning, D., Tudor, K., Radley, L., Dalrymple, N., Funk, J., Vainre, M., Ford, T., Montero-Marin, J., Kuyken, W. and Dalgleish, T. (2022), 'Do mindfulness-based programmes improve the cognitive skills, behaviour and mental health of children and adolescents? An updated meta-analysis of randomised controlled trials', *Evidence Based Mental Health*, 25, (3), 135–142.

Durlak, J. A., Weissberg, R. P., Dymnicki, A. B., Taylor, R. D. and Schellinger, K. B. (2011), 'The impact of enhancing students' social and emotional learning: A meta-analysis of school-based universal interventions', *Child Development*, 82, (1), 405–432.

Dweck, C. S. (2007), 'The perils and promises of praise', *Educational Leadership*, 65, (2), 34–39.

Dweck, C. S. (2012), *Mindset: Changing the Way You Think to Fulfil Your Potential*. London: Robinson.

Dylan Wiliam Centre (2014), 'Is the feedback you're giving students helping or hindering?', www.dylanwiliamcenter.com/2014/11/29/ is-the-feedback-you-are-giving-students-helping-or-hindering

Education Endowment Foundation (EEF) (2021), 'Cognitive science approaches in the classroom: A review of the evidence', https://

educationendowmentfoundation.org.uk/public/files/Publicati ons/Cognitive_science_approaches_in_the_classroom_-_A_rev iew_of_the_evidence.pdf

Eisenberg, N. and Fabes, R. A. (1990), 'Empathy: Conceptualization, measurement, and relation to prosocial behavior', *Motivation and Emotion*, 14, (2), 131–149.

Ellis, A. (1962), *Reason and Emotion in Psychotherapy*. New York: Lyle Stuart.

Emerson, R. W. (1965), *Selected Writings of Ralph Waldo Emerson*. New York: Penguin Classics.

Emmons, R. (2008), *Thanks! How Practicing Gratitude Can Make You Happier*. New York: HarperOne.

Emmons, R. (2010), 'Why gratitude is good', Greater Good Science Center, https://greatergood.berkeley.edu/article/item/why_gratit ude_is_good

Ferguson, S. J. and Goodwin, A. D. (2010), 'Optimism and well-being in older adults: The mediating role of social support and perceived control', *International Journal of Aging and Human Development*, 71, (1), 43–68.

Foreman, J., Salim, A. T., Praveen, A., Fonseka, D., Shu Wei Ting, D., He, M. G., Bourne, R. R. A., Crowston, J., Wong, T. Y. and Dirani, M. (2021), 'Association between digital smart device use and myopia: A systematic review and meta-analysis', *The Lancet*, 3, (12), E806–E818.

Foresight Mental Capital and Wellbeing Project (2008), 'Final project report – executive summary', Government Office for Science, www. gov.uk/government/uploads/system/uploads/attachment_data/ file/292453/mental-capital-wellbeing-summary.pdf

Foster, R. (2022), *Life Time*. London: Penguin Life.

Foulkes, L. (2022), *What Mental Illness Really Is… (and What It Isn't)*. London: Vintage.

Fowler, J. H. and Christakis, N. A. (2010), 'Cooperative behavior cascades in human social networks', *Proceedings of the National Academy of Sciences of the United States of America*, 107, (12), 5334–5338.

Frankl, V. E. (1946), *Man's Search for Meaning*. Boston, MA: Beacon Press.

Fredrickson, B. L. (2013), 'Positive emotions broaden and build', *Advances in Experimental Psychology*, 47, 1–53.

Fredrickson, B. L., Cohn, M. A., Coffey, K. A., Pek, J. and Finkel, S. M. (2008), 'Open hearts build lives: Positive emotions, induced through loving-kindness meditation, build consequential personal resources', *Journal of Personality and Social Psychology*, 95, (5), 1045–1062.

Gebremariam, M. K., Bergh, I. H., Andersen, L. F., Ommundsen, Y., Totland, T. H., Bjelland, M., Grydeland, M. and Lien, N. (2013), 'Are screen-based sedentary behaviors longitudinally associated with dietary behaviors and leisure-time physical activity in the transition into adolescence?', *International Journal of Behavioral Nutrition and Physical Activity*, 10, (1), 9.

Geirland, J. (1996), 'Go With The Flow – Interview with Mihaly Csikszentmihalyi', *Wired*, www.wired.com/1996/09/czik

Gerhardt, S. (2014), *Why Love Matters: How Affection Shapes a Baby's Brain*. Abingdon: Routledge.

Goldman, R. and Papson, S. (1998), *Nike Culture: The Sign of the Swoosh*. London: SAGE Publications.

Goleman, D. (2015), *A Force for Good: The Dalai Lama's Vision for Our World*. London: Bloomsbury.

Gopnik, A. (2016), *The Gardener and the Carpenter: What the New Science of Child Development Tells Us About the Relationship Between Parents and Children*. London: The Bodley Head.

Gottman, J. M. (1994), *Why Marriages Succeed or Fail*. New York: Fireside.

Gowin, J. (2015), 'Why your brain needs water', Psychology Today, www.psychologytoday.com/intl/blog/you-illuminated/201010/why-your-brain-needs-water

Grenville-Cleave, B., Guðmundsdóttir, D., Huppert, F., King, V., Roffey, D., Roffey, S. and de Vries, M. (2021), *Creating the World We Want to Live In*. Oxfordshire: Routledge.

Gutman, L. M. and Vorhaus, J. (2012), 'The impact of pupil behaviour and wellbeing on educational outcomes', DfE research report DFE-RR253, https://assets.publishing.service.gov.uk/government/uploads/system/uploads/attachment_data/file/219638/DFE-RR253.pdf

Hale, L. and Guan, S. (2015), 'Screen time and sleep among school-aged children and adolescents: A systematic literature review', *Sleep Medicine Reviews*, 21, 50–58.

Hamilton, D. R. (2017), *The Five Side Effects of Kindness: This Book Will Make You Feel Better, Be Happier and Live Longer*. London: Hay House UK.

Han, K. T. (2009), 'Influence of limitedly visible leafy indoor plants on the psychology, behavior, and health of students at a junior high school in Taiwan', *Environment and Behavior*, 41, (5), 658–692.

Hanson, R. (2009), *The Buddha's Brain: The Practical Neuroscience of Happiness, Love, and Wisdom*. Oakland, CA: New Harbinger.

Hanson, R. (2014), *Hardwiring Happiness: How to Reshape Your Brain and Your Life*. London: Rider.

Harvey-Craig, A. (2020), *18 Wellbeing Hacks for Students: Using Psychology's Secrets to Survive and Thrive*. London: Jessica Kingsley Publishers.

Health and Safety Executive (2022), 'Work- related stress, depression or anxiety statistics in Great Britain 2022', www.hse.gov.uk/statistics/causdis/stress.pdf

Hedgcock, W. M., Luangrath, A. W. and Webster, R. (2021), 'Counterfactual thinking and facial expressions among Olympic medalists: A conceptual replication of Medvec, Madey, and Gilovich's (1995) findings', *Journal of Experimental Psychology: General*, 150, (6), e13–e21.

Hickman, C., Marks, E., Pihkala, P., Clayton, S., Lewandowski, R. E., Mayall, E. E., Wray, B., Mellor, C. and van Susteren, L. (2021), 'Climate anxiety in children and young people and their beliefs about government responses to climate change: A global survey', *The Lancet*, 5, (12), E863–E873.

His Holiness the Dalai Lama and Cutler, H. C. (1999), *The Art of Happiness: A Handbook for Living*. London: Hodder and Stoughton.

Hughes, K. et al. (2018), 'Sources of resilience and their moderating relationships with harms from adverse childhood experiences', *Report 1: Mental illness. Welsh ACE and Resilience Study*.

Hulleman, C. S. and Harackiewicz, J. M. (2009), 'Promoting interest and performance in high school science classes', *Science*, 326, (5958), 1410–1412.

Hume, D. (1826), *The Philosophical Works of David Hume (Volume 3)*. Edinburgh: Adam Black and William Tait.

Humphrey, J. and Hughes, D. (2021), *High Performance: Lessons from the Best on Becoming Your Best*. London: Penguin Random House.

Hutchinson, J. K., Huws, J. C. and Dorjee, D. (2018), 'Exploring experiences of children in applying a school-based mindfulness programme to their lives', *Journal of Child and Family Studies*, 27, 3935–3951.

Hwang, Y., Bartlett, B. Greben, M., and Hand, K. (2017), 'A systematic review of mindfulness interventions for in-service teachers: A tool to enhance teacher wellbeing and performance', *Teaching and Teacher Education*, 64, 26–42.

Institute of Child Education and Psychology (ICEP), *Teaching Happiness: Positive psychology for behaviour and learning, Module 2: Positive psychology in the classroom*.

Institute of Child Education and Psychology (ICEP), *Teaching Happiness: Positive psychology for behaviour and learning, Module 3: Mobilising motivation and signature strengths*.

Institute of Medicine (2013), 'Educating the student body: Taking physical activity and physical education to school', Washington, DC: National Academy of Sciences, www.nationalacademies.org/hmd/Reports/2013/Educating-the-Student-Body-Taking-Physical-Activity-and-Physical-Education-to-School/Report-Brief052313.aspx

Jenkin, M. (2014), 'How two minutes of mindfulness can calm a class and boost attainment', *Guardian*, www.theguardian.com/teacher-network/teacher-blog/2014/jun/03/mindfulness-class-students-education

Kabat-Zinn, J. (2013), *Full Catastrophe Living: Using the Wisdom of Your Body and Mind to Face Stress, Pain, and Illness (revised edn)*. London: Piatkus.

Kahneman, D. (2011), *Thinking, Fast and Slow*. London: Penguin.

Kahneman, D., Fredrickson, B. L., Schreiber, C. A. and Redelmeier, D. A. (1993), 'When more pain is preferred to less: Adding a better end', *American Psychological Society*, 4, (6), 401–405.

Kaplan, S. (1995), 'The restorative benefits of nature: Toward an integrative framework', *Journal of Environmental Psychology*, 15, (3), 169–182.

Kardefelt Winther, D. (2017), 'How does the time children spend using digital technology impact their mental well-being, social relationships and physical activity? An evidence-focused literature review', UNICEF Innocenti, www.unicef-irc.org/publicati ons/925-how-does-the-time-children-spend-using-digital-tec hnology-impact-their-mental-well.html

Kaufer, D. (2011), 'What can neuroscience research teach us about teaching?', Berkeley Graduate Division, https://gsi.berkeley.edu/ programs-services/hsl-project/hsl-speakers/kaufer

Killingsworth, M. A. and Gilbert, D. T. (2010), 'A wandering mind is an unhappy mind', *Science*, 330, (6006), 932.

King, V. (2016), *10 Keys to Happier Living*. London: Headline Home.

Kuo, M., Browning, M. H. E. M., Sachdeva, S., Lee, K. and Westphal, L. (2018), 'Might school performance grow on trees? Examining the link between "greenness" and academic achievement in urban, high-poverty schools', *Frontiers in Psychology*, 9, 1669.

Kuyken, W., Weare, K., Ukoumunne, O. C., Vicary, R., Motton, N., Burnett, R., Cullen, C., Hennelly, S. and Huppert, F. (2013), 'Effectiveness of the Mindfulness in Schools Programme: Non-randomised controlled feasibility study', *The British Journal of Psychiatry*, 203, (2), 126–131.

Lally, P., van Jaarsveld, C. H. M., Potts, H. W. W. and Wardle, J. (2010), 'How are habits formed: Modelling habit formation in the real world', *European Journal of Social Psychology*, 40, (6), 998–1009.

Langer, E. J. and Rodin, J. (1976), 'The effects of choice and enhanced personal responsibility for the aged: A field experiment in an institutional setting', *Journal of Personality and Social Psychology*, 34, (2), 191–198.

Layard, R. (2011), *Happiness: Lessons From a New Science*. New York: Penguin.

Layard, R., Clark, A. E., Cornaglia, F., Powdthavee, N. and Vernoit, J. (2013), 'What predicts a successful life? A life-course model of well-being', Centre for Economic Performance, https://cep.lse.ac.uk/ pubs/download/dp1245.pdf

Lehrer, J. (2012), *Imagine: How Creativity Works*. New York: Houghton Mifflin Harcourt.

Li, Q. (2019), *Into the Forest*. London: Penguin Random House.

London Playing Fields Foundation (2016), 'Coppermile: Implementing a daily exercise programme at Coppermill Primary School', https://thedailymile.nl/wp-content/uploads/2017/01/Coppermile-report.pdf

Lutz, A., Brefczynski-Lewis, J., Johnstone, T. and Davidson, R. J. (2008), 'Regulation of the neural circuitry of emotion by compassion meditation: Effects of meditative expertise', *PLoS ONE*, 3, (3), e1897.

Lykken, D. and Tellegen, A. (1996), 'Happiness is a stochastic phenomenon', *Psychological Science*, 7, (3), 186–189.

Lyubomirsky, S. (2006), 'Is it possible to become lastingly happier? Lessons from the modern science of well-being', in *The Vancouver Dialogues*. Vancouver: Truffle Tree Publishing, pp. 53–56.

Lyubomirsky, S. (2007), *The How of Happiness: A Practical Guide to Getting the Life You Want*. London: Piatkus.

Lyubomirsky, S., Sheldon, K. M. and Schkade, D. (2005), 'Pursuing happiness: The architecture of sustainable change', *Review of General Psychology*, 9, 111–131.

MacLean, K. L. (2004), *Peaceful Piggy Meditation*. Illinois: Albert Whitman & Company.

MacLean, K. L. (2009), *Moody Cow Meditates*. Massachusetts: Wisdom Publications.

Maguire, E. A., Gadian, D. G., Johnsrude, I. S., Good, C. D., Ashburner, J., Frackowiak, R. S. J. and Frith, C. D. (2000), 'Navigation-related structural change in the hippocampi of taxi drivers', *Biological Sciences*, 97, (8), 4398–4403.

Main, E. (2017), 'Does mindfulness training affect levels of self-regulation in children aged 8–11?', undergraduate, University of Portsmouth.

Martela, F., Lehmus-Sun, A., Parker, P. D., Pessi, A. B. and Ryan, R. M. (2022), 'Needs and well-being across Europe: Basic psychological needs are closely connected with well-being, meaning, and symptoms of depression in 27 European countries', *Social Psychological and Personality Science*, DOI: 10.1177/19485506221113678.

McGaugh, J. L. (2004), 'The amygdala modulates the consolidation of memories of emotionally arousing experiences', *Annual Review of Neuroscience*, 27, 1–28.

McGaugh, J. L., Introini-Collison, I. B., Cahill, L. F., Castellano, C., Dalmaz, C., Parent, M. B. and Williams, C. L. (1993), 'Neuromodulatory systems and memory storage: Role of the amygdala', *Behavioural Brain Research*, 58, (1–2), 81–90.

McGlone, M. S. and Tofighbakhsh, J. (2000), 'Birds of a feather flock conjointly(?): Rhyme as reason in aphorisms', *Psychological Science*, 11, (5), 424–428.

Mills, J. S., Musto, S., Williams, L. and Tiggemann, M. (2018), '"Selfie" harm: Effects on mood and body image in young women', *Body Image*, 27, 86–92.

Mindfulness All-Party Parliamentary Group (MAPPG) (2015), 'Mindful Nation UK', https://mindfulnessinschools.org/wp-content/uplo ads/2017/09/Mindfulness-APPG-Report_Mindful-Nation-UK_Oct2 015-1.pdf

Montgomery, C. (2015), *Happy City: Transforming Our Lives Through Urban Design*. London: Penguin.

Moore, L. L., Lombardi, D. A., White, M. J., Campbell, J. L., Oliveria, S. A. and Ellison, R. C. (1991), 'Influence of parents' physical activity levels of young children', *The Journal of Pediatrics*, 118, (2), 215–219.

Moore, L. and Raws, P. (2021), 'Exploring happiness with life online among children in the UK', What Works Wellbeing, https://wha tworkswellbeing.org/blog/exploring-happiness-with-life-onl ine-among-children-in-the-uk

Morita, E., Imai, M., Okawa, M., Miyaura, T. and Miyazaki, S. (2011), 'A before and after comparison of the effects of forest walking on the sleep of a community-based sample of people with sleep complaints', *BioPsychoSocial Medicine*, 5, (13), DOI: 10.1186/1751-0759-5-13

NHS Choices (2015), 'Benefits of exercise', www.nhs.uk/Livewell/fitn ess/Pages/whybeactive.aspx

NHS Digital (2021), 'Mental health of children and young people in England 2021 – wave 2 follow up to the 2017 survey', https://digital.nhs.uk/data-and-information/publications/statistical/mental-health-of-children-and-young-people-in-england/2021-follow-up-to-the-2017-survey

Nitschke, J. B., Nelson, E. E., Rusch, B. D., Fox, A. S., Oakes, T. R. and Davidson, R. J. (2004), 'Orbitofrontal cortex tracks positive mood in mothers viewing pictures of their newborn infants', *Neuroimage*, 21, (2), 583–592 .

Norris, E., van Steen, T., Direito, A. and Stamatakis, E. (2019), 'Physically active lessons in schools and their impact on physical activity, educational, health and cognition outcomes: A systematic review and meta-analysis', *British Journal of Sports Medicine*, 54, (14), 826–883.

Nussbaum, D. and Dweck, C. S. (2008), 'Defensiveness vs. remediation: Self-theories and modes of self-esteem maintenance', *Personality and Social Psychology Bulletin*, 34, (5), 599–612.

OECD (2017), 'Are students happy? PISA 2015 results: Students' well-being', PISA in Focus, No. 71, Paris: OECD Publishing, www.oecd.org/pisa/PISA-in-Focus-No-71-Are-students-happy.pdf

OECD (2019), 'What do we know about children and technology?', www.oecd.org/education/ceri/Booklet-21st-century-children.pdf

Ofcom (2021), 'Online Nation 2021 report', www.ofcom.org.uk/__data/assets/pdf_file/0013/220414/online-nation-2021-report.pdf

Ofcom (2022), 'Children and parents: media use and attitudes report 2022', https://www.ofcom.org.uk/__data/assets/pdf_file/0024/234609/childrens-media-use-and-attitudes-report-2022.pdf

Office for National Statistics (ONS) (2020), 'Online bullying in England and Wales: Year ending March 2020', Census 2021, www.ons.gov.uk/peoplepopulationandcommunity/crimeandjustice/bulletins/onlinebullyinginenglandandwales/yearendingmarch2020

Oliner, S. P. (2002). 'Extraordinary acts of ordinary people: Faces of heroism and altruism', in S. G. Post, L. G. Underwood, J. P. Schloss, & W. B. Hurlbut (eds), *Altruism and Altruistic Love: Science, Philosophy, and Religion in Dialogue*. New York: Oxford University Press, pp. 123–139.

Oliver, M. (1992), *House of Light*. Boston, MA: Beacon Press.

Orben, A., Dienlin, T. and Przybylski, A. K. (2019), 'Social media's enduring effect on adolescent life satisfaction', *Psychological and Cognitive Sciences*, 116, (21), 10226–10228.

Oxford Impact (2020), 'Wellbeing impact study: The impact of promoting student wellbeing on student academic and non-academic outcomes: An analysis of the evidence', https://oxfor dimpact.oup.com/home/wellbeing-impact-study

Park, N. and Peterson, C. (2006), 'Character strengths and happiness among young children: Content analysis of parental descriptions', *Journal of Happiness Studies*, 7, (3), 323–341.

Park, N. and Peterson, C. (2009), 'Strengths of character in schools', in Gilman, R., Huebner, E. S. and Furlong, M. J. (eds), *Handbook of Positive Psychology in Schools*. New York: Routledge, pp. 65–76.

Park, S., Kim, S., Lee, J. and Heo, B. (2022), 'Evolving norms: Social media data analysis on parks and greenspaces perception changes before and after the COVID 19 pandemic using a machine learning approach', *Scientific Reports*, 12, 13246.

Parry-Langdon, N. (ed) (2008), 'Three years on: Survey of the development and emotional wellbeing of children and young people', Office for National Statistics, https://lx.iriss.org.uk/sites/default/files/resources/child_development_mental_health.pdf

Peterson, C., Park, N. and Sweeney, P. J. (2008), 'Group well-being: Morale from a positive psychology perspective', *Applied Psychology*, 57, 19–36.

Prince, T. (2017), *100 Ideas for Primary Teachers: Mindfulness in the Classroom*. London: Bloomsbury Education.

Public Health England (2014), 'The link between pupil health and wellbeing and attainment: A briefing for head teachers, governors and staff in education settings', https://assets.publishing.service.gov.uk/government/uploads/system/uploads/attachment_data/file/370686/HT_briefing_layoutvFINALvii.pdf

Public Health England (2017), 'Health matters: Obesity and the food environment', www.gov.uk/government/publications/health-matters-obesity-and-the-food-environment/health-matters-obesity-and-the-food-environment--2

Quoidbach, J., Wood, A. M. and Hansenne, M. (2009), 'Back to the future: The effect of daily practice of mental time travel into the future on happiness and anxiety', *The Journal of Positive Psychology*, 4, (5), 349–355.

Ratey, J. J. (2003), *A User's Guide To The Brain*. London: Abacus.

Ratey, J. J. (2012), 'Run, jump, learn! How exercise can transform our schools', TEDx Talk, www.youtube.com/watch?v=hBSVZdTQmDs

Ratey, J. J. and Hagerman, E. (2010), *Spark! How Exercise Will Improve the Performance of Your Brain*. London: Quercus.

Recchia, F. et al. (2023), 'Physical activity interventions to alleviate depressive symptoms in children and adolescents', JAMA Pediatrics, 177 (2), 132.

Richardson, T. and Murray, J. (2016), 'Are young children's utterances affected by characteristics of their learning environments? A multiple case study', *Early Child Development and Care*, 187, (3–4), 457–468.

Richerson, P. J. and Boyd, R. (1998), 'The evolution of human ultra-sociality', in I. Eibl-Eibisfeldt and F. Salter (eds), *Indoctrinability, Ideology, and Warfare: Evolutionary Perspectives*. New York: Berghahn, pp. 71–96.

Rilling, J., Gutman, D., Zeh, T., Pagnoni, G., Berns, G. and Kilts, C. (2002), 'A neural basis for social cooperation', *Neuron*, 35, (2), 395–405.

Roberts, M. (2022), 'School mindfulness lessons don't work for teenagers, study says', BBC News, www.bbc.co.uk/news/health-62126567

Robertson, J. (2014), *Dirty Teaching: A Beginner's Guide to Learning Outdoors*. Carmarthen: Independent Thinking Press.

Robinson, K. (2006), 'Do schools kill creativity?', TED Talk, www.ted.com/talks/ken_robinson_says_schools_kill_creativity

Robinson, K. (2010), *The Element: How Finding Your Passion Changes Everything*. London: Penguin.

Roslund, M. I., Puhakka, R., Grönroos, M., Nurminen, N., Oikarinen, S., Gazali, A. M., Cinek, O., Kramná, L., Siter, N., Vari, H. K., Soininen, L., Parajuli, A., Rajaniemi, J., Kinnunen, T., Laitinen, O. H., Hyöty, H., Sinkkonen, A. and ADELE research group (2020), 'Biodiversity intervention enhances immune regulation and health-associated commensal microbiota among daycare children', *Science Advances*, 6, (42), eaba2578.

Russell, B. (2014), *Do Nice, Be Kind, Spread Happy: Acts of Kindness for Kids*. Brighton: Ivy Press.

Ryan, R. M. and Deci, E. L. (2000), 'Self-determination theory and the facilitation of intrinsic motivation, social development, and well-being', *American Psychologist*, 55, (1), 68–78.

Ryan, R. M. and Powelson, C. L. (1991), 'Autonomy and relatedness as fundamental to motivation and education', *The Journal of Experimental Education*, 60, (1), 49–66.

Scanlan, D. and Savill-Smith, C. (2021), 'Teacher Wellbeing Index 2021', Education Support, www.educationsupport.org.uk/media/qzna4 gxb/twix-2021.pdf

Schnall, S. and Roper, J. (2011), 'Elevation puts moral values into action', *Social Psychological and Personality Science*, 3, (3), 373–378.

Schwartz, B., Ward, A., Monterosso, J., Lyubomirsky, S., White, K. and Lehman, D. R. (2002), 'Maximizing versus satisficing: Happiness is a matter of choice', *Journal of Personality and Social Psychology*, 83, (5), 1178–1197.

Segal, Z. V., Williams, J. M. G. and Teasdale, J. D. (2002), *Mindfulness-Based Cognitive Therapy for Depression: A New Approach to Preventing Relapse*. New York: The Guildford Press.

Selhub, E. (2022), 'Nutritional psychiatry: Your brain on food', Harvard Health Publishing, www.health.harvard.edu/blog/nutritional-psy chiatry-your-brain-on-food-201511168626

Seligman, M. (2002), *Authentic Happiness: Using the New Positive Psychology to Realise Your Potential for Lasting Fulfilment*. New York: Atria Paperback.

Seligman, M. (2011), *Flourish: A New Understanding of Happiness and Wellbeing – and How to Achieve Them*. London: Nicholas Brealey Publishing.

Seligman, M. E. P. and Csikszentmihalyi, M. (2000), 'Positive psychology: An introduction', *American Psychologist*, 55, (1), 5–14.

Seligman, M., Ernst, R. M., Gillham, J., Reivich, K. and Linkins, M. (2009), 'Positive education: Positive psychology and classroom interventions', *Oxford Review of Education*, 35, (3), 293–311.

Seligman, M., Steen, T. A., Park, N. and Peterson, C. (2005), 'Positive psychology progress: Empirical validation of interventions', *American Psychologist*, 60, (5), 410–421.

Service, O., Hallsworth, M., Halpern, D., Algate, F., Gallagher, R., Nguyen, S., Ruda, S. and Sanders, M. (2015), 'EAST: Four simple ways to apply behavioural insights', The Behavioural Insights Team, www.bi.team/wp-content/uploads/2015/07/BIT-Publication-EAST_FA_WEB.pdf

Sheldon, K. M. and Lyubomirsky, S. (2007), 'Is it possible to become happier? (And if so, how?)', *Social and Personality Psychology Compass*, 1, (1), 129–145.

Siegel, D. J. and Bryson, T. P. (2012), *The Whole-Brain Child: 12 Proven Strategies to Nurture Your Child's Developing Mind*. London: Robinson.

Sivarajah, S., Smith, S. M. and Thomas, S. C. (2018), 'Tree cover and species composition effects on academic performance of primary school students', *PLoS ONE*, 13, (2), e0193254.

Slatcher, R. and Pennebaker, J. W. (2006), 'How do I love thee? Let me count the words: The social effects of expressive writing', *Psychological Science*, 17, (8), 660–664.

Smith, J. L., Harrison, P. R., Kurtz, J. L. and Bryant, F. B. (2014), 'Nurturing the capacity to savor: Interventions to enhance the enjoyment of positive experiences', in Parks, A. C. and Schueller, S. M. (eds), *The Wiley Blackwell Handbook of Positive Psychological Interventions*. Hoboken: Wiley-Blackwell.

Snel, E. (2014), *Sitting Still Like a Frog: Mindfulness Exercises for Kids (and Their Parents)*. Boulder, CO: Shambhala Publications.

Soneson, E., Puntis, S., Chapman, N., Mansfield, K. L., Jones, P. B. and Fazel, M. (2022), 'Happier during lockdown: A descriptive analysis of self-reported wellbeing in 17,000 UK school students during Covid-19 lockdown', *European Child and Adolescent Psychiatry*, DOI: 10.1007/s00787-021-01934-z.

Speer, M. E. and Delgado, M. R. (2017), 'Reminiscing about positive memories buffers acute stress responses', *Nature Human Behaviour*, 1, (5), 0093.

Sport England (2022), 'Active Lives Children and Young People Survey: Academic year 2021–22', www.sportengland.org/research-and-data/data/active-lives

Suttie, J. (2012), 'Can schools helps students find flow?', *Greater Good Magazine*, https://greatergood.berkeley.edu/article/item/can_schools_help_students_find_flow

Szeto, A., Nation, D. A., Mendez, A. J., Dominguez-Bendala, J., Brooks, L. G., Schneiderman, N. and McCabe, P. M. (2008), 'Oxytocin attenuates NADPH-dependent superoxide activity and IL-6 secretion in macrophages and vascular cells', *American Journal of Physiology, Endocrinology and Metabolism*, 295, (6), E1495–1501.

Tallis, H., Bratman, G. N., Samhouri, J. F. and Fargione, J. (2018), 'Are California elementary school test scores more strongly associated with urban trees than poverty?', *Frontiers in Psychology*, 9, 2074.

Tamir, M., Schwartz, S. H., Oishi, S. and Kim, M. Y. (2017), 'The secret to happiness: Feeling good or feeling right?' *Journal of Experimental Psychology*, 146, (10), 1448–1459.

Teacher Tapp (October 2022) 'Teacher poll, sample size: 8001'.

The Children's Society (2021a), 'The Good Childhood Report 2021', www.childrenssociety.org.uk/information/professionals/resources/good-childhood-report-2021

The Children's Society (2021b), 'The state of children's wellbeing in 2020', www.childrenssociety.org.uk/information/professionals/resources/good-childhood-report-2020#state

The Children's Society (2022), 'The Good Childhood Report 2022', www.childrenssociety.org.uk/sites/default/files/2022-09/GCR-2022-Full-Report.pdf

The Daily Mile (2018), 'Health and wellbeing', https://thedailymile.co.uk/category/research-articles/

UCL Institute of Education (IOE) (2020), 'Research shows "a sense of belonging" is important for pupils' learning and behaviour', www.ucl.ac.uk/ioe/news/2020/nov/research-shows-sense-belonging-important-pupils-learning-and-behaviour

UK Government (2017), 'Childhood obesity: A plan for action', www.gov.uk/government/publications/childhood-obesity-a-plan-for-action/childhood-obesity-a-plan-for-action

Ulrich, R. S. (1984), 'View through a window may influence recovery from surgery', *Science*, 224, 420–421.

United Nations (UN) (2018), '68% of the world population projected to live in urban areas by 2050, says UN', Department of Economic and Social Affairs, www.un.org/development/desa/en/news/populat ion/2018-revision-of-world-urbanization-prospects.html

University of Cambridge Research (2022), 'One in three young people say they felt happier during lockdown', www.cam.ac.uk/research/ news/one-in-three-young-people-say-they-felt-happier-during-lockdown?utm_campaign=research&utm_medium=social&utm _source=twitter

Vickery, C. E. and Dorjee, D. (2016), 'Mindfulness training in primary schools decreases negative affect and increases meta-cognition in children', *Frontiers in Psychology*, 6, (10), 2025.

Waters, E., Wippman, J. and Sroufe, L. A. (1979), 'Attachment, positive affect, and competence in the peer group: Two studies in construct validation', *Child Development*, 50, (3), 821–829.

Way, B. M., Creswell, J. D., Eisenberger, N. I. and Lieberman, M. D. (2010), 'Dispositional mindfulness and depressive symptomatology: Correlations with limbic and self-referential neural activity during rest', *Emotion*, 10, (1), 12–24.

Weng, H. Y., Fox, A. S., Shackman, A. J., Stodola, D. E., Caldwell, J. Z. K., Olson, M. C., Rogers, G. M. and Davidson, R. J. (2013), 'Compassion training alters altruism and neural responses to suffering', *Psychological Science*, 24, (7), 1171–1180.

What Works Centre for Wellbeing (2017), 'Sport, dance and young people', https://whatworkswellbeing.files.wordpress.com/2017/ 06/dance-sport-wellbeing-briefing-22june.pdf

Wiking, M. (2019), *The Key to Happiness: How to Find Purpose by Unlocking the Secrets of the World's Happiest People*. London: Penguin Life.

Williams, M. and Penman, D. (2011), *Mindfulness: A Practical Guide to Finding Peace in a Frantic World*. London: Piatkus.

Wilson, E. O. (1984), *Biophilia*. Cambridge, MA: Harvard University Press.

Winnicott, D. W. (1962), *The Child and the Family: First Relationships*. London: Tavistock.

Winston, R. (2014), *What Goes On In My Head? How Your Brain Works and Why You Do What You Do*. London: DK Children.

Wolke, D., Lee, K. and Guy, A. (2017), 'Cyberbullying: A storm in a teacup?', *European Child and Adolescent Psychiatry*, 26, (8), 899–908.

World Meteorological Organization (2022), 'United in Science 2022', https://public.wmo.int/en/resources/united_in_science

Wu, P.-C., Chen, C.-T., Chang, L.-C., Niu, Y.-Z., Chen, M.-L., Liao, L.-L., Rose, K. and Morgan, I. G. (2020), 'Increased time outdoors is followed by reversal of the long-term trend to reduced visual acuity in Taiwan primary school students', *Opthalmology*, 127, (11), 1462–1469.

Youth Sport Trust (2021), 'Wellbeing survey March 2021', www.well-school.org/t/well-school-evidence/78/4

Youth Sport Trust (2022), 'PE & school sport: The annual report 2022', www.youthsporttrust.org/news-insight/research/pe-school-sport-the-annual-report-2022

Index

Index

Praise for *Wellbeing in the Primary Classroom: The updated guide to teaching happiness and positive mental health*

'If you want healthier, happier children, this book is for you. Yet again, Adrian Bethune demystifies the theory of wellbeing and turns it into clear, practical advice we should all implement in our classrooms and schools.'

Ben Levinson OBE, Executive Head Teacher at Kensington Primary School @mrlev

'This is a helpful guide for teachers to think more about their and their students' wellbeing.'

Laurie Santos, Professor of Psychology at Yale University and host of The Happiness Lab podcast @lauriesantos

'The timely publication of this new edition demonstrates Adrian's authorial authority as well as the impact his original work had. 'Tales from the Classroom' shows the practical application of sound research into happiness and wellbeing and the chapter on 'Neuroplasticity' will be essential reading as schools develop their understanding of the mechanics of the maturing brain. A publication be well-thumbed and bookmarked!'

Andrew Cowley, author of The Wellbeing Toolkit and The Wellbeing Curriculum @andrew_cowley23

'Adrian's book is one of those books that I genuinely recommend to teachers and head teachers all the time! This updated guide is a brilliant synthesis of valuable research and is brimming with practical ideas that will make a positive and life affirming difference to children and teachers alike! For schools and educators right now, this is the book you need; this is essential reading!'

Rae Snape, Headteacher at Milton Road Primary School and author of The Headteacher's Handbook @RaeSnape

'This gem of a book is a must have for all who support the wellbeing of children in the primary classroom. Practical, totally accessible and full of 'positive psychology' tools which really work!'

Dr Tina Rae, Educational and Child Psychologist and author of A Toolbox of Wellbeing @DrTinarae

'I thought I knew a lot about wellbeing in the classroom until I read this book, I learnt so many useful strategies that I can use not just in school, but for me as a person and a professional. I loved that the practical suggestions were backed up with research and evidence, I really think everyone working with children should read it - I'll be ordering all of our staff a copy! It's a 10/10 again for the wellbeing in schools guru!'

Dave McPartlin, Headteacher Flakefleet Primary School @Dave_McPartlin

'This is a wonderfully humane and useful book for teachers. Idea by idea it shows how the skills for living can be taught in practice. Beautifully written by a teacher who walks the talk.'

Lord Richard Layard, Chairman of Action for Happiness

'Wellbeing is more important and relevant than ever; Adrian's book brings this to the forefront of discussion whilst giving so many fun ideas you can incorporate into your classroom and practice.'

Emily Weston, Year 5 and 6 Teacher @primaryteachew